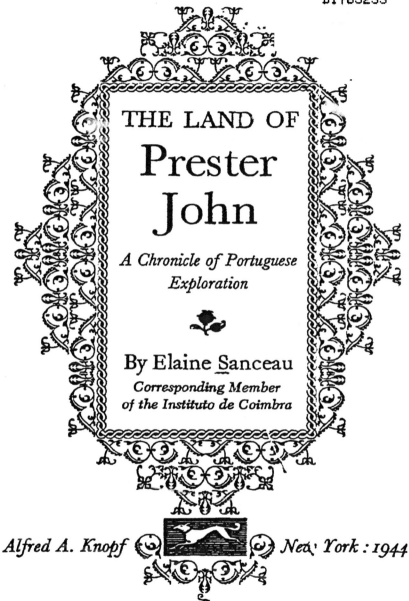

THE LAND OF
Prester John

A Chronicle of Portuguese Exploration

By Elaine Sanceau

*Corresponding Member
of the Instituto de Coimbra*

Alfred A. Knopf *Ne₥ York : 1944*

Contents

PART I

HOW PORTUGAL SOUGHT PRESTER JOHN

PART II

HOW PORTUGAL SAVED PRESTER JOHN

Contents

PART III

THE PARTING OF THE WAYS

MAPS AND ILLUSTRATION

Introduction

The modern traveller, killing time at Estoril while waiting for a passage on the Clipper, does not often give much thought to the country he is passing through. A kindly people, and a sunny sky — some bathing, and some golf perhaps — a smokeless city drenched in light hanging picturesquely from precipitous hills above a broad blue river — may well be all that Portugal will stand for in his memory. He is far too apt to forget the world history that was prepared beside these smiling shores.

He may not realize that he owes it to Portugal that he should be a modern traveller at all! This blue estuary shining in the sun was the highway that first led ships to the world's end. The simple courteous people that he sees around descend from pioneers. They are a nation that has lived adventurously and made its mark upon the earth.

Its traces may be found over four continents. Portugal has had an African adventure, as witnessed by the battlemented towers she left beside Moroccan beaches, by the names she wrote on the map, and the vast territories of Angola, Mozambique, and Guinea, where she is mistress still.

She had an American adventure too, and founded a great nation on the far shore of the Atlantic to grow amid the riches of the forests and the mountains of Brazil.

Introduction

Her Indian adventure can still be traced today by ruined fortresses at all strategic points around the Indian Ocean, and her language is spoken still throughout the Orient where men of Portuguese descent are found among the native races from East Africa to the spice archipelagoes of the Pacific.

There was an Abyssinian adventure as well, of which fewer traces remain – a side-line it turned out to be – and yet in many ways it was the strangest and the most heroic of all.

It was not intended as a side-line when first embarked upon – quite the contrary. Henry the Navigator and the kings who continued his task looked to the Christian Empire of Ethiopia as the cornerstone of their great enterprise. To understand their dream we must go back to mediæval times and remember the Holy War waged by Christians against the Moslem hordes, for ever threatening to engulf Europe.

Portugal as a nation was born of the Crusades. When, in 711, the Moors overran the Iberian Peninsula, a handful of Gothic warriors with their King withdrew to the Asturian mountains. From that impregnable stronghold the armies of the Cross defied Islam and set out to reconquer by degrees the land that they had lost. It took them seven hundred years, and crusaders from many European countries came to bear a part.

Thus in the eleventh century a French prince carried arms against the Infidel under the King of Castile and León. As a reward he was given in fief the lands that he had conquered from the Moors, by the Atlantic Ocean. So Portugal came into being, and some decades later threw off her allegiance to the Castilian crown and stood, and fought, alone.

This independence was not won without a struggle. Castile, three times more powerful, resented the emancipation of the younger realm, but Portugal held firm. After a terrible dynastic crisis during which annexation appeared imminent, she defeated her enemy in 1385 and so saved her existence as a nation. .

The Moorish Kingdom of Algarve – last Moslem stronghold in the south of Portugal — had been conquered a century earlier. But the Moors still remained at Granada and in North Africa — a potential menace always, a peril that had been exorcized, but lurking only just behind the door.

The Paynim horde outside the gate — that was the spectre that haunted mediæval Christendom upon its southern and its eastern borders. If the Moslems of Africa and Asia should one day unite, all would be up with Christian Europe. That is why the mediævals thought so lovingly of Prester John — Christian King in Africa who might protect their flank. Why *Prester* and why *John* historians and Orientalists have not made clear, but whatever its origin, men of the fifteenth century were convinced that the Emperor of Abyssinia bore this title.

Little was known about his empire except that it was vast and, though in the heart of the Moslem world, it had always been Christian. To find this isolated champion of the faith, to make alliance with him against the common foe, to make contact through him with the Nestorian Christians in the spice lands of the Orient, became the aim of Portugal, born a crusading nation.

The story of this quest, undertaken in faith and carried through tenaciously in spite of every hardship and setback, is one of the most romantic in history. It all turned out quite differently from what had been expected and hoped for, but the strange fruitless adventure of Portugal in search of Prester John remains a high light in the records of human endeavour.

PART I

HOW PORTUGAL SOUGHT PRESTER JOHN

1

The Wandering Myth

A world of phantoms floated around mediæval Christendom. Europe saw itself as a small oasis — a spot of light where true religion reigned and life was normal, while mystery and magic veiled everything beyond.

To the west surged the ocean which no man had crossed, impassable and enigmatic as infinity; to the east and south all trailed away into the outer dark. The earth went on, men knew, but none could say just how. It was a wonderful and wicked world that lay beyond the Christians' ken — a world of paynims and of infidels, of sorcery and enchantment. Strange stories filtered through from time to time like echoes from another planet; strange apparitions now and then broke forth, as when a man of unknown race from the world's end was seen on the confines of Christendom, or else sometimes a Christian, greatly daring, would himself disappear into the shades. At other times, more terrible than all, was heard the gallop of horses bearing wild yellow warriors across the eastern steppe, and Europe trembled lest she might be swamped by those demoniac hordes let loose from some region of nameless horror.

The Crusades served to lift a corner of the veil. The crusaders, touching the fringe of the unknown, heard and saw many things. Thus Europe was made aware of Far Cathay and the Great Khan, the Old Man of the Mountain and his Assassins, and so it was that from the dim light of far away there rose and grew the tale of Prester John.

Nobody was sure exactly where might be the realm of Prester John, sole Christian ruler in a heathen continent, but no one doubted his existence. There was no king on earth like Prester John. His robes were washed in fire and woven by the salamander. He lived in an enchanted palace in the mountains, and in front of it a magic mirror stood where he could see his vast dominions at a glance. Seven kings waited constantly on Prester John, as well as sixty dukes, three hundred and sixty counts, and knights and noblemen beyond compute. Thirty archbishops sat at his right hand, and twenty bishops on his left. A king and abbot was his cook, a king bishop his butler, an archimandrite his master of horse, an archbishop his pantler. Surrounded by menials of such exalted rank, how could he also style himself a king? Besides, this mighty potentate was perfect, therefore humble. So he was known as Presbyter or Prester John.

His kingdom was the land where dreams come true. The Fountain of Youth flowed there and subterranean streams of gems. There might be picked up the magic stone that gives sight to the blind or makes a man invisible. No poor were in the land of Prester John, nor misers, nor thieves, nor murderers, nor even flatterers. There all men spoke the truth, and vice did not exist. It was the earthly paradise that no man has yet found.

Such was the mirage that shone before the eyes of the twelfth century. Its colours faded as the years passed by, but still the myth endured. As a night wanderer follows a will-o'-the-wisp, mediæval imagination pursued Prester John, whose kingdom in like manner moved from end to end of Asia. Sometimes it was alleged to lie beyond the Persian mountains, sometimes in India, and sometimes on the far-off Mongolian steppes near China.

By the fourteenth century it had travelled west. The fact

4

had dawned on Europe that a Christian kingdom existed in Africa. Abyssinian pilgrims sometimes visited the Holy Land, but nobody was certain where they came from. Inaccessible mountains, it was rumoured, locked their kingdom round. What could it be if not the land of Prester John? Prester John of the Indies they called him still, the vague geography of the time confusing India with east Africa.

The realm of Prester John had ceased to be a synonym for fairyland, but it remained alluringly remote. This outpost of the faith, lost and cut off, was almost as appealing to imagination. When mediæval dreams gave way to the pursuit of facts, then men set out to seek for the reality.

It was a prince of Portugal who led the way. Henry the Navigator stood between two worlds – the dying Middle Ages and the dawning Renaissance. The mysticism of the one and the insatiable curiosity of the other were the driving forces which controlled his life. He was a crusader and a man of science rolled into one.

Dom Henrique was born in 1394 – the end of an age – to a nation on the threshold of new destinies. He was third son of the King João I, that valiant bastard who had upheld the independence of the realm against the armies of Castile and so won for himself his father's crown.

The revolution of 1382 and the long wars that followed had shaken Portugal to her foundations but left her spiritually renewed. An old order had been swept away with the corrupt court of the late King Fernande; a new dynasty sat on the throne, a new generation of statesmen gathered around it; new ideas were in the air, new energies were stirring in the blood – it was a nation's springtime.

The Infante Dom Henrique inherited the martial instincts of his father, and the earnest devotion of his mother, Philippa of Lancaster, the daughter of Chaucer's "good Duchess Blaunche." He was, moreover, the grandson of John of Gaunt, patron of letters, and the descendant of Alfonse el Sabio of Castile, and Dom Diniz, who founded Coimbra University.

5

Thus there was intellectual ancestry on either side; Dom Henrique and his brothers developed a thirst for knowledge at an early age, and from childhood they read and collected books.

The influences of their environment, however, were against mere contemplative cultivation of the mind and soul. João and Philippa's five brilliant sons were born in the hour of triumph in a country that had just been fighting for its life. They were surrounded by men of action, and it was the heroes who had won the victory that were the guides and models of their boyhood. Between these and their mother, the young princes were brought up in an atmosphere of practical piety and high-minded militarism. The late war had been of the defensive order — "a just war to obtain peace," the Constable Nunalvares Pereira had defined it, which reminds us of the modern slogan "a war to end war."

The total end of war, however, was a utopia of which mediævals rarely dreamed. All knights and gentlemen had to be soldiers, but Henrique's generation had inherited a tradition of fighting for the right. Their fathers' swords had won their country's freedom; the sons who grew up in a land at peace aspired to win their maiden spurs in the defence of a good cause.

For men of the Iberian Peninsula, a good cause was never far to seek. Their kingdoms were the buffer states of Christendom against the Moslem hordes outside the pale. Close to their gates still raged a holy war, which had known intervals of truce, but never peace, during six hundred years. It is true that the Moor had been pushed out of Portugal, but across the narrow straits, beyond the sea, his palmy cities flourished almost within Christian sight. When Dom Henrique and his brothers wished to win their knightly spurs, it seemed to them that a high and holy enterprise would be the conquest of Ceuta.

Queen Philippa backed up her sons' suggestions to their father. "Since God in His mercy has been pleased to give them strength of mind and body," said she, "I would not for

6

the world that they should fail to execute works such as these, however difficult!"[1]

So it was that, carrying with them a dying mother's blessing, Dom Henrique and his brothers sailed across the straits and were knighted by their father in the conquered Moorish town.

That hour fixed a nation's destiny. A young man with an inquiring mind had his first taste of Africa, and found that he was gazing at a mystery.

Ceuta was the fairest town along the Moorish coast. It overflowed with lovely things from far away. It was rich with pearls from the Persian Gulf, with rubies from Ceylon, perfumes of Syria, and silks of Egypt. Within the flat-roofed houses faced with coloured tiles were carpets from the Persian looms and embroideries from India. Behind the houses there were mosaic courts, scented with orange trees and musical with fountains; behind the town were fields of sugar-cane, orchards, and trailing vines; behind the orchards were the hills, and then behind those – what?

Ceuta, divided from the Christian world by a few leagues of sea, was the last link of a long chain that began in the totally unknown. And this chain could be followed back, Henrique knew, to Satan's seat – those lands where Islam reigned unchallenged and supreme. For centuries the Infidel had held the key to the earth's richest treasures. Now that the young prince saw Ceuta mosque transformed into a Christian church, he dreamed of new and greater triumphs for the Cross. Should not the warriors of Christ pursue the "abominable sect of Mohammed" across the world and tear it like an evil thing from its Far Eastern stronghold? Ceuta should be only a beginning – Ceuta between the desert and the sea, with a vast unknown continent behind. How far into this mysterious land did the accursed Crescent hold its sway? Had Africa an end, or did it run from pole to pole? Where beyond those hills of darkness lay the realm of Prester John, that isolated champion of the faith who would surely welcome help

7

against the common foe? If Prester John could but join forces with the Christians of the West, could they not then destroy Islam? And the land of Prester John was on the way to India, that fabled treasure-house of spice and gold. Had not St. Thomas found his way to India and planted there a Christian church?

Dom Henrique went home with his mind full of questions. How to reach Prester John and get in touch with that mysterious India that Alexander's armies had seen long ago? The land routes of the Orient were closed to Europe. Everywhere the Crescent barred the way, and so to reach the Christians of the East, Dom Henrique chose the path of the Dark Ocean.

That was a fearsome undertaking. "No man sailing south of Cape Bojador returns alive!" declared mediæval wisdom. A region of nameless horror stretched beyond. The Middle Ages formulated theories and left the matter there, but the Renaissance was seized with the desire to prove. Intellectually, Dom Henrique was of the Renaissance though he lived and died a generation earlier. When he began to wonder, then he must find out.

He gave his life up to this end. He established his abode in the far south of Portugal, on the Cape of Sagres, the last point of Europe. There, "where two seas, the Mediterranean and the Great Ocean, fight together," he set himself to solve the riddle of the universe and so "attain the purpose that he had in mind, to discover from the western side the navigation to Oriental India."

Pleasure, political power, even family ties meant nothing to the recluse of Sagres, and all the revenues of the Order of Christ, of which he was Grand Master, were devoted to his quest. Upon his windswept rock the Infante gathered about him a unique court: mathematicians, astronomers, cartographers, makers of instruments of precision, builders of ships, collected there from far and wide, each contributing his own particle of skill or wisdom to the task. With the men of theory came the men of action — all the seamen, pilots and adventurous young *fidalgos* of Portugal, as well as foreign wanderers out to see the world and seek their fortune. And mingling with the sages and the sailors of the West were more exotic types. The Infante by his largesse lured into his orbit pilgrims from the Levant who came to visit Occidental shrines — Syrians and Copts and other dwellers on the confines of Christendom who carried with them echoes of the world beyond. From such he gathered news about the Arab trade with the Far East, and how their treasure-laden *djelbas* sailed up to Suez bringing the spices of India to Alexandria and Cairo. But the strangest tales were brought by captives such as the Moor Adahu, who told of inland seas far in the heart of Africa, of how salt caravans crossed the Sahara into the Sudan, and how hundreds of camels laden with gold went down to the Red Sea from Timbuktu.

Thus surrounded by "men of diverse nationalities," the Infante Dom Henrique spent his days and nights co-ordinating all his clues, meditating upon travellers' reports, poring over old maps, compiling others, wrestling with mathematics, studying the stars, and from all this deducing a new science — how men might find their path on trackless seas. And continually he sent forth ships — each year more ships — with orders to sail farther and farther south until they found the end of Africa.

They sailed cautiously at first — for might not any kind of monster haunt the South Atlantic? — and then with reckless ease, for after all no bogy put in an appearance, and though they sailed into the tropics, the ocean never boiled as those supposed to know affirmed it would. They even found out with a shock that Ptolemy — that oracle of all learned mediævals — "the illustrious Ptolemy, who wrote so well of many things," says one of Dom Henrique's men, "was quite mistaken here!" Ptolemy had declared the tropics to be "uninhabited because of the great heat, and we found quite the contrary!" [2] Such was the crumbling up of preconceived ideas. Even the demon Cape Bojador turned out to be an overrated

9

terror. It is true that a ship could not sail home against the
current that ran down the coast, but the answer was to lose all
sight of land and sweep a circle out to sea.

The Dark Ocean soon ceased to frighten Henrique's navi-
gators. They engulfed themselves far from all continents and
found the lovely islands lost in the Atlantic. They defied one
by one the capes of Africa — Bojador, Branco, Palmas, and
beyond. They saw the desert shores give way to tropic green,
they saw all Arab traces fade away and Berber types succeeded by the genuine Negro — yet the intriguing coast ran
on and on, apparently for ever.

Dom Henrique never showed signs of discouragement. He
colonized Madeira and the Azores; he built fortresses and
trading factories on the coast of Africa, and sent his caravels
far out to sea towards the unknown west. Whether they
reached the Antilles forty years in advance of Columbus, or
Brazil fifty years before Cabral, is a question that historians
are debating still. It is certain that the Infante sought to penetrate the undiscovered world in all directions, but he never
lost sight of the East and Prester John.

Exactly how much he did upon the eastern side is wrapped
in even deeper mystery than the Atlantic explorations that he
organized. His messengers must have succeeded in some pen-
etration overland, if we may judge by Azurzra's enigmatic
chronicle. "He joined East to West," says this writer, who died
in 1474, twenty-four years before the sea route to the East
had been discovered. And in one of his bursts of rhetoric this
same chronicler paints a glowing picture of how the inhabitants of the Nile Valley might now be seen wearing the Infante's armorial device and decked in jewels and finery from
Portugal. "What brought this about," he cries, apostrophizing
his hero, "if not the liberality of thy expenditure and the labours of thy servants moved by thy virtuous intelligence,
through which were carried to the farthest Orient things fash-
ioned in the West?" It has been pointed out that Azurzra, in
common with most of his contemporaries, believed the Niger

to be a branch of the Nile. That may be so, but both he and they knew East from West and could not possibly describe as *"fins do Oriente"* the west coast of Africa.

Even more intriguing is a document discovered not long ago in the Chancelaria of Afonso V. Here we find mention of a certain Jorge, "ambassador of Prester John," who was in Portugal in 1452. Nothing more is known about this personage. No chronicler, contemporary or subsequent, ever refers to him, and when, sixty years later, a messenger from Abyssinia arrived at Dom Manuel's court, he was welcomed as the first ambassador from Prester John.

Who, then, was Jorge, and what? Was he some Abyssinian pilgrim to Rome or Jerusalem that Henrique's agents had waylaid and persuaded to visit Portugal? Such an explanation seems quite probable, but why then call him an ambassador?

It was in 1454, two years after this mysterious visit, that we find Afonso V bestowing upon the Order of Christ, of which Henrique was Grand Master, spiritual jurisdiction over Guinea, Nubia, and Ethiopia.[3]

We can speculate as freely as we choose about all this. It is a puzzle with too many pieces missing to be reconstructed otherwise than by imagination.

When Dom Henrique died, in 1460, the problems that he had set himself were still mostly unsolved. The land of Prester John had hardly ceased to be a legend. The dream of a sea route to India was not substantiated yet. But in his lifetime Dom Henrique had changed the world. His hand had swept away for ever the phantoms with which men's imagination peopled the Atlantic. A nation had lost all terror of the ocean. And the nation that the Infante had trained in seamanship was young and strong — a people yet unspoiled by luxury, who had lived by agriculture and the sword. Their fathers had bequeathed to them a great fighting tradition. Few in number, they were used to overcoming fearful odds. Sons of the vanquishers of both Moors and Castilians, they felt themselves to be invincible. As for the perils of the deep, a sea voyage was no longer a haphazard adventure, but a problem to be worked out by the rules of an exact science. Portugal thus faced the unknown world and feared it not at all.

The great quest was carried on. Afonso V, the African, engrossed though he was in the conquest of Morocco, did not forget it altogether; and his son, the future Dom João II, on attaining manhood, brought to bear upon the problem all the vigour of his restless intellect. "He was determined," we are told, "to pursue the discovery of the Guinea coast that his predecessors had begun, for by that coast it seemed to him that he would find the land of Prester John of which he heard reports, and by that way he might reach India."[4]

So the little ships continued seeking new horizons. In 1471 Alvaro Esteves had crossed the Equator. In 1484, a stone pillar was erected near the Congo River by Diogo Cao. Finally, in 1486, Bartolomeu Dias struck boldly out to sea and sailed far south of the discovered world. For thirteen days his fifty-ton caravels ran blindly before wild winds and raging seas, and the long-sought cape was turned at last, unknowingly amid the shrieking storm. "Cape of Tempests," the sailors called it when they saw the giant upon their homeward way. "Call it rather Cape of Good Hope!" said Dias, with visions of the golden East before his eyes, and so the name remained. But they had gleaned no news of Prester John upon those savage shores.

At home in Portugal, meanwhile, the King, Dom João II, was speeding on the enterprise in another direction. While Bartolomeu Dias was seeking Prester John on the east coast of Africa, two men had been sent forth from Santatem upon an equally stirring adventure.

Afonso de Paiva and Pero da Covilham were to travel from Egypt inland, gathering all the information that they could about the trade routes of the East and India. They were to reach Ethiopia by some means and bear a letter from their King to Prester John.

2

The Lost Forerunner

Dom João II of Portugal was no star-gazing mystic. Chasing shadows did not in the least appeal to that brisk and Machiavellian monarch. If he sent messengers into the blue, it was that he felt fairly certain that they would find substance at their journey's end.

His pioneers had been collecting dues for some time past. The men who braved the terrors of the deep would not be daunted by the equatorial forest. They plunged in and explored. Strange black kingdoms were found below those steaming shades, all savage realms of Ju-Ju worshippers; but even from such depths of heathen night were gathered hints of something else beyond.

Twenty moons' journey towards the rising sun, declared the woolly-pated men of Benin, there ruled the great King Ogané. The chiefs of Benin regarded this Ogané with almost religious veneration as a being far above themselves. None of them had ever seen him; they sent him their ambassadors when they acceded to the throne, and that was all. Nor did even the ambassadors see Ogané, for curtains always veiled the august one from profane gaze. All that the envoys of Benin ever saw of him was just one foot, protruded once only for them to feast their eyes upon before they left. On this same happy occasion Ogané would present his visitors with a shining brass helmet for their King, and a brazen cross for him to hang about his neck. Without these insignia no king of Benin could reign lawfully.

The ambassador also would receive his gift before he wandered back across the heart of Africa. He took away with him a little cross, a small model of that sent to his master. The proud possessor of this trophy was endowed with special privileges when he reached home.

Twenty moons' journey to the east — that meant 250 leagues, more or less; the Portuguese calculated from what they knew of the native rate of progress in the bush. Dom João called for his experts and his maps, and they studied the matter. The land of Ogané lay to the south of Egypt, it would seem, and surely Ogané was Prester John!

Dom João resolved to conjure this mysterious and inaccessible greatness from its splendid isolation and draw it into touch with his own little kingdom of the West. Prester John would help him find the way to India, he felt sure. Meanwhile, to break the silence of the ages and communicate across the intervening unknown space seemed almost like sending messages to Mars.

Dom João left no stone unturned. Countless black prisoners were let loose down the west coast of Africa. All had been treated well. All were laden with gifts and richly clad. They should have glowing tales to carry to their inland homes about the marvellous realm beyond the sea, the birdlike ships which sailed so far, and the greatness of the King who owned them. Some echoes of all this might cross the wilderness to Prester John.

Dom João also tried more direct means. His first attempt was unsuccessful. Two monks, who felt their zeal enough to compensate for all deficiencies, plunged boldly into the breach. But the good men had underestimated the difficulty of travel in the Middle East without a word of Arabic to help them. They got no farther than Jerusalem, whence they turned back discouraged.

Dom João was not the man to repeat a mistake. He selected a new pair of messengers — practical laymen this time, with an easy flow of Arabic at their command.

Pero da Covilham, a linguist with an adventurous soul, already had behind him a chequered career. He had served the Duke of Medina Sidonia in Castile as a youth, but when war broke out with his native land, he went home. He accompanied King Afonso V to France on his famous visit to Louis XI; he became successively guardsman to Dom João II, a spy across the border in Castile, and ambassador to Morocco. He negotiated treaties with the King of Tlemcen, arranged for the return from Fez of the bones of the martyred Infante Dom Fernando, and purchased horses for the future King Dom Manuel, then Duke of Beja. In all these things he had served faithfully, Dom João suavely said, and he was lucky also. Now he must undertake a great thing for the crown. Let him, with Afonso de Paiva for companion, travel east to find the realm of Prester John! Dom João would give him a letter to that enigmatic personage, who would doubtless be able to inform them from which of the Indian ports the spices came that reached Venice via Alexandria and Cairo.

Pero da Covilham and Afonso de Paiva bowed before the royal commands. The King handed them a planisphere on which to mark the land of Prester John, when its site should be discovered. He also gave them 400 cruzados, partly cash and partly letter of credit on the Medicis' bank, for travelling expenses, and his blessing. So equipped, on May 7, 1487 the dauntless pair started from Santarem.

Only the bare outlines of their adventures are recorded. From Barcelona they embarked for Naples, where they cashed their cheque before proceeding to Rhodes. Two compatriots, Knights of St. John, welcomed the travellers into their house, and there they stayed awhile. Bidding farewell to these kind hosts, the companions turned their backs upon the friendly island of the Hospitallers — the last of their familiar world that either would ever see — and, disguised as merchants with honey to sell, they crossed to Alexandria. Both nearly died of fever there, but as soon as they were better they pushed on to Cairo. Adopting Moslem garb, they joined some Moors from Maghreb, whom they accompanied to Aden.

Beside the arid hills upon the desert edge the two friends said good-bye. Pero da Covilham embarked upon an Arab dhow sailing for India. He was following the spices to their fountainhead while Afonso de Paiva crossed the strait to journey to Ethiopia and to Prester John. At a later date agreed upon by both, they were to meet at Cairo.

So each man went his lonely way. Afonso de Paiva's wanderings never will be known. Whether he reached Ethiopia after all and what befell him, there are no records to tell. We only hear that he got back to Cairo first and there he died alone.

Pero da Covilham meanwhile visited the countries where the spices grew. He disembarked at Cannanore, the port for ginger. He saw, moreover, Calicut — strange gorgeous city of thatched houses and half-naked men, of coco palms beside the beach, of gold and jewels and elephants and pepper. Especially pepper! Pepper may not mean much to us, but in that age it ranked with precious stones. Men risked the perils of the deep and fought and died for pepper. We find that hard to understand, perhaps, for the romance of pepper has now faded from the earth.

Tearing himself from the dazzling spectacle of Calicut, Pero da Covilham went on to the lordly town of Goa, where the Moslem dynasty of Bijapur held sway. Thence he embarked for Sofala and Madagascar — the Arabs called it Island of the Moon. To complete his tour of Indian Ocean ports, he took ship to Ormuz, the richest city all around those coasts. Having admired the splendours there, the wanderer returned to Aden. He kept his tryst at Cairo in due course, but found he was too late. There was nothing left but to go home.

At this juncture two Jews appeared upon the scene. Rabbi Abraham from Beja, and Joseph, a shoemaker of Lamego, were inquiring secretly for him. Rabbi Abraham had letters from the King, and Joseph of Lamego was to take the answer back.

Pero da Covilham studied the instructions of his lord and master. If he had been to all the places indicated and collected all the information that the King required, the monarch said benignly that he might return. If, however, he had not yet found Prester John, then let him spare no effort till that was achieved. No difficulty ought to dismay him, added Dom João, in that tone of encouragement so easy to assume when spurring on another.

This was not all. Rabbi Abraham, a travelled man, had heard about the glories of Ormuz, and informed Dom João, who wanted to know more. Before proceeding to Abyssinia, Pero da Covilham would therefore escort the rabbi to Ormuz and send him back to report to the King.

Pero da Covilham, as it happened, wanted to go home. He was tired of wandering in outlandish parts. The heather and pines of Portugal, the cool slopes of his native Serra da Estrels, seemed infinitely more alluring than the scorched rocks of Aden or the blazing Persian Gulf. Besides, he had a wife — by now it might be that he had a child — at Covilham.

But orders were orders. If Portuguese kings asked a great deal of their subjects, it must be said that they met with a magnificent response. Pero da Covilham turned his face from the home he never was to see again and travelled to Aden and Ormuz. He left his Hebrew companion there with letters for the King. Rabbi Abraham would join a caravan and return via Aleppo. Pero da Covilham, meanwhile, sailed back to the Red Sea.

He visited Jidda while he was about it, and Mecca and Medina, thence to Tor and after down to Zeila, where he plunged inland and up the mountains. And so at last, in 1494, he reached the court of Prester John.

Alexander, Lion of Judah, King of Kings, received the foreigner with open arms. He was flattered to have been sought out by a brother Christian monarch far away. Pero da Covilham's difficult mission was at last accomplished. Soon he might travel triumphantly home.

But while he waited for his dispatch the Emperor Alexander died. His brother Naod, who succeeded to the throne, was very pleasant to the stranger, but ignored Dom João's messages. Pero da Covilham then craved for leave to go, but the monarch refused. It was not the custom of his country, he declared, to let a foreigner depart. Pero da Covilham thus found himself marooned.

He was not badly treated. They gave him an Abyssinian bride and broad acres of land. One writer [1] says they even held out hopes that he might have leave to go if he produced and left behind a son!

Pero da Covilham hastened to oblige, but still he was detained. Dom João must be dead, said they, so why return? Let him remain in the employment of his lands and rear his half-caste family.

Pero da Covilham accepted his fate. He gave up hope of seeing Portugal again, or the wife that he had left at Covilham. He learned to speak and write the language like a native, and lived like an Abyssinian nobleman on his estate.

He seems to have been influential in the land and always very well received at court. The Dowager Queen Helena especially enjoyed his conversation. She liked to hear accounts of Portugal. Also, one gathers that his artistic taste was appreciated by the lady, for when she built a church, Pero da Covilham, at her request, designed the altar.

She might have had more competent advice. The Portuguese traveller, it appears, was not the only European at that time immured in Abyssinia. A Venetian painter, Nicola Bianca Leone, was also there. How or why or whence he came, nobody knows. He must have lived in Abyssinia over fifty years. One who met him in his advanced old age describes him patronizingly as "a very worthy person and great lord, although a painter"! [2] It was in his professional capacity that he once

18

had scandalized the Abyssinians when decorating a church for Alexander's father. He depicted the Virgin with the Holy Child on her left arm! This struck the natives as almost sacrilegious, but the Negus evidently liked the picture, for it stayed.

We are not told if the two stranded Europeans found consolation in each other's company; neither do we know anything about the meeting which, presumably, took place in 1508 between Pero da Covilham and two compatriots of whom we shall hear later. Certainly all such voices from the world that he had lost were few and rare, and when, in 1521, Dom Rodrigo de Lima's embassy reached Abyssinia, the exile wept with joy to see his fellow countrymen. He was particularly glad of the opportunity to confess himself to the chaplain who accompanied the delegates. For over thirty years, he told Father Francisco Alvares, he had remained unshriven. The reason was that the secrecy of the confessional was ill observed in Abyssinia, and Pero da Covilham, a cautious soul, would take no risks. He simply went to church, said he, and told his sins to God.[3]

Dom Rodrigo would have taken him back home with them, but the exile refused. It was too late, he said; "I am too old!" But he expressed the wish to send one of his many sons to Portugal to see the King. This young man, aged twenty-three, "the colour of a russet pear," would claim the reward that should have been his father's due. Also, the latter was not sure, perhaps he had another son at Covilham. If that should be so, the half-caste youth would bear with him twenty ounces of gold to give to his white brother.[4] If such a person did indeed exist, we cannot tell, nor what had been the fate of the young wife left waiting so many years for a husband who never returned. We only know that the brown boy died before he reached the shores of the Red Sea, and the gold that he carried was sent back inland to his father. Thus the gulf that cleft a life in two was never bridged.

Pero da Covilham died in Abyssinia.

3

The Odyssey of Matthew

The years that Pero da Covilham remained lost in the Abyssinian mountains had been eventful in the outer world. In 1497 Vasco da Gama had sailed round the Cape to Calicut, and the gateway of the East at last stood open wide. The Portuguese built fortresses in India and East Africa and took possession of the Indian Ocean. Only faint echoes of all this penetrated the inland fastnesses of Abyssinia.

But Portugal had not forgotten Prester John. Messengers might die, and messengers might disappear, but Portugal was bent on getting into touch with Prester John, and the Portuguese are a tenacious race. In 1506 a third attempt was made. João Gomes and João Sanches, with Sid Mohammed, a Tunisian Moor, to be their guide, sailed with Tristao da Cunha's fleet and were landed at Malindi in due course. Thence, it would seem, they failed to make progress, "because around Malindi the Kaffirs of the bush are very wild and fierce, so they decided that it would be better to strike inland from somewhere nearer to the Straits." Thus it was that, in March 1508, a certain Francisco de Tavora, captain of a unit of the Indian Ocean fleet, found them still waiting at Malindi and took them off with him to his commander.

The great Afonso de Albuquerque, at that time chief cap-

tain of the fleet off the Arabian coast, was cruising in the
neighbourhood of Guardafui. Having himself been present
when João Gomes had disembarked in Africa more than a
year before, he was amazed to see the party reappear. Since
they had not travelled via Malindi, he inquired of Sid Mohammed, what route they did propose. The Moor said that
it would be best to strike inland from Berbera or Zeila and
then return to Portugal via Timbuktu.

Albuquerque gave them letters for Prester John in Arabic
and Portuguese and fifty seraphims for their travelling expenses; more than that the canny Moor refused to take —
money, he said, was the worst enemy a wayfarer could have.
Nor, apparently, did he think much of João Gomes as a travelling companion. The man was an unceasing chatterbox! Sid
Mohammed feared that he might get the party into trouble
if he could not hold his tongue.[1]

All three were put ashore on the Somali coast near Guardafui, all posing as Moslem merchants whom the Portuguese
had robbed, and so they walked away into the blue and off
the map. Thenceforward they are no more than wandering
names — seen here by some, reported to be there by others,
but they never come into the light again. In 1510 João Gomes
seems to have been met by two Castilian Jews at Suakin.[2] The
Moor was with him still, but João Sanches was dead. The surviving pair were setting off for Cairo when a quarrel parted
them. Sid Mohammed vanished into the desert, and João
Gomes sailed for Jidda alone. The Jews said that his intentions were to make for Alexandria and Venice. That is the
last we ever hear of him.

It is certain, however, that he had reached Abyssinia. More
than that, we know he was received at court. The Emperor
at that date was under twelve years old, the kingdom being
governed by his step-grandmother, Queen Helena, a devout
and very learned lady who composed works of theology in her
spare time. The Regent was interested in the Portuguese, and
so she caused to be drawn up this edifying letter:

In the name of the Father, the Son, and of the Holy Ghost, Three Persons, and One God, grace and blessing rest upon our beloved brother King Manuel, Rider of the seas, Subjugator and Oppressor of infidels and Moslem unbelievers — may the Lord Christ prosper you and give you victory over your foes. May He enlarge and extend your dominions through the intercession of those messengers of Christ, the four evangelists, John, Luke, Mark, Matthew, may their sanctity and prayers preserve you!

We would inform our beloved brother how two messengers arrived here from your great and lofty house. One was named João, who said he was a priest, and the other João Gomes. They said: we require provisions and men. We are therefore sending Matthew, our ambassador, with orders to reach one of your Indian ports and tell you that we can supply you with mountains of provisions, and men like unto the sands of the sea!

We have news that the Lord of Cairo is building ships to fight your fleet, and we shall give you so many men . . . as to wipe the Moors from the face of the earth! We by land, and you, brothers, on the sea!

The lady further on bursts into prophecy:

Now is the moment come [she cries] for the fulfilment of the promise made by Christ and Holy Mary, His Mother, that in the last time there would arise a king among the Franks who would make an end of all the Moors!

Everything that Matthew, our ambassador, may tell you, believe as from ourselves, for he is the best man that we have, and if we had another who knew or understood more than he we should have sent him. We would have entrusted our message to those of your subjects who came here, but we feared that they might not represent our case as we desire.

With this ambassador, Matthew, we are sending a cross made of the wood of that on which Our Lord was crucified. It was brought me from Jerusalem, and I had two crosses made out of it, one for us, and the other one for you. The said wood is black and has a little silver ring attached to it. We could have sent you much gold, but we feared that the Moors might steal it on the way.

If you are willing, we should be very glad to have your daugh-

22

ters in marriage for our sons, or — better still — if you would marry your sons to our daughters. With which no more, save that salvation and grace of Our Redeemer Christ and Our Lady the Holy Virgin rest on your estate, upon your sons and daughters, and on all your house! Amen. We moreover add that were we to muster all our people we could fill the world, but we have no power on the sea. May Christ Jesus help you, for certainly the things that you have done in India are miraculous! [3]

This affectionate and pious letter was written in both Arabic and Persian. It has been surmised that Pero da Covilham assisted in its composition; but if that were so, surely he would have appended a Portuguese translation, and no such thing accompanied the letter. Such as it was, the document was signed and sealed, and delivered to the Matthew aforesaid.

This man's identity would seem a little vague. An Armenian, says one contemporary; a Christian merchant resident in Cairo, says another; a recently converted Moslem, affirms a third; the brother of the Coptic Patriarch of Cairo and married to a kinswoman of Prester John, apparently declared Matthew himself.[4] All these statements may be true — most of them are not incompatible. What we know for certain is that the man was white, of distinguished appearance, and middle-aged. There was a boy travelling with him — his brother-in-law, Matthew explained, and also an ambassador, though too young to take a personal share in any negotiations. The lad's function in Matthew's train was therefore purely ornamental.

Both arrayed themselves as Moslem merchants, the precious cross was inconspicuously wrapped up in an old rag, and they set out for Zeila. Orders were to sail from there to India and ask the Portuguese Governor for a passage with the homebound fleet.

It certainly was uphill work for Portugal and Abyssinia to communicate. If the voyages of Pero da Covilham and João Gomes had been adventurous, that of Matthew in the other direction was just as bad. It may have been even more difficult, for while the Portuguese had travelled unencumbered, Matthew had brought with him at least one wife.

Accompanied by this lady and her maid, or understudy — contemporary opinion seems uncertain which was which, or what — the ambassadors arrived at Zeila, where they were robbed and imprisoned before they could proceed.[5] Managing to get away from Zeila at last, they took ship to Dabul — from the frying-pan, as it turned out, into the fire.

Dabul was a port belonging to the Moslem kings of Bijapur, and commanded by a captain of the famous Ismail Adil Khan. Devout follower of Islam though Matthew seemed to be, something went wrong. His mission was discovered or suspected, and Matthew found himself in prison once again, while the captain took possession of his goods. The latter sent word to his master, Ismail Adil Khan: exactly what was he to do with Matthew? The crown of Bijapur had recently lost Goa to the Portuguese and did not wish to see the enemy strengthened by any new alliance.

Happily for Matthew, Goa was near Dabul, and it happened that Afonso de Albuquerque, then Governor of India, was at the moment there. He had just inflicted a smashing defeat upon another one of Ismail's officers. The Governor heard about Matthew and sent a message to Dabul: This man had come to speak to him and was on no account to be detained. If Matthew were not released immediately, then Albuquerque would be obliged to do that which he would rather not.

The captain of Dabul did not inquire what "that" might be, though certainly he was between the devil and the deep sea. He had not yet had his reply from Ismail Adil Khan, but he dared not argue with the conqueror of Goa and Malacca. He preferred to set Matthew at liberty, returning all the stolen goods, "without a bodkin missing"! An unfortunate mistake, the captain suavely explained; had it occurred to him that Albuquerque might want to see this man, he would have speeded him to Goa. He proceeded so to do, for which compliance his own angry lord nearly cut off his head.

Agreeably aware that Ismail Adil Khan was foaming at the mouth, Albuquerque welcomed Matthew ostentatiously. The messenger from Prester John could not have arrived at a more significant moment.

It was December of 1512, just over six years since Afonso de Albuquerque had flashed into the Orient and set himself immediately to laying the foundations of an empire. During those six years, first as commander of the fleet off the Arabian coast, and then as Governor of India, he had established Portuguese supremacy from Ormuz to Malacca. Already Persia courted him, Calicut was fawning at his side, the Turkish lords of the Deccan were lashed to heel, and the Moslem kingdom of Cambay was apprehensively polite. There was no longer any power in India that would care to challenge him, and he had just returned from conquering Malacca and bringing the chief kingdoms of the archipelago under Portuguese sway. All this was the progressive working out of a tremendous plan. Uniting the fervour of an imperialist to that of a crusader, Albuquerque dreamed of an empire for his country vaster than the worlds conquered by Alexander that would bring about the triumph of the Cross over the Crescent once for all.

Afonso de Albuquerque, whose birth nearly coincides with the death of the Infante Dom Henrique, is another instance of a man whose whole soul is bound up in an idea to the exclusion of all human aspirations after private happiness or physical repose. Of the two, the case of Albuquerque is perhaps the more remarkable because, even more versatile and many-sided than was the Infante in his gifts, and more complex in character, he equals him in singleness of aim. To Albuquerque his work was life — apart from it he seemed to wish for nothing. If he desired honours, it was only to give him more authority in Asia; he only wanted wealth that he might meet public expense out of his own coffers when funds failed to arrive from home; and the chief reward that he hoped for his services was to be permitted to die at his post.

He knew quite well that he might not live long enough to fulfil his program, and until that was accomplished he could have no rest. As Governor, he worked both day and night, bringing to his task a tenacity that few men have equalled, a military genius that made the hardest conquest seem a simple thing, and a capacity for ruling native races that never failed to win the conquered people's hearts. Albuquerque was, moreover, one of those few men who combine with a vision that sees far into the future a practical realism that takes in little things of every day. We find him dwelling upon grandiose schemes such as that of uniting with the Shiah Shah of Persia to destroy Sunnite Islam and so to reconquer Jerusalem, and giving his attention to homely details such as the packing of cargo for ships, or the distribution of rice rations to poor children of the schools founded by himself for little natives. No design was too magnificent for his imperial edifice, but the smallest stone to be fitted into its structure was worth thought and care.

With all this, no empire-builder ever had scantier material resources at his command. King Manuel of Portugal had large ambitions: he sent elaborate and exacting orders to his captains overseas, but when it came to furnishing the necessary supplies, he seems to have expected the Lord to provide! Shortage of men, of ships or armaments and money was the problem that faced Albuquerque at every turn of his career. In 1507 he had sailed to conquer Ormuz with six ships and 400 men, equipped, as he himself describes, with "weapons few and rotten, the stock of sail-cloth, cables, and ropes depleted, wet gunpowder, few bombardiers, one or two carpenters and coopers, lances all rotten, crossbows without any arrows, and a hundred and fifty men sick unto death . . . we may have had food and water for eight days."

With such a fleet he conquered Kalyat, Kurhat, Muscat, and Sohar on the Oman coast, and finally Ormuz, queen city of the Persian Gulf.

As Governor of India he was scarcely better supplied. "I

entreat Your Highness, send me arms," we find him writing in October 1510. "Many lances, many pikes . . . I have never seen a more pitiful sight than these fortresses — there is not a lance to be found in them!"

He conquered Goa a few weeks later, none the less, with 1,680 men against 10,000 to 12,000 well-armed Turks who held the town for Ismail Adil Khan.

Eight months after this, Albuquerque seized Malacca, with 1,000 against 20,000 men, and the rotten old ship in which he sailed to do the deed broke in two and sank beneath him on the return voyage. He arrived in India with two leaky ships and a handful of men, but even so his name was quite sufficient to dismay the troops sent by Adil Khan to besiege Goa in the conqueror's absence. Albuquerque, with the reinforcements that arrived from Portugal that year, ejected the Moslems from their stronghold at Benastarim by one of those audacious military manœuvres in which he excelled. Ismail saw his last hope of recovering Goa fade away and sent his messengers to ask for peace.

Albuquerque was satisfied with the way that his plans were working out. He held the chief strategic points along the Indian coast, and he had fortified Malacca at the gate of the Far East. Portugal commanded all the trade routes of the Orient except that of the Red Sea. This corner of the map was the weak point and danger spot of Portuguese dominion.

During the past twelve years the Portuguese had come to view the Indian Ocean as their private lake. Their ships patrolled its waves in every direction, challenging any native craft that dared to navigate without the Governor's permit. But the Red Sea was an enigma still. No European fleet had ever sailed into the Arabs' "Enclosed Sea," where "ships of Mecca" bolted into safety. Between the desert shores beyond Bab-el-Mandeb the Crescent reigned supreme, and the Soldan of Egypt was still the chief hope of his co-religionists. The Portuguese had once destroyed his fleet, but it was expected that he would launch another. "The Lord of Cairo is building ships to fight yours," wrote Queen Helena to Dom Manuel. The rumour had reached India before Matthew came, and Suez was said to be the Soldan's naval base. The only menace to Portuguese sea power was Egypt, and Egypt might at any moment be incorporated in the still more dangerous rising empire of the Turk. If Portugal could once obtain control of the Red Sea, then the spice trade would be entirely in her hands, and all the forces of Islam smitten to death.

"I must enter the Straits this year," wrote Albuquerque to his King, and after defeating the troops of Adil Khan he prepared to do so. Matthew's arrival at this moment from those very shores with offers of an Abyssinian alliance was strangely opportune. "If Your Highness could but see," the Governor wrote jubilantly, "what is going on in India since it became known that this was an ambassador from Prester John, it would seem to you as the portent of some great change, so dismayed are the people of India. May it please Our Lord that this should be the beginning of the ruin of the house of Mecca."

Matthew's welcome at Goa was accordingly elaborate.

We received the ambassador with a procession [writes Albuquerque], and went with him to church. There, a sermon was delivered by a preaching friar who showed us the True Cross and held it out for us to kiss, and we touched many jewels with it. Afterwards I accompanied the ambassador to his lodging, where I ordered that he should be well provided for and served. I gave him two slave girls, his countrywomen, for his service and that of his wife, and I also gave him two boys from his country who could speak our language.

Between the tribulations of the past and those that lay before him, Matthew's brief stay at Goa must have been a pleasant interlude. He fared sumptuously in the best rooms of the palace at Goa, waited upon like a great lord. Presents were daily showered upon him and his — at some inconvenience, we imagine, to his hosts. Articles appropriate for complimentary gifts were lacking from Portuguese government stores, to judge by documents that inform us how such objects were collected when occasion arose. Any person possessing something of value might be called upon to hand it over, subject to payment at a future date, sooner or later according to the uncertain ebb and flow of the exchequer.

From records of the settlements of such accounts we learn how, among other things, Matthew was given two gold rings set with rubies, relinquished by one of those Jews who had reported the passage of João Gomes at Suakin; an unknown João Mendes provided a piece of brocade; and a length of damask cloth, two pouches of musk, and a silken girdle were contributed by one Gomes Teixeira. A velvet tunic went to swell Matthew's wardrobe from that of Bastiam Rodrigues, and a similar brocaded garment from João Machado. A "Portuguese mattress, large and good," [6] was taken from another person to soften the ambassadorial slumber, and — public funds being, as usual, low — the Governor advanced 177 cruzados of his own to buy the honoured guest further unspecified requirements. Some gold pieces were also pressed upon Matthew, but "as there were not many of them," writes Albuquerque in a letter to the King, "I made out that I was merely sending him a few samples of the coinage of Your Highness." [7]

Thus enriched and gratified, Matthew sailed for Cannanore together with a letter from the Governor ordering the ambassador to be embarked for Portugal with every honour.

"Ambassador indeed!" sniffed Jorge de Melo, captain of Cannanore, and eyed the unfortunate Matthew askance. It did not really concern Jorge de Melo whether this was an ambassador or not; the matter with him was that he had had a difference of opinion with the Governor and wanted to get his own back in some way.

As Matthew's ill luck would have it, Jorge de Melo was not the only man at Cannanore just then who happened to be in that frame of mind. Francisco Pereira Pestana had not seen eye to eye with his chief regarding the amount of pay that was his due, and felt besides that his own prowess on the battlefield was insufficiently admired. He was now about to sail for Portugal in a very bad temper, and he and Jorge de Melo shook their heads in unison.

Stirring the soup of their resentment was a third party, by the name of Gaspar Pereira. Besides being a professional intriguer, Gaspar Pereira also considered himself to be an injured person. The Governor had proposed taking him to the Red Sea, and Gaspar Pereira did not wish to go. He announced that he was far too ill for such adventures and so lingered at Cannanore with someone else's wife, engaged in his favourite pastime of raising hornets' nests.

Poor Matthew was made into Albuquerque's scapegoat by these three. They seized upon the wretched Armenian's reputation and tore it to shreds. This man, said they, was never sent by Prester John. An Abyssinian should be black, as everybody knew, and Matthew was quite white. He was nothing but a Moslem spy in the service of Egypt; his morals were unspeakable; his credentials were forged. If Afonso de Albuquerque had not been so puffed up with pride he would have seen through the imposition. He had simply let himself be diddled by this man! Such tales were spread till Cannanore bubbled with righteous indignation, and the Moslem traders of that port were only too happy to fan the fire.

The women of Matthew's establishment were also brought into the intrigue. It seems certain that he was not an ideal husband, and between him and his wife (or wives) there was little love. If she would testify against him, one of them was told, the Governor would send Matthew to the stake and have her married to a Portuguese. This dazzling prospect drew the lady, for the conquering strangers enjoyed a huge success among the fair ones of the Orient. Wife and slaves joined in the conspiracy against their lord.

It was Matthew himself, however, who put the fat into the fire by threatening to beat one of his women one fine day. She promptly retaliated by screaming out for all to hear that this man really was a spy and every evil thing that had been said.

Jorge de Melo and his friends rushed to the spot. They drew up documents and signed indictments. The truth was out at last, they cried. The villain was unmasked!

"Our Lord has been pleased to awaken the understanding of Jorge de Melo and his friends that they might know the truth about this dog . . ." piously exclaims one who signs himself João Afonso de Azevedo [8] in a letter to the King. But no message was dispatched to Goa to enlighten the deluded understanding of the Governor.

Was he indeed deluded? some people hinted darkly. He knew about it all the time! asserts Gaspar Pereira, who also hastened to write home this spicy bit of news. The Governor had hushed up the swindle to gain credit for himself. It seemed a great thing to send the King an ambassador from the long-sought and elusive Prester John. "He says that for this service alone Your Highness will make him a count."

No attempt was therefore made to shatter Albuquerque's alleged illusions before he sailed for the Red Sea, nor did they dare to disobey the orders he had sent to Cannanore concerning the ambassador. "Let the chastisement of his villainy rest with Your Highness," Matthew's accusers enjoined the King, and then embarked the criminal after the manner that the Governor commanded.

A document informs us how fifty planks and three hundred nails were supplied to make a store-cupboard and chicken-coop adjoining Matthew's cabin, and that four kitchen basins were provided him as well as a hatchet, a spit for roasting, and two loaves of soap.[9] "He was given a big cabin," writes Albuquerque's secretary, Gaspar Correa,[10] "in which he and his women and servants were well accommodated." This was on board the ship commanded by Bernaldim Freire, a feather-pated youth who swallowed every tale that he was told about his passenger.

Poor Matthew had an awful voyage to Portugal. Bernaldim

Freire, assisted by Francisco Pereira, made a nightmare of his life. They cast him into irons at Moçambique. They boxed his ears and plucked his beard, abused him as a Turkish spy who had deceived that fool Afonso de Albuquerque, and finally appropriated to themselves his wife and slaves.[11]

If, as all contemporaries affirm, it was merely to spite the Governor that his enemies behaved like this, it was an extraordinarily stupid intrigue. For the fact remained that Matthew really had been sent by Queen Helena and carried with him genuine letters. In Portugal, when he presented his credentials to the King, their authenticity was recognized at once.

Dom Manuel was overjoyed. Prester John at last! The King "received the cross upon his knees, with tears in his eyes, thanking God for bestowing such a gift upon him as well as letters and ambassadors from so great a king as that of Abyssinia, so remote and far distant from Europe. . . ."[12] Matthew was welcomed as a heaven-sent messenger. Dom Manuel wrote at once to Rome about his glad arrival, and the despised Armenian now became the hero of an ecstatic correspondence between the Holy Father and the King.

We can imagine how awkward all this was for Bernaldim Freire and Francisco Pereira. Some say that they escaped to Castile, others that the King imprisoned them in Lisbon castle. It is certain that Albuquerque's enemies had overreached themselves for once.

He himself, meanwhile, knew nothing of what had occurred at Cannanore. No one told him until five months later when on the island of Kamaran in the Red Sea. "I was," he wrote the King, "the most astonished man on earth." Why should doubt be thrown upon the veracity of Matthew's mission? Certainly not because he had travelled in Moslem disguise. Had not João Gomes done the same, and his companions? There was no other way of entering or leaving Abyssinia. "If they wish to go out through Zeila, Zeila belongs to Moors. If they wish to pass by Dahlak, Dahlak is Moorish, and if they want to leave by the island of Suakin, Suakin is also of the Moors. . . ."

That Prester John should desire to communicate with Portugal was nothing strange. An alliance would be to their mutual interest. Albuquerque admits that he did not overhaul the envoy's papers to ascertain their authenticity, but then: "It is not for me to cross-examine ambassadors from kings and princes of these parts when they are on their way to you, nor to open their letters and instructions without a special warrant, signed and sealed by you, authorizing me to do so."

As for the suggestion that the man might be a spy from Cairo – why on earth should the Soldan seek information in such a devious and complicated manner? "I have men from Cairo constantly about me, and every day they come with merchandise from overland." And if it was Lisbon that the enemy desired to spy upon: "Are there not in Portugal scores of Venetians, Italians, Florentines, Genoese, and men of other nationalities who have continual dealings with Alexandria and Cairo?"

When, however, on his return to India, Albuquerque inquired into the origin of all the trouble, he ceased to wonder much. "The Lord knows that all this disorder was worked up in the belief that they were hitting me direct." He was used to such tricks from Gaspar Pereira, and: "I am not surprised at Francisco Pereira doing what he did, for he bears me a grudge . . . besides which, *Senhor*, he is a very trying man." As for Francisco's travelling companion: "I am not surprised at Bernaldim Freire, for he is young, and anybody can lead him astray."

It was a relief to learn that the ambassador had been received with honour by the King. Albuquerque was much preoccupied with Prester John since his return from the Red Sea. That voyage had not been wholly a success. Aden had not been captured in the one assault attempted as the fleet passed by. Shortage of water on the ships had left no time to repeat the attack, and lack of wind had made it quite impossible to reach Suez. But Albuquerque had not wasted a minute of the three months and a half that he had spent in the Red Sea. He had made careful observations, he had acquired much useful information, and the appearance of the Portuguese in those waters had shaken the Moslem world with fear. Albuquerque intended that their terror should be justified in the near future. He had his plan of campaign ready, which he expounded to the King.

Prester John was an important figure in the scheme.

4

A Dream in the Desert

The dreary island of Kamaran, "all flat and almost level with the sea," twisted its stunted mangroves within sight of the Arabian coast. The steaming swamps were lost in hot dry sand drifting beside abandoned mosques and large stone buildings that were stately once, erected, it was said, by merchants who in days gone by had traded with the land of Prester John for gold. No one knew when or how or why the town had died; but as a commercial centre Kamaran had ceased to be, and its halls were deserted. In the shadow of the noble ruins a few Arabs built their shacks, for there was water on the island still, and tufts of grass. The dwellers on the desert mainland brought goats and camels there to graze and supplied provisions to passing ships.

In the sheltered port of Kamaran, which looks towards Arabia, Albuquerque's fleet had hung at anchor for eight weeks — from May till July 1513. All day long a hot wind blew feebly across the sea from the Sudan; at night a still more burning breeze moved down the desert coast some leagues away. The east wind, which could have borne the fleet to Jidda or Suez, had taken them to Kamaran and ceased to blow. Twice the fleet had left the island on the wings of a deceitful breeze that died at once, leaving the ships to float between the sandbanks and desert isles. Their sails flapped drearily to fitful puffs from the north-west. Neither bark, nor boat, nor bird flitted across the dead horizon. The shining sea was transparent and very still.

A sailing-ship within the Strait of Bab-el-Mandeb between April and July was rather like a creature in a cage. She could not navigate up channel on the north-west winds prevailing at that season, nor could she sail out of the Red Sea into the monsoon. There was nothing for it but to stay at Kamaran, and there the Portuguese careened their ships. They fed upon stray camels left upon the island, they cast their nets for fish, and caught and ate the weirdly bright-blue or green crabs that swam in the translucent water. They whiled away the time by playing chess or cards, and every day they saw their comrades die. The summer months at Kamaran were not healthful for Europeans.

While his men counted the days, and cursed their fate, their commander discussed the land of Prester John with an interesting prisoner who introduced himself as Lord of Massawa and Sheik of Dahlak. This elderly and distinguished-looking "Moor," captured with a nephew at Kamaran, seems to have had plenty to say about himself and others. He airily explained his own presence on the island by the fact that he had killed his cousin's father. The cousin, not unnaturally incensed, had obtained assistance from the Sheik of Aden, and so dislodged the Sheik of Dahlak from his lands and sent him into exile across the sea.

Albuquerque and the Sheik appear to have entertained each other very well during their stay at Kamaran. Having been forcibly ejected from the opposite coast, the Sheik had no secrets to keep about those parts and answered every question asked with a grim satisfaction. The island of Massawa, he said, was so close to the Abyssinian mainland that "a man could shout and be heard on the other shore," and the Sheik had all his life had intercourse with the Ethiopians of the coast. He was so informative that Albuquerque proposed sending him to Portugal along with other prisoners, but on their way to India the man died. His nephew, "who knows the language of Prester John and that of Dahlak," was dispatched to the King instead, together with an Arab pilot whose wife and children lived at Jidda — "a marvellous man, by whom Your Highness may be better informed."

Two genuine Abyssinians were also added to the collection of distinguished foreigners gathered in the Red Sea and sent home for the information of His Highness. Abyssinian slaves — poor simple wretches kidnapped by Arab traders in the hinterland of Massawa — were common enough in India, but these two men were educated Abyssinians. They had been pilgrims on their way to Jerusalem when they were taken prisoner by the Moslems of Suakin. Having escaped, they joined the Portuguese at Aden, and Albuquerque easily persuaded them to visit Portugal instead of Palestine. "They are men versed in our doctrine," he tells the King; "one of them knows how to write his language very well, and I also send Your Highness an Abyssinian youth who was slave of the Soldan's factor at Jidda. I send him as interpreter for the two others, who cannot speak Arabic, which he speaks very well, besides the language of his own country."

With information gleaned from such as these, added to his own observations, Albuquerque studied the political problems of the Red Sea. For Portuguese supremacy in those waters, he told the King, all that was necessary would be to occupy Aden and Massawa.

The shores of the Red Sea in 1513 had many masters, some nominal and others real. On the African side, from Bab-el-Mandeb up to Suakin was theoretically subject to Prester John. In practice, however, the Emperor's authority was slight over the Moslem tribes that occupied long stretches of the coast. They paid him tribute, it is true; but Abyssinia, having no navy, could not control a single port.

Ethiopian rule, such as it was, expired at Suakin. The desert shores above, where roamed wild tribes of Bedouin, belonged to the Soldan of Egypt. The only town upon this coast was the abandoned city of Kosseir, "with ruined churches bearing signs of crosses on their walls, and Greek inscriptions that appear to indicate that it was once inhabited by Christians."

Suez was the Soldan's chief port and naval base. There in his shipyards lay the half-finished ships that were intended to eject the Portuguese from India. The Soldan could not look forward to the realization of this pleasant hope in the immediate future, however, for the wood destined to build his fleet had been captured at Rhodes by the Knights of St. John.

Egyptian rule on the Arabian side of the Red Sea extended as far south as Jidda, the port at which the faithful disembarked to visit Mecca. The Sheriff of Jidda and Mecca, who held the desert inland, "may have three hundred horsemen and no more, and some of these are Bedouin mounted on camels." South of Jidda was the Sheriff of Jizem — "six hundred horse, no more" — and from Kamaran to the mouth of the Straits was the dominion of the Sheik of Aden.

After the Soldan, the great power of the Red Sea was indisputably the Sheik of Aden. Not only was he Lord of the Gulf, but, thanks to his intervention at Dahlak, he controlled all those islands. The Sheik of Aden had not given his help for nothing, and the exile of Kamaran's usurping cousin had gained little but a barren title with his revenge. He was allowed to live at Massawa on a pension while the Sheik of Aden placed a servant of his own to collect the revenues of the pearl fisheries that lay all around the islands of Massawa and Dahlak. These revenues were considerable, for Arabs came in *djelbas* to fish there from all parts of the coast, and, added to the duties that they paid, the first and last two days of each man's fishing belonged entirely to the island lord.

It was Aden that supported Zeila, just outside the Straits: "The Lord of Zeila and Berbera is a very small thing — he cannot have two hundred horse; he is maintained by charitable offerings from the hinterland of Aden and those parts, because he makes continual war upon the Christians of Prester John."

A Dream in the Desert

The Sheik of Aden could afford to spend his money upon such pious works for, between the pearls of Dahlak and the port of Aden, he must have been doing very well.

Aden [Albuquerque informs the King] has become a great port since Your Highness entered India, because your fleet prevents the ships of Jidda and Mecca from navigating at the proper season. As they leave late, they cannot enter the Straits and have to discharge their merchandise at Aden. They sell it there and buy other goods that are brought there from Jidda and those parts, and the merchants of Aden send the goods to Jidda later on in their ships. In Aden are many merchants from Cairo who have great riches in the town. Many merchants from Jidda have also come to live at Aden because their ships cannot reach the port of Jidda at the right time. For this reason Aden has grown much more important than it used to be. It is reputed to be the wealthiest place out here; most of the gold of Prester John goes into Aden, and all merchandise from the land of Prester John.

Aden commands the mouth of the Straits, and all the ships of India on their way to Jidda pass by Aden during the months of November, December, and January and February. . . .

The strategic advantages of holding such a place were obvious, besides which "Your ships would have a marvellous port there, sheltered from every wind — thus a fortress at Aden would be a sound and profitable thing."

Equally sound and profitable would be the fortress at Massawa. A territorial base was necessary for a permanent naval force to be maintained in the Red Sea, and that was where the land of Prester John came in. The "men like unto the sands of the sea," so lavishly offered by Queen Helena, are not the foundation on which Albuquerque's calculations are drawn up; he had lived in the Orient quite long enough to know what value might be set upon figures of speech. The Abyssinians, he says, "are renowned as very brave, and esteemed by the Moors, who know them to be valiant men." Their help would no doubt come in useful to the garrison of Massawa, but he lays no special stress on the man-power of Abyssinia.

Massawa "would be a good port for our ships, because it touches the land of Prester John, is the principal port of his country, and replete with provisions, and reinforcements of men if necessary, or any other thing that we might need. . . ." The Portuguese could also barter pepper and other Indian merchandise for gold from Abyssinia, and exploit the pearl fisheries of Dahlak.

He [the Sheik of Dahlak] told me that Prester John had often tried to gain the island of Massawa, but had no means of crossing over. He had already attempted to fill up the arm of the sea between the island and the mainland, but could not. Moreover, he told me that Prester John greatly desired to see us and have intercourse with us and he believed that if a captain of Your Highness went there with the fleet, Prester John would come to visit him in person, and to see Your Highness's ships.

A Portuguese fortress at Massawa, backed by the power of Prester John, would dominate the whole of the Red Sea to the Soldan's complete undoing. "All the riches of the world will be in your hands," Albuquerque tells Dom Manuel. Besides the gold and pearls to be collected, there would be no more leaking out of spices to the West through Moslem channels, "and you could moreover prevent any merchandise from Cairo and those ports from entering India except in your ships." As for the Egyptian navy — sole menace to Portuguese supremacy in Eastern waters — "Once we have gained a footing in the Red Sea, the smallest fleet that visits Suez, if anything is breeding there, can burn as many ships as they can launch before they are armed or equipped."

As a seaman Albuquerque was fully aware that the type of vessel designed for sailing the Atlantic and the Indian Ocean was unsuitable for permanent service in the Red Sea. The sixteenth-century Portuguese *nau*, with her towering superstructure, her enormous square sails, and depth of keel requiring at least three fathoms to float safely, was the most awkward thing to navigate among the shoals and shallows of those

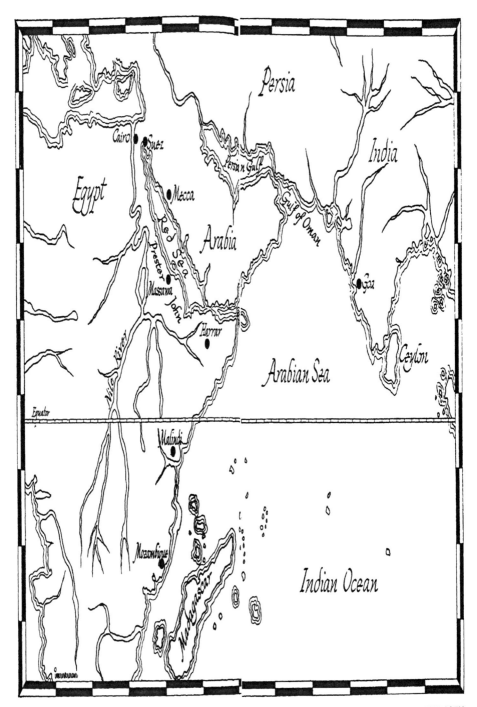

RELATIONSHIP OF PORTUGUESE INDIA TO THE LAND OF PRESTER JOHN

land-locked waters. "If the Lord please that we should establish ourselves on the Red Sea," writes Albuquerque, "and explode this menace of Suez and the Soldan's fleet, Your Highness must exchange the square-rigged ships for galleys, with perhaps three or four *naus* among them. Galleys," he explains, "can be beached and repaired anywhere, and enter any place."

This question, however, could be studied later. The first steps to be taken were "to settle the affair of Aden, and build a fortress at Massawa. . . . I should fortify myself in those two places," he advises the King, "and spread no further for the present until these two things are settled."

After that, there was no limit to the possibilities! One need only look around and take one's choice:

Once Your Highness has a base in the land of Prester John, you can decide what you want to do with Zeila. Perhaps Prester John would like you to destroy it, but, having a fortress at Aden, we shall have to draw provisions from Berbera and Zeila, for Aden is supplied from there with corn, butter, sheep, maize, and honey. . . .

As for the island of Suakin . . . it will be useful for the gold that comes not through it . . . fifty men can hold the place quite easily.

Zeila and Suakin were mere side issues — Jidda was more important. Once Massawa was Portuguese, however, then Jidda would be theirs:

For neither spice, nor merchandise, nor food could reach it from outside, and if the Soldan would maintain a garrison, he could not feed the men, for he would have no source of supply; whereas Your Highness can hold the place and draw provisions from the land of Prester John, just opposite.

Prester John would also furnish the Portuguese with mounts — "there are many good horses in the land of Prester John." These could be shipped across to Jidda, and in one lightning raid their riders would burn Mecca to the ground. To destroy Mecca strikes Albuquerque as very easy, nor would many men be necessary to do the deed. The Sheriff was not powerful, and in Mecca itself were no men-at-arms, only a few devotees "with henna-stained nails, and rosaries in their hands." Nor was Egypt likely to help the holy city, for

the succour the Soldan could send to Mecca would not be much. He has seven thousand horsemen within his fortress, which has a wider enclosure than that of Evora. He will not part with any of these, for they are his bodyguard, and every now and then some of those alguazils who succeed to the throne attack them and thrust them out. His Emirs, which are his chief captains, will not give up any of their own men, nor yet themselves leave Cairo. Neither the Lord of Damascus, nor that of Aleppo and those other fortresses near Shah Ismail's frontiers would leave them unprotected. Therefore it seems to me that the Soldan might send a thousand horse, and to provide those for the march would mean ten thousand camels and a constant supply of provisions from Cairo, which would be very difficult to organize from such a distance. But let us say that he sends two thousand horse — could not five or six hundred Portuguese, on a good day and in a fortunate hour, fight against two or three thousand Moorish horsemen and defeat them and put them all to flight? And if it seemed to us that there was any risk about it, there are so many good horses in the land of Prester John that it would be an easy thing to mount a thousand Portuguese, the more so that the passage is so short. . . . I have in mind greater things than these that we could do if once we gain a footing there, and make alliance with the land of Prester John.

He did not forget that Abyssinia held the upper reaches of the Nile. Therein lay certain victory over Egypt:

If the King our Lord would send out some of those engineers who make cuttings through the mountains of Madeira, they could divert the flood of the Nile and turn it aside from watering the lands of Cairo — thus in two years Cairo would be undone, and the whole country ruined. . . .

A thrust at Islam such as Albuquerque proposed would have meant the deliverance of Christendom from the spectre that had haunted it for seven centuries. To understand the full significance of that we must view it through the eyes of those who lived four hundred years ago, when the capture of Constantinople by the Turks was still a living memory. Panic-mongers in modern times have talked about the yellow peril, but the Moslem menace to Europe of that day was no alarmist's scare. It was a palpitating and hideous reality. Pressing hard on the confines of Christendom all through the Middle Ages were the dreaded scimitars wielded by Moor, Arab, or Turk — an alien race, an alien faith, an alien civilization — ever waiting to bear down and swallow up. How many times they really had swept over, how often the fate of the Western world had trembled in the balance, we have only to read our history books to recollect. The tide had been held back, but not yet turned. The great Christian empire to be built in the East — Portugal backed up by Prester John — would deal the death blow in the foeman's flank, and win the final victory for the Cross. It is not strange that Portuguese imperialists felt themselves to be workers on a design approved by God.

On a dark night in the Red Sea, when the fleet lay at anchor outside the harbour, hoping for a breeze, a brilliant cross rose in the sky and shone over the land of Prester John. It was clearly seen from each one of the ships, and all the men fell on their knees. "I took it that Our Lord had sent this sign," wrote Albuquerque, "to show that He would have us go that way." But still no wind arose that could have blown the fleet over to Massawa.

Albuquerque's duties as Governor of India obliged him to return there after the monsoon. The fleet from Portugal reached India between August and October, and there were all the mails to be received and answered, the homebound fleet to be dispatched, and hundreds of other matters to be looked into. Shortage of time to get through all the work that rested on his shoulders handicapped Albuquerque as seriously as the shortage of more material things. In 1513 he returned to India from the Red Sea in September, fully determined to sail back again early the following year: "I must leave for the Straits in January," he told the King, "if any profit is to come of it." But he found his ships were quite unfit to navigate so soon; their wooden sides were warped and blistered and burst open by the scorching sun of the Red Sea. By great good luck all except one survived the return voyage, but none of them could sail again without wholesale repair. That fort of Massawa on which so much depended could not be built just then.

The project became the fixed purpose on which Albuquerque's mind was bent for the remaining two years of his life. He thought of it all through 1514 in India as he took a hand in the intricate game of Indian politics. When, in 1515, a number of circumstances obliged him to build a fort at Ormuz instead of sailing into the Red Sea, he only postponed Prester John and Massawa to the next year.

"We have no unsettled question left in India now but that of Aden and the Red Sea," he wrote from Ormuz to the King on September 22, and: "May it please Our Lord," he says upon another page of the same letter, "that we should fix ourselves at Massawa — the port of Prester John." By that date Albuquerque must have realized that he himself had little chance to do it; yet when, on November 8, desperately ill, he left the Persian Gulf for India, it appears that he clung to his idea still. "He told me," writes the captain of the Ormuz garrison, "that on the 1st of January I was to send part of the fleet and men to him for entering the Straits. . . ." If he had made any sort of recovery, it is clear that he meant to waste no time in convalescing, but somehow to drag himself to Massawa and build that fort!

And if he had done so — what then? Could the rest of his program have been carried out? Would it have been possible to destroy Mecca and give Egypt to the desert — to change the history of the world and alter the face of the map?

It certainly seems wild, but there was never anything of the unpractical visionary in Albuquerque. He showed at all times a firm grasp of fact and a keen sense of reality. Anything he set himself to do he did, and much of what he achieved appeared impossible. Whether this last scheme was workable we speculate in vain, for the only man whose genius might have realized the dream died at the zenith of his glory, and the brilliant vision was extinguished with his light.

5

A Frustrated Mission

One day at Evora — so runs the tale — the King, Dom Manuel, ordered a tunic to be made out of a rich Oriental cloth.

The tunic turned out a success. Dom Manuel was pleased with his appearance when he put it on. He disported himself in his new garment before all the courtiers, who dutifully went into ecstasies. Duarte Galvão, the elderly historian, alone gazed with a disapproving eye. Not thus, he observed austerely, had Dom Manuel's predecessors on the throne of Portugal behaved. Duty was what engrossed those kingly minds, not dress!

Dom Manuel responded to this admonition by appointing Duarte Galvão ambassador to Prester John upon the spot.

The tunic story may be fact or fiction, but that the sequel was the King's revenge is certainly untrue. Court gossips might well represent it in that light. To be torn away from the amenities of palace life and embark for the wilds of Abyssinia would be a grim chastisement to these butterflies, but it is certain that Duarte Galvão did not view it so. We have it on his own authority that there was nothing that he more ardently desired. He felt that such an embassy would be a unique opportunity for serving God. "I should be very happy," he wrote to his friend Afonso de Albuquerque, "if the King would send me." He might be rather old for an undertaking of that nature, but: "There is neither old age nor weakness in the service of God, so long as there are devotion and good will. . . ."

This letter is undated, but we gather from the context that it was written in 1513. Matthew had not yet arrived in Portugal, but it was already known that he was on the way, and the idea of an embassy to Prester John was being earnestly discussed.

The envoy's warm reception when his ship came in at last has already been seen. For a year Matthew was entertained in Portugal, together with his young companion, whose name was Jacob, we are told. Receiving ambassadors was expensive in those days. Not only had one to lodge and feed one's guests, but to dress them as well. Dom Manuel played the host in style. The strangers lived in luxury at his gorgeous court, and their wardrobe was renewed every few months.

The King, meanwhile, prepared a fitting answer to his long-sought ally Prester John. Matthew would return to Abyssinia in the train of a fully equipped Portuguese embassy, complete with present. The latter was an offering worthy of one great king to another. To enumerate all the beautiful and costly objects mentioned in the list that has come down to us would take too long. It must have required a miracle of packing, but the desirability of travelling light was not considered in those spacious days.

Chief among the rich collection figured a lordly bed — a bed of ample size we gather from the fact that the four fine linen sheets that went with it were nearly five yards long. The sleeper reclining upon this couch would be sheltered by blue and yellow taffeta curtains, with a tastefully painted canopy above. An emperor with a crown upon his head sat there aloft, in the act of crowning a queen, while four men sounded trumpets in the corner. Six large mattresses stuffed with merino wool were provided for this super-bed; the bolsters and the pillows, also stuffed with wool, were embroidered in gold. For chilly nights a woollen blanket, embellished with the ar-

47

morial bearings of Dom Manuel, was thoughtfully supplied.
The bed-cover was of yellow damask and black velvet inter-
woven with gold threads, and there was also a white embroidered counterpane. As a suitable background for such a bed
were Flemish cloths of silk and gold to hang upon the bedroom wall. Rich cushions of all kinds were added to the gift,
and a brocaded chair studded with silver nails.

Not only Prester John's bedroom but also his dining-room
was to be furnished by Dom Manuel. He had a beautiful table
made in finest marquetry for his royal brother, with a cloth of
silk and gold to spread upon it. A complete dinner-service
went with this, including knives, fruit-dishes, and several sets
of tablecloths, each over eight yards long – napkins and hand-
towels as well, all embroidered in gold.

Two complete costumes – "everything required to dress a
man from shirt to cloak" – were likewise offered, one in silk
and gold, the second in damask; rich suits of armour, swords,
shields, harness for horses – everything in gold, silver, and
finest steel.

After supplying Prester John the wherewithal to sleep,
dress, dine, and fight in dazzling elegance, his spiritual and
intellectual needs were contemplated. All things pertaining
to religious service and the complete equipment of a church
were provided: devotional pictures, candles, altar-pieces,
vestments, organs, bells, illuminated missals, and Legends of
the Saints in Portuguese. Thirty books of catechism were
moreover added, and finally a thousand children's reading-
books.

These are only a few items of Dom Manuel's tremendous
gift.

It took some preparation, but there was plenty of time.
Matthew's unpleasant voyage from India had been particularly long. Though he had left Cannanore in January 1513, he
only disembarked in Lisbon thirteen months later. The fleet
for India always sailed in the spring. It was too late to join the
1514 voyage, but the embassy was organized to leave the fol-

lowing year. In 1515 Duarte Galvão hoped to see his heart's desire fulfilled. Duarte Galvão was a man of letters and his delight took literary form. He sat down happily and penned a stirring Exhortation, urging all men to join the holy enterprise of Christian expansion overseas.

The King's choice of ambassador was sound in many ways. Duarte Galvão had experience and learning, and we have seen that he took a serious view of life. He had been secretary to Afonso V and counsellor to both Dom João II and Dom Manuel. Foreign affairs seem to have been the special sphere of his activity, and his diplomatic talent had been proved on more than one occasion when he was sent on embassies to Louis XII of France, the Emperor Maximilian, and the Pope. Oriental affairs also interested him, and when, in 1500, Pedralvares Cabral had sailed for Calicut, the letter in Arabic and Portuguese which he carried for the Samorin had been drafted by Duarte Galvão.

Against all this has to be set his age. Duarte Galvão was seventy. A less optimistic generation might have thought he was too old to travel so far, but the sixteenth century showed a superb disregard for such material details. That same year Dom Manuel was appointing to be Governor of India a man subject to epileptic fits. If an infirmity of that kind were no obstacle to occupying a strenuous post of high command, then a healthy septuagenarian might well go to Abyssinia!

The other members of the Ethiopian mission were Lopo de Vilalobos, who was to act as secretary; Lourenço de Cosmo, in charge of the present; and the chaplain, Padre Francisco Alvares, of later fame as the first European to write a book on Abyssinia. Duarte Galvão's young son Jorge also went east with him, not as a delegate, but to serve in India, where his brother Ruy already had spent several years.

Our friend Matthew, of course, accompanied the embassy, as well as the boy Jacob. Each one received for parting gift a complete new outfit of apparel: breeches, doublets, tunics, cloaks, several pairs of shoes, slippers, and hosen; six fine

linen shirts and six pairs of pants for Matthew, two of each for
the boy — all of these garments packed in a handsome leather
trunk closed by two locks.

What had happened to Matthew's wife (or wives) by then
we cannot say. The chronicles are silent and the documents
refer to them no more. His retinue included a number of
slaves and servants, and we now hear of an Abyssinian friar.
Where the latter had been picked up is not explained. It
seems that Matthew introduced him as a very holy man of
exalted connections in his native country.

So the two ambassadors set sail — and quarrelled all the
way. It is difficult to tell whose was the fault. Perhaps we
should not blame either too severely — a six months' voyage,
cramped quarters in a little ship, nothing to do, and the same
faces every day! It could be a strain on anyone's good nature,
and Matthew had a very peculiar temper, while Duarte Galvão was a peppery old gentleman. To add to the general un-
pleasantness, Matthew and his holy man fell foul of each
other. This was no good Christian but a Moslem, Matthew
said, and the holy man resented the insult. Finally, by way
of climax to a disagreeable voyage, the youth Jacob became
very ill.

When the fleet came into port at Goa, matters did not im-
prove. It is important to remember that this fleet had sailed
under the command of Lopo Soares de Albergaria, an inca-
pable and rather stupid epileptic, chosen by the King to su-
persede a genius. The series of petty intrigues that had led to
his appointment as Governor of India do not concern us here.
What bore directly upon the embassy to Prester John was the
fact that Lopo Soares's sense of inferiority found expression
in a black and bitter hatred for everything connected with
his mighty predecessor. It was well known that Albuquerque
had attached great importance to Matthew and his mission;
consequently Lopo Soares frowned on both. He appears to
have had a certain respect for Duarte Galvão, but Galvão had

been Albuquerque's friend, which was quite enough for the new Governor to dislike him.

The fleet made the briefest call at Goa — not much longer than was necessary for Lopo Soares to make his entry in the town as Governor. Correct procedure would have been to wait till Albuquerque's return from Ormuz and take over from him, but when dealing with his rival Lopo Soares did not care to be correct. It would be humiliating for Albuquerque to arrive and find that he had been dispossessed, so Lopo Soares assumed control at once.

While the Governor was ashore introducing himself to the unenthusiastic Goanese, he received a letter from Duarte Galvão, who had not disembarked: the Abyssinian boy was getting worse. Sixteenth-century ships did not cater for invalids, and Duarte Galvão, at Matthew's request, begged Lopo Soares to have him received into Goa hospital for treatment. Lopo Soares took no notice at all, nor would he even trouble to have a physician sent to the patient on board.

The fleet sailed for Cochin via Chaul and Cannanore. Poor Jacob's condition became desperate, and between Baticala and Cannanore he died. Matthew was devoted to the boy, and his grief was pathetic. Duarte Galvão, irascible though he might be, was a kind soul. He forgot that he and Matthew could not bear each other, and sat by the dying Jacob, says Padre Francisco Alvares, "until the end, consoling the ambassador and expounding to him the doctrines of Holy Mother Church."

The colleagues seemed completely reconciled. Jacob was "buried honourably" at Cannanore, and Father Francisco remained some days ashore with Matthew to arrange for Masses for the dead boy's soul. Matthew decided to buy a palm grove to endow the church to this effect, and had a note sent to Duarte Galvão on the ship requesting him to come ashore and give advice.

All would have been quite serene if Padre Francisco had

not added to the letter his petition that the Abyssinian monk, who had also fallen very ill, should be brought ashore and interned in the hospital.

Duarte Galvão came at once, bringing the invalid, whereupon, to everyone's surprise, Matthew went off into a purple fury. They had let Jacob die, he cried, and they would save this Moslem monk!

"If he were either Moor or Jew," replied Duarte Galvão, "why on earth did you bring him with you from Portugal and say that he was such a holy man?"

Matthew's answer was a burst of Arabic that the interpreter absolutely declined to translate.

Duarte Galvão beat a dignified retreat. "When he is calmer," said he to the interpreter, "tell him that I withdrew to trouble him no further." [1] But Matthew showed no signs of calming down. He turned upon Padre Francisco. How had he dared send for that monk? When Prester John heard of it, he would have Padre Francisco cut up into slices, bit by bit, and when Jacob's father knew, he would kill all the Portuguese!

In Portugal, remarked the interpreter reprovingly, one did not speak like that to one's father confessor! Whereupon the mercurial Matthew, suddenly repentant, threw himself at the chaplain's feet and kissed his hand, begging for his forgiveness and his blessing. Father Francisco gave him both at once like a good Christian, but to make peace with Matthew's enraged colleague was more difficult. There seem to have been further passages of arms between them, for Lopo de Vilalobos, the secretary, states that, dropping into Matthew's lodging he found him in tears: Duarte Galvão had been calling him a Moor, wailed Matthew, and it was a lie!

Unfortunately, there was too much time for this sort of thing. Lopo Soares did not propose to sail for the Red Sea before January 1517. Meanwhile the embassy was at a loose end.

It must have been a very unpleasant year in India. Everybody seems to have been quarrelling with someone else, and the Governor made no attempt to put things right. He himself was in a sour temper. The triumph that he had looked forward to did not come off. His enemy had indeed returned from Ormuz in December, but the man perversely died before he disembarked! Lopo Soares felt himself foiled, and more than ever viewed the Abyssinian delegation with a jaundiced eye. Matthew declares that he treated him "worse than a captive," while Duarte Galvão complains of the Governor's curt and offhand manner towards himself. On his side, Lopo Soares told the old man that his character was very difficult!

Duarte Galvão was hurt. Never, said he stiffly, had such a thing been suggested before! Three kings of Portugal had he served and he had had dealings with many others of Christendom, to say nothing of emperors and popes. Never had any of these exalted personages found him otherwise than easy to get on with. "I rise and depart," said he majestically, "happy in the esteem in which the aforesaid princes have ever held me."

Beyond this consoling thought he found solace in the study of the Abyssinian alphabet, two copies of which he made out for Dom Manuel. "I am very pleased with them," he writes, "and so will Your Highness be when you see them." His enthusiasm for his mission remained quite undamped. He told the King that he had never been so keen on any other, "though this one is more difficult and I am older. . . ."

When 1517 at last came round he was one of the minority who did not embark plunged in profoundest gloom. The Red Sea cruise was organized with two objectives: to land the embassy upon the African coast and then to seek out and fight the Turkish fleet wherever it might be. This was the year when Salman Rais, the Turkoman, embarked on his career of conquest. Already his men were occupying the Red Sea ports and building themselves ships. The veterans of India had not the least objection to fighting the Turk; the trouble was that they did not wish to go with Lopo Soares. As one of their number has set on record: "The men of India had no pleasure in serving under Lopo Soares, seeing that he was hostile to everything connected with Afonso de Albuquerque, whom they all loved with all their hearts."

It would have been difficult to love Lopo Soares. They say that he seldom spoke to anyone, and when he did, it was ungraciously. His subordinates in India acted much as they liked — one gentleman even took possession of a ship and set up as a pirate on his own account — but in the Governor's presence no man might sit, nor cover his head save on the rare occasions when requested so to do. This, Lopo Soares felt, was discipline!

The men of India were not used to being treated like that. The late Governor had never hedged himself round with such ritual. He had ruled them with a rod of iron and worked them off their feet, but he had always been their comrade none the less, and even his enemies admit that he had pleasant manners. He had been a martinet, no doubt, but he was a martinet with a sense of humour, and though his rebukes were withering, they also made one laugh. In Lopo Soares there was not a gleam of fun. He was a stick, and very disagreeable.

Duarte Galvão, thrilled to the core at the prospective fulfilment of his sacred mission, thought it a pity that anyone should sail reluctantly. He caused his Exhortation to be circulated in the fleet, to see if that would cheer them up. It was, one reader observes admiringly, "a very substantial treatise, setting forth the praise and honour due to the conquerors of India . . . and the great merit before God of those who lost their lives in such a war. . . ." Duarte Galvão was a historian, and noble examples from the past flowed from his pen. None of these, he affirmed, were equal to the achievements in India, which were miraculous, the greatest in the world, and brought about by God! The effect of this disquisition upon the temperamental souls who read it was dynamic. A flame of enthusiasm leaped in every breast "because the happenings in India being quite modern and of recent memory, many felt that these praises applied to them." In a happy glow of self-satisfaction, retrospective and prospective, all put out to sea,

As for Matthew, he sailed in an angelic frame of mind. Before embarking he had sought out Duarte Galvão and "begged to be forgiven for the love of God." They ought to be good friends, said Matthew, since they were bound on such a holy errand — Father Francisco's words, no doubt; the good priest seems to have been working hard in the interests of peace between the two ambassadors, for "both are my spiritual sons," says he benignly. Duarte Galvão agreed to draw a veil over the past, but he and Matthew wisely embarked on different ships. Padre Francisco, at Duarte Galvão's request, went with his fiery penitent, "so that I might consolidate their friendship."

It was a good thing for poor Matthew that the chaplain remained by him. The ship's captain, a nephew of Lopo Soares, showed himself worthy of his charming uncle by being unpleasant to his passenger. More than once Padre Francisco intervened to prevent the Armenian's being cheated of his rations. Despite such provocation, Matthew's advance in grace continued to surprise his ghostly father: "He who used to be like a furious lion now showed himself as gentle as a lamb." After all, said Matthew philosophically, he would be at home in a few weeks. It hardly was worth while to make a fuss.

Before entering the Straits, the fleet halted at Aden. The Sheik was panic-stricken when he saw so many ships — thirty-eight — sailing all together! The fleet that had passed in 1513 was not much over half that size. He sent a messenger on board at once with the keys of the town to offer to Lopo Soares.

Lopo Soares waved them aside with many thanks. He had no time, said he, to go into this matter. All that he wanted now were pilots and provisions. On his return from the Red Sea he would be happy to accept the town.

The *fidalgos* gasped, the messenger was just a little stag-

gered — and Afonso de Albuquerque must have turned in his
grave!

The Sheik could scarcely believe in his luck. He sounded
trumpets and lit bonfires on the hills. He covered the sea with
boatloads of provisions for the fleet and sent them all the pilots
that they required. Thus they were speeded on their way and
the Sheik no doubt thumbed his nose when he saw them
depart.

Red Sea navigation was never easy for deep-draught sail-
ing-ships. Albuquerque had found too little wind, Lopo Soares
encountered too much. To make matters worse, against the
advice of the pilots, he refused to anchor by night. The whole
fleet nearly came to grief in consequence, and one smaller
boat completely vanished. Some forty men, including Duarte
Galvão's son Jorge, had been on board. It was surmised that
they had run aground and might yet reappear, but for Jorge's
father the suspense was cruel.

Following this loss the old ship *Frol da Rosa* broke in two.
The crew was rescued, but some valuable artillery remained
on board. It was suggested to the Governor that a ship go
alongside and save it. "Tonight," answered Lopo Soares.
"However," says Gaspar Correa, "the ship did not wait till
then, but sank."

Meanwhile the ship *São Pedro,* with Father Francisco and
Matthew, had dropped behind and then been blown away.
They found themselves entangled among the reefs and islands
between Suakin and Dahlak. They remained three weeks before this island, not knowing what had happened to the rest
of the fleet.

At Dahlak Matthew had the pleasure of meeting several
acquaintances, both Christian and Moslem. He seems to have
enjoyed his own prestige as envoy newly returned from the
court of the great King of Portugal, and he let his public know
that a magnificent present was on its way to Prester John. In
spite of all this he urged the captain not to stay at Dahlak.
The inhabitants, he said, were treacherous and unsafe. Let

them anchor rather near Arkiko, whence they could get into touch with the Bahr Nagach who ruled the land near the sea-coast for Prester John. Padre Francisco volunteered to go and seek that dignitary himself with a few others. The captain, however, like his uncle, was determined to pay no attention to anything that Matthew might suggest.

Two caravels appeared about this time, one of them in charge of Lourenço de Cosmo. The Governor had sent them to reconnoitre the coast. The captain of *São Pedro*, anxious to get rid of Matthew, promptly transferred him to Lourenço de Cosmo's ship and sailed to join his uncle's fleet at Kamaran.

Matthew, left behind under protest, continued to urge Lourenço de Cosmo and the other captain not to stay at Dahlak. They preferred to listen to the slippery Grenadine interpreter who came with them, and arranged that they should land and parley with the Sheik of the island. Matthew refused to disembark with them, and therein showed that he was wise. Lourenço de Cosmo and two others were killed, while the rest managed to escape. Admitting too late that the Armenian had been right, the survivors sailed back to Kamaran.

Matthew's colleague had not been having a more satisfactory time. Duarte Galvão's ship had continued to follow the fleet, and Lopo Soares announced that Jidda was his first objective. It was suggested that the fleet was short of water and it might be well to take on supplies at Kamaran before proceeding farther, but the Governor scouted the idea. Were not the Turks installed at Jidda with eighteen newly-built galleys? Lopo Soares would not turn back for anything until he had burned those Turkish ships! They were no true knights, but Jews and cowards, who would do otherwise. To Jidda he would go!

And to Jidda he went, full sail. There were the Turks all right, also the galleys, and plenty of artillery besides, which fired on the ships as they zigzagged into port. Regardless of the fire, the fleet manœuvred in and out of the sandbanks and narrow channels, while the Turks looked on amazed at such a display of seamanship. It was an impressive prelude. Everyone expected something thrilling to be staged next day. The *fidalgos* waited breathlessly for their commander to propound to them his plan of attack.

Three days passed. The fleet lay at anchor in the port of Jidda. The Portuguese looked at the Turks, who watched them with interest. Absolutely nothing happened. Then, one fine morning, signalling to his fleet to follow, Lopo Soares calmly sailed away. The captains swore and cursed, Duarte Galvão remonstrated, while the Turks howled with joy. Fernão Gomes de Lemos, who had fought with elephants at Malacca, disregarded the command and hung behind. He started firing at the galliot nearest to him, but the galliot simply fled, so Fernão Gomes got no fun.

Lopo Soares locked himself up in his cabin. "Go away and do not disturb me!" he told Duarte Galvão. But acoustics are good on wooden ships, and the old-timers waxed reminiscent just outside his door. Lopo Soares could hear the most withering comparisons drawn between him and his predecessor.

Duarte Galvão supposed that now, at any rate, the embassy would be escorted to the opposite coast, but Lopo Soares said that it would be imprudent to divide the fleet. On the other hand, to leave the Red Sea was impossible, the monsoon season having started in the Indian Ocean. They therefore made for Kamaran — a nightmare voyage.

The water supply had all but given out. A quarter of a pint was each man's daily allowance, and that in a blazing heat "that burned men's bodies up." They died cursing the Governor for dragging them to Jidda uselessly.

The dismal island of Kamaran was welcomed as a haven of salvation. Water was there! Men, half crazy with thirst and heat, threw themselves bodily into the blessed element, and lingered in it "until they fell and died."

Following the agony of sailing thirsty over a burning sea came that of starvation on the desert sand. Kamaran had been described as purgatory in 1513, but this year it was hell. On the previous occasion there had been at least camels to eat. This time the island offered absolutely nothing. One small ration of boiled rice was dealt out daily, and men had to subsist on that. In 1513 Albuquerque had succeeded in obtaining occasional provisions from the Yemen coast. Lopo Soares tried to do the same, but failed. "Return to Jidda!" he was told derisively. That absurd performance was the joy of all the sheiks by the Red Sea. Never was a commander's prestige more completely gone. Lopo Soares scarcely dared to come ashore, his own men cursed him so. They wrote insults upon the walls, and swam out to his ship at night merely to shout abuse. They had endured hardship before, but never without glory. It was bitter to have been brought to such a pass merely to look like fools.

Thus the long, empty days passed by while starving men gasped out their lives beneath a blazing sky, before a sea of brass.

And Duarte Galvão, the scholarly intellectual, the counsellor of kings, who had so gladly sacrificed the ease of his declining years to link up Christendom with Prester John? He who had come so far in pursuit of a dream now saw it dying with himself upon the arid shores of Kamaran. He waited for news of his son, which never came, and he waited to be sent upon a mission that was not to be fulfilled. He begged Lopo Soares to let him cross to Massawa, but the Governor refused. He did dispatch the caravels to reconnoitre, as has been seen; but he would not allow the ambassador to go with them. When Lourenço de Cosmo had reported, he said, then Duarte Galvão might go.

A day came when the old man gave up hope. His son was lost for ever, and he himself would not see Prester John. He had travelled all that weary way merely to die of grief on this forsaken isle.

Father Francisco arrived at Kamaran shortly before the end. "Padre," said Duarte Galvão, "you ask me how I am, but you do not tell me of the death of my son!"

"Sir," answered the good priest, "if God please, he may be at some port of the country from which we have come."

"I am far more certain," said the dying man, "that he and all those on his ship are now in paradise, where Our Lord will in His mercy surely take them, since they died in His service and that of the King."

Duarte Galvão joined his son on June 9, and he was buried in the sand at Kamaran. Nine years later Padre Francisco disinterred his bones, and they were carried back to Portugal.

Lopo Soares saw himself relieved of the necessity of going to Massawa. It is true that he still had Matthew on his hands, but he did not mean to trouble about him. He sent word to the Armenian that he might be left at Aden, Berbera, or Zeila. Matthew declared quite truly that at none of these Moslem ports was it safe for him to land. On his side he suggested three alternatives: if Lopo Soares did not wish to send him over to Arkiko, let him then return to India, or — remembering the good time he had enjoyed there — to Portugal! The Governor permitted him to remain with the fleet, but announced that he would leave him at Ormuz.

On the return voyage Lopo Soares attacked and burned Zeila, to feel that he had done something after all. He called at Aden once again, but the obliging offer of five months before was not renewed. The fleet seems to have dispersed about this time. There was great shortage of food and drink and "each captain went to seek for both where he thought fit." Their commander made no attempt to round them up. Times had changed since they went cruising under Albuquerque, when the fleet was counted from the flagship masthead every morning and no unit dared to venture out of sight!

Matthew fiercely refused to disembark at Ormuz, so he and Padre Francisco landed together at Cochin — sole members of a mission that had fizzled out. Duarte Galvão, the principal, lay in a solitary grave at Kamaran, Lourenço de Cosmo had been beheaded at Dahlak. Lopo de Vilalobos, the only one of the party who appears to have been in the Governor's good books, was sent home to explain what had occurred as plausibly as could be managed.

Padre Francisco Alvares remained at Cochin awaiting orders from the King. "I beg Your Highness," he writes, "if you send another message to Prester John, that I may not be left behind."

Poor Matthew was not very happy nor well treated, but, says Father Francisco, "he was much consoled by the letters from Your Highness which I read to him every day."

As for the present — the magnificent and multifarious present, consisting of such exquisite works of art, and estimated at a value of more than 30,000 cruzados — in the damp heat of the tropics it rotted away. "All was lost through the fault of Lopo Soares," says Gaspar Correa, "and Lopo Soares never paid for it"!

6

The Improvised Embassy

✠

Give a dog a bad name and hang him, says the proverb. It may well be cited in poor Matthew's case. The charge of being a false ambassador, first invented by Gaspar Pereira for ulterior motives, continued to shadow his career. In spite of all proofs to the contrary, people would persist in doubting him. Even Dom Manuel, by whom he had been received with open arms and treated as an honored guest, is said by some to have expressed misgivings about Matthew. The only persons, in fact, who had always seemed quite certain that he was genuine were Padre Francisco Alvares, who heard him in confession, and Albuquerque, who seldom, if ever, failed to size up any man correctly. But the first of these two had little power to help, and the second was dead.

Matthew tells the King that Lopo Soares gave him poison at Cochin. "My Lord, you are a saint," he writes entreatingly, "and you know everything. Do not give ear to Lopo Soares, since he tried to kill me, which God did not permit." Matthew had an excitable imagination. It is unlikely that Lopo Soares really attempted to poison him, but it is certain that the Governor made his life unpleasant. The wretched ambassador must have been delighted when Diogo Lopes de Sequeira came to take Lopo Soares's place at the end of 1518.

Diogo Lopes had not much more confidence in Matthew

than most people had. All the same, he was quite willing to repatriate him, and in 1520 took him with the fleet to the Red Sea.

At the time that Diogo Lopes had left Portugal, Duarte Galvão was supposed to be in Abyssinia. The new Governor was therefore under orders to proceed to Massawa and learn what answer Prester John had given to Dom Manuel's message. We do not know what fresh instructions the King sent out when he heard of Duarte Galvão's death and the complete collapse of the embassy. Whatever they were, Diogo Lopes sailed for the Straits on January 8, 1520, taking with him not only Matthew but Padre Francisco Alvares, who still was dreaming of the land of Prester John. A few of the skilled craftsmen and musicians who had originally come out with the delegation seem to have gone as well, all of which looks as if the Governor had definite intentions with regard to Abyssinia.

Like his predecessor, however, Diogo Lopes's first idea was to reach Jidda and chastise the Turks. But this time the capricious wind of the Red Sea refused to take them there, so the fleet fetched up at Massawa instead.

"Massawa is a very beautiful place," the Sheik of Dahlak had informed Albuquerque at Kamaran. Perhaps it was, as Red Sea standards went; but what the Portuguese saw on arriving there does not answer such a description: a little bay sheltered from every wind, and a little island with a cluster of stone houses and a mosque. No springs of water were there, and no wells, only twenty-two cisterns sunk into the ground to catch the rain. The mainland could be seen close opposite, and the village of Arkiko, consisting of straw houses fenced around by thorns. There was another islet in the bay, overgrown by wild scrub — and that was all there was to Massawa! Yet this port was known to be an important trade emporium by the shores of the Red Sea. The Arab ships, after passing Bab-el-Mandeb, would call at Dahlak first and then at Massawa, where they bartered Indian produce for gold, ivory, butter, wax, and Abyssinian slaves kidnapped inland.

There was no sign of such activities when Diogo Lopes's fleet swung into harbour. Throughout the village not a creature could be seen. It might have been an island of the dead. All the inhabitants had obviously been seized with panic and bolted when they saw the ships appear.

Two men were discovered at last, in hiding on the smaller island, and they were brought to Matthew, who conversed with them in their own language, after which, slightly reassured, their companions came out. We owe a grim description of these people to Gaspar Correa: they were tall and black, with very little on, and "from the time that they are born they neither cut nor comb their hair, which becomes like a cap of matted wool, and they carry oiled and pointed sticks thrust into it with which they scratch the lice underneath, because their fingers cannot reach the scalp, and their sole occupation," concludes our writer tersely, "is scratching their heads."

These unprepossessing persons told Matthew that the Bahr Nagach was two days' journey inland. The Bahr Nagach was the Governor who ruled the lands by the seacoast for Prester John. A letter was dispatched immediately, informing him of Matthew's arrival with the Portuguese. The Bahr Nagach replied at once — he would be coming very soon. Meanwhile the local chieftain of Arkiko, wearing a burnous draped over a Moorish shirt, rode up to pay his respects to the visitors.

Confidence being restored, the mainland woke to life. Some seven monks appeared upon the scene. "Black and thin," they were, according to description, "decent men and of few words." But they said sufficient to express their joy. They came from the monastery of Bizan, several days' journey inland. The news of the arrival of a Christian fleet had filled them with such happiness that, breaking their custom, they had travelled during Holy Week.

The worthy men were greeted with an enthusiasm equal to their own. There were congratulations and rejoicings all round. Portugal and Abyssinia wept on each other's necks, for, says the chronicler, "no one could restrain his tears at the pious thought of how two Christian peoples, one Oriental and the other Occidental, so far removed, so different in civilization, customs, and religious rites, should yet be joined in ties of spiritual brotherhood by the sign of the cross, which filled them thus with faith and love and charity."

Wiping their eyes, they adjourned to the abandoned mosque of Massawa. This edifice was consecrated, and Portuguese and Abyssinians celebrated a thanksgiving Mass.

With all this poor Matthew came into his own. Those who still persisted in believing that he was an impostor could now observe that to these people he was a great man. The ruler of Arkiko and the monks had greeted him with deepest reverence, kissing first his hand and then his shoulder as a token of respect. The Bahr Nagach, when he appeared, embraced him cordially, and they talked long together. Everyone was properly impressed. "Now all could see," says Father Francisco triumphantly, "that Matthew was a real ambassador." We wonder why they had been so hard to convince. At any rate, they seem to have been glad to find themselves mistaken, and beamed at Matthew benignly while tears of joy were trickling down his beard. These were emotional half-hours.

The Bahr Nagach, it must be owned, was not an especially imposing figure: "Badly dressed," observes Gaspar Correa, as were also the two thousand men who followed him. Matthew, no doubt, looked splendid in comparison, for he had "noble clothes which he had brought from Portugal." That was five years ago, but materials were more lasting in that age and clothes remained "noble" longer than they do today!

Diogo Lopes had pitched a lordly tent upon the beach in which to meet his Abyssinian colleague, but the shy Ethiopian would not venture in, so the interview had to take place outside. It went off very well. Each sitting on his carpet spread upon the ground, Diogo Lopes and the Bahr Nagach exchanged compliments. Diogo Lopes spoke fluent Arabic. The Bahr Nagach was pleasant and polite. Everyone expressed appropriate sentiments about this happy meeting, and, each in the name of his own country, the two principals swore everlasting friendship on the cross. All the cannon of the fleet then fired a joyous salvo, which might have caused a very serious incident. A projectile fell right among the Abyssinians, ricocheting three times. Diogo Lopes, much alarmed, apologized profusely, but fortunately no one had been hurt, and the Bahr Nagach was not at all perturbed. Safety, said he devoutly, depended solely on the will of God. There was a little more amicable conversation, and the party broke up "because the heat was such that they could do nothing else."

All felt that the intercourse with Prester John had made a good beginning, and it seemed a pity not to follow it up. Diogo Lopes held rapid consultation with his captains. Now that Matthew would be really going home, an ambassador ought to be sent with him. Everybody volunteered for this exciting post, and so the embassy was quickly organized.

Dom Rodrigo de Lima would take Duarte Galvão's place, with Jorge de Abreu as second fiddle. João Escolar would be secretary and João Gonçalves treasurer to the party. A physician, Mestre João, was to accompany the delegation, and the arts were represented by Lazaro de Andrade, "a good painter," Manuel de Mares, an organist who carried several instruments with him, and Estevão Palhares, a skilful fencer, besides sundry other craftsmen and mechanics. Needless to say, Padre Francisco Alvares was chaplain and much to the fore. "Dom Rodrigo," said the Governor, "I am not sending Padre Francisco Alvares with you, but you with him!"

Having improvised an embassy, it was further necessary to raise a present, and to this end they combed the fleet. As a result there were collected four pieces of Flemish tapestry, a sword with golden hilt, a gold-embellished dagger, some crimson velvet cuirasses, a helmet, and, not to forget the Emperor's education, "a *mappamundi*, for Prester John to understand the roundness of the earth." Certainly, as Padre Francisco has remarked, this present "was not so good as that which the King had sent out with Duarte Galvão," but that one was "already ruined at Cochin through Lopo Soares." It would not do to explain this to Prester John. Dom Rodrigo was to tell him that the worthier offering had been on board the ship Santo Antonio, which had sunk between Aden and the Straits; but Dom Manuel would send another gift next year. Meanwhile, "You will present these things to him as from me," writes the Governor in Dom Rodrigo's *regimento* (paper of instructions, "and tell him that I send them as a token that I am his servant, and that which the King was sending him will follow next year."

Diogo Lopes seems a trifle apprehensive lest Dom Rodrigo might be tackled on a subject still more awkward to explain. "If, on arrival, Prester John's ambassador's should complain that he was not treated and honoured here as became an envoy from so great a prince, you will say that it was owing to certain doubts and intrigues sown by the Devil; but all is to be amended, if it please Our Lord."

Having conveniently shelved this responsibility upon the enemy of all mankind, Diogo Lopes bade the embassy farewell on April 30. The Bahr Nagach provided mules and camels, and so the party struck inland, on the road to Asmara.

The Bahr Nagach was to have been their guide, but Matthew had his own idea in mind. Matthew was very happy, not to say above himself. His long exile was ended, his character was cleared, everyone deferred to him, and he was going home! He meant to get there by the route he chose, and that was via Bizan. He had left most of his belongings at the monastery of Bizan, it appears. The Bahr Nagach objected that Bizan was out of the way, but Matthew did not care. Neither did the Bahr Nagach! He parted from the delegation and continued his own road.

Matthew declared that he knew the country better than anyone else and they must follow him. He was quite rude to the Bahr Nagach's brother-in-law, a pleasant youth who met the travellers shortly afterwards and offered courteously to put them on their way. Forging ahead, the Armenian led them by breakneck goat-tracks across "diabolical mountains and forests" where nobody could ride. The sun blazed, the scorched rocks burned, the camels shrieked "as though they were possessed." "Truly," exclaims Francisco Alvares, "devils walked at midday in those woods, where wild beasts abounded." So they stumbled on through a fantastic inferno, along a path that they feared would not lead anywhere.

After three days, when the travellers felt quite certain that they were lost, signs of human life appeared at last. Herds of goats and cows roamed the mountain-side, led by men so scantily attired that "there was little of them that could not be seen." The women, Padre Francisco notes with some relief, "were better covered, but not much." All these people were "very black and Christian."

Some monks appeared likewise. They were very old, and as thin as sticks, wherefore, Padre Francisco says ambiguously, "at first sight they seem to be of holy life." They came from the little convent of St. Michael, not far from Bizan. There the travellers were lodged, and one by one they all fell ill, beginning with the doctor. Mestre João, however, was a competent physician. Nothing dismayed, he "bled and purged himself, and so got well and then attended to the others."

Matthew, who ought to have been accustomed to the climate, was as ill as anybody else. Mestre João treated him successfully, and all might have been well, but as soon as he felt better the patient insisted upon packing up and moving on. No one could have restrained him, for Matthew "was very fond of his own way," says his father confessor. The consequence was what might be expected. He had not been gone long before an urgent message summoned Mestre João and the chaplain to his side. They found him dying half-way between St. Michael and Bizan. It was too late for the physician to do anything, but Padre Francisco heard his last confession and wrote the Portuguese translation of his will. Queen Helena was to inherit all that he possessed. In this manner, upon May 23, the first ambassador from Prester John passed out.

Poor Matthew, with his changing moods, his caprice and his temper, his bursts of piety and penitence, his uncertain matrimonial state, the very certain love he bore his young companion Jacob, the tribulations of his Odyssey, and tragic death when he was nearly home, remains a pathetic and intriguing figure to the last. He met with much injustice and misunderstanding, yet we feel that he brought some of it upon himself. He was certainly a most peculiar person. If we knew more about his origin and antecedents it might be easier to make him out. As it is, he stands as an enigma on the page of history — an enigma to which Francisco Alvares alone possessed the key, but that was under the seal of the confessional, and so he has not passed it on.

Matthew was buried at the monastery with every honour, and the embassy remained a few weeks longer at Bizan. For some reason the monks appeared annoyed that they should leave at all and did everything they could to hinder their departure. In spite of obstructions, however, the party got away on June 18. Father Francisco, if no one else, had passed an interesting month at this religious house, and has much to write about its rules and observations. "Some of these friars are very good, devout, and honourable — others are not so" is his final verdict on his African colleagues.

More precipitous paths up rocky mountains, and the expedition found itself on a high tableland. The soil seemed fertile here, "with cultivated fields, and others lying fallow as in Portugal," the travellers observed approvingly.

They were now at Debaroa, capital of the province ruled by the Bahr Nagach. This gentleman had been all smiles to Diogo Lopes de Sequeira; but Diogo Lopes had had armed troops at his side, cannon that thundered from the sea, and a great fleet swinging at anchor off the shore. To twelve or four-

teen lonely foreigners completely cut off from their kind he
did not think it necessary to be so pleasant. The Bahr Nagach
was not sure he approved of foreigners; at any rate he did not
see why he should be the one to put them up! When the Portuguese arrived at Debaroa, he inhospitably withdrew to the
neighbouring village of Addi Baro.

Dom Rodrigo followed him there. He needed beasts of burden and he needed guides. Matthew was no longer there to
help the party, and it was difficult to wander across Abyssinia unaccompanied by anyone who knew the ropes. Accordingly, Dom Rodrigo with the chaplain and a few others, when
they had said their prayers at the Addi Baro church, presented themselves at the ruler's palace — "We thought that he
would speak to us at once" — but they were told that the great
man was asleep. As far as Dom Rodrigo was concerned, he
did not wake that day, and the ambassador with his companions were packed into a goat-pen for the night. "We could
only just squeeze into it," Padre Francisco says.

Next morning found them once again outside the not very
palatial palace. It was a one-storeyed building consisting of
a number of rooms opening into one another — which rooms,
the observing eye of Father Francisco did not fail to note,
"were very seldom swept." At the entrance of the house three
porters barred the way. They would not let the strangers pass
without exacting a tip, and the gratification they desired
was pepper!

We are not told if Dom Rodrigo went about with pepper in
his pocket, but somehow they got through, only to be held
up by three more porters with whips. Mopping their brows,
they waited half an hour, and "it was hot enough to kill us."

Dom Rodrigo's patience began to wear thin. Were they to
be admitted or were they not? he asked the porter, because
if not, he would go. The porter took the message and returned
to say that they might come in.

The Bahr Nagach sat on a couch, "draped with poor curtains," and his wife sat by his side. They could see that he was

70

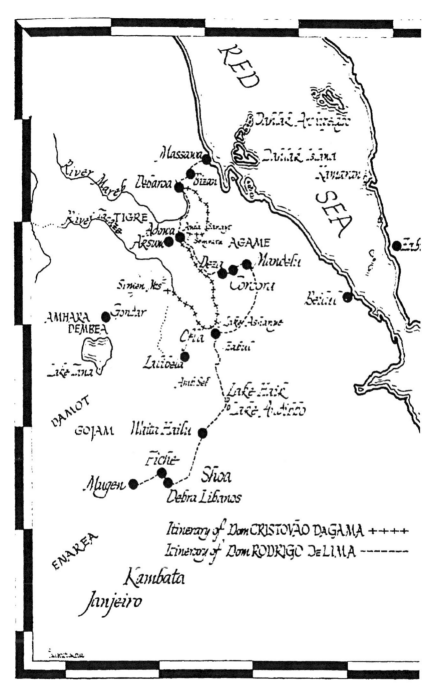

MAP OF ABYSSINIA SHOWING ITINERARIES OF DOM
CRISTÓVÃO DA GAMA AND DOM RODRIGO DE LIMA

suffering from eye disease. Anxious to make himself agreeable, Dom Rodrigo offered the assistance of his doctor, but "I have no need of him," the Bahr Nagach replied ungraciously.

Could he provide oxen and asses for their journey, Dom Rodrigo asked, and mules for them to ride? Oxen and asses, yes, said the Ethiopian, but no mules. These must be bought.

At the conclusion of a rather chilling interview the visitors were led into an outer room. There it seemed that they were to be refreshed before departing. Straw mats were laid for them to sit upon the floor, a horn of honey wine was brought, and a large basin of food. This contained an uncooked paste of roasted barley flour and water.

Dom Rodrigo and his comrades gazed upon this chickenfeed with feelings of dismay. The more they looked at it, the more their courage failed. No one could bring himself to eat the stuff, and so the feast was left untasted.

But they were not suffered to escape so easily. The Bahr Nagach might be indifferent whether his guests ate or not, but his mother took it very much to heart. The lady felt that her housekeeping was slighted, and she sent more food after the departing strangers. Five large wheaten loaves, another horn of honey wine, and some more of that sticky concoction which had defeated them before. Good manners left no loophole this time. They set their faces and they ate it up.

Debaroa proved no easy place to leave. The Bahr Nagach was anything but helpful, and beasts and carriers were difficult to find. The latter would load up and progress for a few leagues, after which they dumped their burdens by the wayside, declaring that they could go no farther and must be relayed. Others never appeared available, and the baggage was thus left in the rain — for the rains were starting by that time, which added not a little to the complications.

The Bahr Nagach — when they could get hold of him, which was not often — would promise anything and then dismiss the matter from his mind. Clearly, he did not wish to be

bothered with the embassy. He had a war with certain neighbouring tribes, and that was what preoccupied him. He was
short of armaments, he said to Dom Rodrigo; would the latter
oblige him with some swords?

Dom Rodrigo gave him "a very good sword" that he was
wearing for the journey, but the Abyssinian was not satisfied.
He wanted Dom Rodrigo's other sword as well, he said – the
beautiful one with an ornamental hilt. Dom Rodrigo did not
wish to part with his best sword. He bought a handsome
gilded sabre from a member of his staff and gave that to the
Bahr Nagach instead. It seems that even that was not enough,
for the following night "two swords and a helmet were stolen
from the house in which the Portuguese slept."

In the end sufficient mules were found, and the Bahr
Nagach gave them three camels, so they got away. The rains
had really set in by then, which made it most imprudent to
proceed. "They never travel at that season," observes Padre
Francisco, "but we hurried off, not knowing the country or
the risk that we incurred."

In spite of everything they struggled on, out of the lands of
the Bahr Nagach into the mountains of Tigré. It was a strange
region that the travellers were now traversing – vertical peaks
all round, rising to meet the sky, and on every mountain-top
a hermitage hung like an eagle's nest on rocks which it seemed
no human foot could climb. Below the mountains – ruins:
stone churches a thousand years old, vast systems of irriga-
tion works, remains of Greeks and Romans scattered among
monuments more ancient still where Sabæans had worshipped the sun before the Christian era.

Not only the aspect of the scenery changed as they pro-
gressed inland, but the people began to be different, in costume and every other way. Costume is hardly the word to
apply to anything so negative as our writer describes. The
women dressed in beads and little else. "In Portugal and
Spain," observes Father Francisco, "men marry for love of a

72

pretty face — the rest is hidden. No such mystery," he adds, attends an Abyssinian "bride."

The reception which the travellers met varied from one village to another. Some places pelted them with stones, others refused to sell them food; but the nuns of Farso welcomed them with almost disconcerting veneration. These were saintly pilgrims from Jerusalem, declared the pious ladies. To acquire merit for themselves, they washed the strangers' feet, drinking the water afterwards and bathing their own faces in it!

The Governor of Tigré showed himself more friendly and hospitable than had the Bahr Nagach. He provided the embassy with guides and an escort numbering five hundred men. The handling of the baggage, however, seems still to have been inefficient. As they travelled towards the mountains of Bernacel, the party was dismayed to find their packs, which had gone on ahead, embedded in the middle of a flooded field.

As they paused, debating how to extricate their property, some men on muleback were seen approaching from afar. One of the riders made straight for the chief man of the Abyssinian escort, seized his bridle-rein, and began belabouring him with a big stick. Dom Rodrigo rushed to the rescue, and the aggressor would have been dispatched if Jorge de Abreu had not caught some words that he cried out in broken Italian. Explanations followed. This was no brigand after all, but a highly respectable if impetuous monk, by the name of Saga Zaab. The Emperor had sent him to meet the visitors and help them on their way. When he saw the mess that Dom Rodrigo's guide had made, he had been moved to wrath.

Saga Zaab provided them with more mules and camels, and he accompanied Dom Rodrigo's party to their journey's end. he proved a useful help, but Dom Rodrigo objected to his system of spending every night upon a mountain-top. It was unhealthful down below, insisted Saga Zaab. That, said Dom

Rodrigo, did not matter. Saga Zaab could climb up if he liked, but they would not trouble to follow him. So the Abyssinian perched aloft while the Portuguese pitched their tents in the plain.

The chiefs that they met upon the way were mostly pleasant. The Ras of Angote, an important personage, gave them a very honourable reception which "consisted principally of drinks," Padre Francisco says. They found the Ras sitting with four large jugs of wine at hand and a crystal goblet standing by each jug. From these he urged his guests to drink, and go on drinking until all were empty. Happily for them, he also did his bit, and his wife with two lady friends was not left far behind. When the liquid gave out at last, the Ras called for more. But the sober Portuguese were horrified at the prospect of further libations. Dom Rodrigo invented an excuse, and so they got away.

They were invited to a Sunday dinner after church next day. Dom Rodrigo accepted, but feeling unequal to face Abyssinian cooking, brought his own meal with him, which unusual procedure apparently gave no offence. Padre Francisco has described the party, which seems to have been a success.

All sat upon the floor on mats around two large trays that served as tables, the Ras in the middle of his guests, his lady modestly screened by a curtain farther off. "Water was brought and we washed our hands, but no towel came to wipe them, neither was there any tablecloth." The Portuguese said grace, which struck the Abyssinians as a pleasing custom, and then the feast began. Bread was placed upon the board, and on every piece of bread were slices of raw meat, which the Ras consumed with evident enjoyment while his guests looked on amazed. Three dishes of black earthenware also appeared, containing each a kind of soup, or stew, made up, it seems, of cow-dung and gall, with bits of bread and butter floating on the top. The shuddering Europeans all decided that "we could not eat such potage." They turned thankfully to the

74

"good roast chickens and boiled beef" which Dom Rodrigo had provided. He offered some of these to his hostess, but if the lady ate or not behind her curtain nobody could see. "She helped well with the drinks, however," the chaplain remarked.

Bidding farewell to this convivial pair, our travellers went on. Already they were in the province of Amhara and approaching their journey's end. It had been a full five months' steady going across this strange townless kingdom of rich churches and poor villages, of barren rocks and cultivated fields, of mountains and of ruins — five months' perpetual moving on through heat and cold, through flood and drought, from airy height to stifling hollow, from panther-haunted jungle into desert, and from desert into populated tableland. The day's march, a halt for the night, and on again next day — it had all grown to seem part of the unchanging scheme of life when at last, on October 10, they sighted far away the tents of Prester John.

Prester John at Last!

Prester John lived in a tent. Throughout the vastness of his empire he had no fixed abode, but perambulated his nomadic court according to the exigencies of politics or war. Lebna Dengel Dawit was this young ruler's name as it figures in Ethiopian chronicles, but his Portuguese contemporaries simplified it to David. As for the fancy title bestowed on him by European imagination, that died hard. "The Moors and Abyssinians call him Emperor and not Prester John . . ." Albuquerque seems to have been the first person to take note of this fact, but Moors and Abyssinians notwithstanding, to the Portuguese he had always been Prester John, and Prester John he would remain to the end.

The Emperor at this time was some twenty years of age. Old Queen Helena's tutelage was a thing of the past. The dowager still lived at court, but in retirement. Young David, like his namesake and alleged ancestor, had embarked early on a military career. Abyssinia, with the independent Moslem tribes of Adel and Harrar seething about her southern frontiers, needed a warrior king. Lebna Dengel at the age of seventeen had buckled on his sword. He had met the famous Emir Mahfuzh on the plains near Zeila. There the terror of Ethiopia lost the battle and his head, which gory trophy the young champion bore away, as well as the green standard and velvet tent presented to the Emir by the Sheriff of Mecca. This victory had placed Abyssinia in a strong position – much stronger than at the time when Queen Helena had written her letter to Dom Manuel. The arrival of an embassy from Portugal therefore caused less excitement than it would have done a few years before.

This does not mean that Dom Rodrigo was not courteously received. The Emperor sent along one of his lords to welcome and accommodate his guests. He also offered for their use a splendid tent – one of his own, they were informed, and of a type reserved for royalty. He further sent them veal pasties and cows and honey wine, all of which things were pleasant; but what seems to have upset Dom Rodrigo was a message that they were at liberty to purchase merchandise and sell their wares. This base insinuation was too much for a *fidalgo's* pride. What did the Emperor take him for? Neither he nor his father, nor his mother, nor any of his ancestors, said Dom Rodrigo loftily, nor those of the other gentlemen who came with him had ever bought or sold! He was amazed that such a thing should be suggested! It is doubtful, however, whether Lebna Dengel could appreciate the importance of this point or understand the aristocratic prejudices of the West.

His own pride was made manifest in dignified delay. To grant an early audience to a foreign embassy was not consonant with his greatness. What most interested him about them was the present which he hoped that they had brought. From Matthew's passage at Dahlak in 1517 the news had percolated into Abyssinia that a magnificent gift was on the way. The Emperor accordingly sent word to Dom Rodrigo that it was his gracious pleasure to receive the offering.

It was sad that reality should fall so short of expectation. Dom Rodrigo laid out what he had as best he could. He added to it four bales of pepper, a commodity as highly prized in Abyssinia as it was in Europe of that day, but even so the effect was not rich. Such as they were, the modest gifts were carried pompously into the Emperor's white and purple camp, while a hundred court officials marched before, scattering the crowd by means of leather thongs.

The whole performance was not unlike a circus. A double row of arches, swathed alternately in white and purple cotton cloth, led up to the imperial tent, and a squadron of two thousand men was lined up on either side. Before the arches sat four mounted guards on steeds caparisoned in silk brocade. In front of these horsemen, two on either side, were four chained lions. Like Christian into Palace Beautiful, the delegates walked up between the lions.

The gifts were taken in to Prester John, but the ambassador was not admitted to the presence. When the offerings had passed before the regal eye, they were brought out again and spread upon the arches for the populace to see. The Chief Justice of the realm got up and made a speech: God should be praised, said he, for having brought about this happy meeting among Christians. Anybody who felt otherwise might weep; those who rejoiced could sing! At this the listening crowd politely bellowed its delight.

Dom Rodrigo hoped for an audience the next day, but he was disappointed. The fact was that Prester John thought nothing of their present. He wanted more and did not hesitate to say so. Would they hand over all the pepper that they had? This Dom Rodrigo was very loath to do. There was no currency in Abyssinia and spices served instead; still, as the Emperor was insistent, he surrendered most of his supply. Further to gratify their host, they decided to give him four of their travelling-chests, because "it seemed to us that he would be pleased with them, and we should find favour in his sight."

Lebna Dengel was not happy yet. There was something else for which he yearned, and since it was not offered him he asked for it. A messenger arrived at Dom Rodrigo's tent to say that the Emperor would like to have a pair of breeches!

Dom Rodrigo sacrificed at once one of his own, and another member of his staff produced a second pair. Their breeches and all other things, said the ambassador politely, were at the disposal of Prester John.

But neither Dom Rodrigo's breeches, nor yet the attractive little leather trunks, nor all the pepper they had given him brought Lebna Dengel to the point. The delegates waited impatiently and in some apprehension. Would they be permitted to deliver their message and depart? None of their predecessors at the Abyssinian court had got away. If foreigners would seek them out, said the Ethiopians, they should remain in Abyssinia altogether! Returning travellers might go about spreading evil reports. They seem to have held a pessimistic view of the impression that their country made upon outsiders and to have been sensitive about it.

It was not from Pero da Covilham that Dom Rodrigo heard all this — the former was resident on his estates and had not yet appeared. His informants were a number of Europeans discovered stranded at the Abyssinian court: two Catalans, a Biscayan, a German, a Greek from Chios, and eleven Genoese. All of these men, escaped from Turkish prisons — some after forty years' captivity — had strange adventures to relate. Unhappily for our curiosity, adventures were at a discount in those days. So many lives were like a serial in the *Boys' Own Paper* that sensational experiences of private persons were scarcely considered worthy of record. All that we know of this particular group of adventurers is that most of them had been confined at Jidda at the time that Lopo Soares passed in 1517. When, to their sorrow, he sailed away without rescuing them they had seized a boat and managed to escape. Finding it impossible to overtake the fleet, they had made for Massawa, whence they went on to Abyssinia. There Dom Rodrigo and his party found them very much at home. They all had learned the language, some of them were married, and Padre Francisco Alvares baptized the half-caste infant of a Genoese. As, beyond their knowledge of Amharic, all these men spoke Portuguese, which in those days was a widespread universal tongue, it may be easily imagined what a blessing they were to the newcomers. All sorts of information was supplied by them, including the disquieting item that his counsellors were advising the Emperor to detain the Portuguese indefinitely.

The suspense was rather trying, the more so that they had several false alarms. One morning at about three a.m. the delegation's cicerone, Saga Zaab, rushed up excitedly. The Emperor wished to speak to them at once! All hastened to get ready, and they had just arrayed themselves in their most splendid clothes when a second messenger appeared to say that the monarch had changed his mind. "We were as sad as the peacock who, having spread his tail, had to close it again," chuckles Padre Francisco, whom nature had blessed with a sense of humour.

Another night — Prester John's habits were apparently nocturnal — a second summons came. They had to wait outside the tent an hour in the teeth of a bitter wind, but this time their best clothes were not put on wholly in vain. Between rows of lighted candles they were led through a series of tents, loudly announced in every one. At last they reached the inner sanctuary, carpeted and hung with rich embroidered cloths. Here they were brought, not before the Emperor, but before the gorgeous curtains behind which he sat! The interview was with an unseen presence, and carried on by messengers that came and went behind the veil. The elusive Prester John, now run to earth, was no more than a voice — a voice that demanded without any preamble where was the present which Matthew had announced?

Clearly the ambassador was suspected of misappropriation. Dom Rodrigo explained all that he could. Everything that he had to give, he said, already had been given, and some more. Dom Manuel's present was at Cochin, waiting to be sent. Dom Rodrigo had only come on a friendly visit and to find out the way. A more official embassy would no doubt follow. But Lebna Dengel seems to have remained suspicious and postponed receiving them in solemn audience.

Meanwhile messages came and returned, and it was all question and answer. The delegates were getting quite accustomed to this. Since their arrival at the Abyssinian court they had been subjected to repeated and searching questionnaires about the Portuguese in general and themselves in particular, their firearms and their fortresses, their allies and their King – was the latter married, by the way, and to how many wives? The Emperor also wished for more details about Dom Manuel and his Queen, how old their children were, and how they took their meals, and where they lived. How many were the Portuguese? What was the size of Portugal? How many fortresses had they in India, and what did they pay their men? How many arquebuses had Dom Rodrigo brought with him? Who taught the Moors and Turks to manufacture artillery; and, finally, which feared the other most, the Moors or the Portuguese? The Portuguese, Dom Rodrigo assured him, were not afraid of Moors; but he piously gave the true faith all credit for that fact. As to how the Turks had learned to use gunpowder – though their spiritual perceptions might be dim, still they were men and they had understanding which permitted them to find out such things for themselves.

Firearms interested Lebna Dengel. He made the delegates bring along their arquebuses and fire a discharge for his benefit. He must have had a peephole in his curtain, for he further wished to see them use their swords; whereupon Dom Rodrigo de Lima and Jorge de Abreu, who were the two most skilled performers, fenced together in great style.

Prester John seemed anxious to put his guests through all their paces. He demanded next that they should dance and sing – a request that might be disconcerting to a modern diplomat, but these belonged to a less self-conscious generation. Without turning a hair, the delegates treated the Negus to an exhibition of their graceful movements and the beauty of their voices.

Having examined the strangers' mundane accomplishments, the Emperor satisfied himself as to their religious

orthodoxy. His royal brother, Dom Manuel, had done exactly
the same thing when visited by Matthew. In matters concerning the faith, both monarchs felt that one could not make too
sure. Matthew, while in Portugal, had been subjected to a
minute catechism on the subject of his beliefs. In Abyssinia,
Padre Francisco Alvares, representing the religion of the delegation, was sounded no less carefully. Not for nothing had
Lebna Dengel Dawit been brought up by the learned Queen
Helena. At his hands Father Francisco underwent a stiff theological examination that was continued and repeated during
many interviews. It seems that the examiner could have carried on indefinitely; not so the unhappy examinee. On one
occasion the latter had to beg "His Highness to have pity on
an old man who had neither eaten nor drunk nor slept since
noon the day before" (it was already about three o'clock).
"He asked me why, since he enjoyed talking to me, I did not
enjoy it too. I answered that hunger, weakness, and old age
did not allow me. Reluctantly the Emperor gave him leave
to go and dine, but as he went a messenger came running after
him. A new and lighter subject of curiosity had seized Lebna
Dengel — might he have Padre Francisco's hat to look at? He
would return it soon. Padre Francisco surrendered his hat
and got away in peace. He reached his tent in a fainting condition, but was summoned back again after an hour and a half.

Padre Francisco acquitted himself of these successive or-
deals with much credit. He held forth upon the doctrines of
the Church, the rites and festivals that she celebrates; and he
explained to everybody's satisfaction the symbolic meaning of
the vestments that he wore. What he seems to have found the
most trying was his examiner's demand for exact figures at
all times. How many, and how much? seem to have been
favourite phrases with Lebna Dengel. How many prophets
were there all together? he inquired. How many foretold the
coming of Our Lord, and how many books did each one write?
How many books did St. Paul write, and the Evangelists?
Padre Francisco pleaded that he had been travelling for six

years and some of these figures had escaped his memory, so though he answered everything, he did not vouch for the accuracy of his replies. How many books were in the Bible all together? the curtained inquisitor demanded next. Padre Francisco boldly guessed that there were eighty-one, and was congratulated upon his good memory. He was really cornered, however, when asked at what date to celebrate the festival of St. Baralam. "I was," said he, "distressed." After searching through every calendar available, he found one which included this exotic saint, and never went to court again without that priceless work of reference to consult.

The divergencies between the Church of Rome and that of Abyssinia were also discussed. Did members of the Latin Church obey the Pope in everything? Lebna Dengel asked, and Father Francisco assured him that invariably they did. Suppose the Pope ordained something unscriptural — what then? young David inquired. If their Coptic Patriarch did so, he added, the Ethiopian would throw the edict in the fire!

Such a case, Padre Francisco answered with conviction, could never occur. The Pope being the Holy Father, his mandates could never be in opposition to Holy Writ. On the contrary, it was the Scriptures that inspired them all. Moreover, he was guided in his decisions by the counsel of doctors, cardinals, archbishops, and bishops, who were enlightened upon these matters by the Holy Ghost. Such learned persons, he added, were sadly lacking in Ethiopia!

The cross-questioning does not appear to have included any definitions of the Trinity. Had it done so, examiner and examinee might have found themselves more seriously at variance. But it seems that this question was not raised, and the fundamental difference between the Roman and the Coptic Churches thus passed unnoticed. As it was, the doctrinal discussions only helped to build mutual esteem. Francisco Alvares concluded that the Abyssinian Church, though ignorant, was devout, while Lebna Dengel pronounced the Portuguese religion to be sound. A spirit of mutual tolerance prevailed which would have been almost impossible a few decades later on when the generation of churchmen reared in the shadow of the Inquisition had grown up. Thus, when the Portuguese were asked by the Ethiopians which was the better of the two, the Roman or the Coptic Mass, "we answered that both were good, since both were to one end, and God was willing to be served in many different ways." In the same spirit, though Father Francisco was a little startled to behold his Ethiopian colleagues "leaping, dancing, and hopping" about the church, when called upon for his opinion he declared that "all was well since it was done to the glory of God"!

With all this, the embassy had only once seen Prester John. Invisibility was part of the royal prestige in Abyssinia. The Emperor showed himself to his people three times a year — at Christmas, Easter, and Pentecost. On every other occasion curtains veiled him from all except the favoured few. Dom Rodrigo and his companions were vouchsafed this privilege when the Emperor gave official audience to the embassy.

It was again at night, and preceded by a very long and very chilly wait — "three hours at the door, where it was very cold and dark." It must be remembered that these were high altitudes.

At last they walked up between the usual row of bright illuminations towards a kind of stage from which a pair of gorgeous curtains were drawn apart. There, raised aloft "after the manner in which God the Father is represented on wall paintings," sat Prester John upon a platform six steps high. His person was richly adorned. A tall crown of gold and silver was upon his head, in his hand he grasped a silver cross, and before his face was held a blue taffeta veil, concealing it up to the nose. Every now and then this veil was lowered, revealing his whole face. He wore a long brocaded robe and silken shirt with ample sleeves, while over his knees was draped a cloth of gold. "In age, complexion, and stature he is a young man, not very black, but chestnut or the colour of a russet apple. Good-looking, of medium height, a round face, large eyes, and a high-bridged nose. His beard is beginning to grow. . . ."

The delegates made deep obeisance, touching the ground with their right hands as they had been instructed was good form. Dom Rodrigo delivered the Governor's letter, of which an Amharic translation had been made. Lebna Dengel glanced through it rapidly. Why had not the King written himself? he asked. He was told that Dom Manuel's letter had been lost in 1517, which it seems was the truth. A few compliments were exchanged. Prester John said that he would be delighted for the Portuguese to build fortresses at Massawa and Suakin, for which he promised to supply provisions. He further invited them to capture Zeila. That, Dom Rodrigo said, would be an easy thing to do. Where the King of Portugal sent his navies in force, the Moors fled from their very shadow! He also suggested that he himself might be captain of the fortress at Massawa. And so with pleasant words the audience ended.

It had gone off very well, and there was nothing left to do but await the answering letters to carry back. These would have to be written in gold lettering, the Emperor said, and might take time. This was a pity. Dom Rodrigo expected the fleet to be at Massawa to fetch him between February and April 1521. If the delegation failed to be at Massawa within the dates prescribed, they knew that they would not be waited for. Any ship lingering in the Red Sea after the end of April would have to remain there for three months until the monsoon ceased — an experience no commander cared to risk. It had been tried in 1513 and again in 1517, with terrible mortality each time. Thus Dom Rodrigo had good reason to urge the Emperor for a prompt reply.

8

A Prolonged Visit

Prester John decidedly did not believe in hustle. Dom Rodrigo had to possess his soul in patience and follow the court about over the mountains.

The court of Abyssinia on the move was no ordinary spectacle. The whole neighbourhood packed up at the same time and followed after. The great lords rode while their rich tents were carried by a regiment of servants. The poor broke up their little shacks and bore them along piecemeal. There were men on foot and men on horseback — oxen, donkeys, camels, all bearing their load. So many people on the march reminded Father Francisco of "a Corpus Christi procession in some large town."

At the centre, in a space kept clear of the mixed multitude, the Emperor rode his mule. A canopy of curtains held aloft concealed the sacred form from profane gaze. His four symbolic lions were led in front, held strongly fettered by a numerous. guard. To the rear his carriers bore upon their heads a hundred jars of raisin wine and a hundred ornate baskets filled with loaves, all to be distributed on the way to those whom royalty might delight to honour.

Thirteen consecrated tents — the Emperor's churches — figured solemnly in the procession. Eight priests were in charge of each one, which they carried in relays of four. Two acolytes walked in front with a cross upheld and censers swinging, while they rang a bell. Any who crossed their path had to dismount and stand aside until the "church" had passed.

The embassy took part in this impressive exodus. An honourable position was assigned the Portuguese, near the Emperor's person. And so they followed him by breakneck mountain paths until a lofty tableland was reached where the court camped to celebrate the Christmas festival.

Pero da Covilham's estates were not far off, and he hastened to court to meet his fellow countrymen. The old exile must have been a most interesting person. He spoke, Padre Francisco tells us, every language — Christian, Moslem, or heathen — and he was a perfect mine of information. Unhappily for us, Pero da Covilham never troubled to write his reminiscences, and what could have been one of the most exciting biographies in history may only be constructed in imagination.

All the exiled Europeans gathered with the Portuguese on Christmas morning to celebrate the festival after the rites familiar to their youth. Prester John had given the embassy the Emir's captured tent to use as a church. It had been duly blessed and exorcized — a precaution recommended by Lebna Dengel "in case some Moor had sinned within it" — and in it Padre Francisco said his daily Mass. The Christmas services were a success. All musical members of the congregation helped. Manuel de Mares presided at the organ (some kind of harmonium, no doubt), while the painter Lazaro de Andrade, Mestre João the physician, João Escolar, secretary of the embassy, a Genoese, and a Catalan named Nicolas, all sang with such effect that an enraptured Abyssinian priest declared "he thought he was in paradise among the angels." The Emperor with his wife and Queen Helena in their tent was also listening and admired. Some Abyssinian ceremonies about this season were rather startling to the Portuguese. Would they like to be baptized? asked the Ethiopians on the eve of the Epiphany. Padre Francisco answered in surprise that all of them had been baptized already and once was enough. "Not at all,"

said the Ethiopians. "We are baptized every year." Padre
Francisco, interested but a little scandalized, witnessed the
performance later on.

If mortification of the flesh can confer merit, there certainly
was merit here. It was a cold night at these altitudes, with
frost upon the ground, but the baptisms began at midnight
in a deep tank filled with water from a mountain stream. In
the middle of this pool an old priest stood, immersed up to his
armpits and "dying of cold," Father Francisco observes feel-
ingly. The Emperor, the royal family, and the Patriarch, each
clad only in a loincloth, took the plunge first in privacy. The
penitents of lesser rank came afterwards — men and women
all stark naked. One by one they passed under the priestly
hands and were made to bow their heads beneath the icy
water. It was broad daylight before the ceremony was over,
and we are not told whether the officiating priest subsequently
died of pneumonia.

"What do you think of it?" asked Lebna Dengel from behind his screen, and Father Francisco answered that he disapproved.

"I quite agree with you," said the Abuna — the Patriarch of
Abyssinia — to our friend in an aside. Repeated baptisms, in
his opinion, were unscriptural. But he had no one to support
him in this view. The Emperor's grandfather had instituted
the system of annual baptism, and from the highest motives.
Since men would not refrain from sinning, this monarch felt
that the cleansing waters should be frequently renewed. So
many souls, he said devoutly, might otherwise be lost! The
Patriarch was not quite happy over the innovation, but the
Emperor had his way.

This Abuna was named Mark and hailed from Alexandria,
the headquarters of the Coptic Church, whence came all
Abyssinia's patriarchs. The post does not appear to have been
greatly coveted, for each time an Abuna died it was very difficult to find him a successor. The Abyssinians were already
considering what would happen after Mark's demise — an

event not likely to be long delayed if, as he told Francisco Alvares, he was a hundred and twenty years old!

Mark was a meek and benevolent old man — "little and bald," and with a beard as white as wool — very pleasant in his speech. He and Padre Francisco became great friends. On their first meeting each had endeavoured to outdo the other in reverent courtesy. Padre Francisco tried to kiss the Patriarch's hand, which the Abuna did not allow, but would have kissed his foreign colleague's foot. In the end they sat down side by side and conversed heart to heart. "Did I not tell you," observed the Patriarch, beaming at Pero da Covilham, "that one day you would see your fellow countrymen?"

Pero da Covilham was enjoying their society, and they found in him a complete guide to correct behaviour at the Abyssinian court. "You must seem more impressed," he enjoined the ambassador. "Admire all that they show you."

The advice was needed, for the Ethiopians were constantly displaying things for Dom Rodrigo's wonder, and Dom Rodrigo did not care to be outdone. "Look at those beautiful hangings in our church," they said. "Is there anything in Portugal to be compared with them?" Certainly there was, said the ambassador, they ought to see Batalha. "Behold the trappings of the Emperor's horse!" cried someone else ecstatically. "Has the King of Portugal harness like that?" Among the objects that Duarte Galvão had been bringing for the Emperor, Dom Rodrigo answered loftily, were harnesses more beautiful than those.

But a point was scored by the Ethiopians when they exhibited all the state umbrellas, each one of which could have sheltered ten men. Did Dom Manuel walk out under such parasols? they asked the chaplain, who had to own that Dom Manuel did not. But the King had no need of such things, he added loyally, for he had many hats! Dom Manuel had, moreover, shady gardens in which to stroll when the sun was oppressive.

It might perhaps have been more tactful not to lay too

much stress upon the glory and riches of Europe, for, observed the Ethiopians gloomily, the present which Dom Rodrigo brought had not been much. Dom Rodrigo was getting tired of having that unhappy present thrown into his teeth.

The King of Portugal, he declared, did not give presents — he received them! All the kings of Asia sent him gifts. Now and then he might offer something to a friend, not as a matter of custom, but as a special token of regard. Prester John had been one of those favoured few. If a series of unfortunate accidents had prevented the delivery of the present, that could not be helped. Besides, all this giving of gifts was not a European custom. Equipped just as they were, Dom Rodrigo and his suite could have presented themselves before any king! They had acquitted themselves of their mission. Why did not the Emperor give them their answer and permit them to depart? Dom Manuel, said Dom Rodrigo in conclusion, had received Matthew with far more honour than Lebna Dengel had shown them.

Ah, replied the Abyssinians, if their embassy had arrived during the reign of David's predecessor they would not have enjoyed such good treatment as that which they had now met — not, that is to say, unless they had brought a really satisfying present! It all came back to the same thing. The present had been a bitter disappointment, and to describe the wonders that Duarte Galvão would have brought only deepened the gloom.

No blame attached to Dom Rodrigo if his offering failed to please. But the delegation indisposed the Emperor in another way which was entirely their own fault. It really was unnecessary to let the Abyssinians see that Dom Rodrigo and Jorge de Abreu were at daggers drawn.

For the inevitable had happened. Even before they reached the Emperor's court the first and second in command had fallen out — "over unimportant things," says Francisco Alvares.

"Maintain good peace and concord, as men visiting a

90

strange land who must be careful how they act" — so Diogo
Lopes wrote in Dom Rodrigo's *regimento*. Diogo Lopes knew
what he was talking about, and to whom. But he must have
been equally aware that he was preaching in the desert. Old
Portugal produced a marvellous race of men. There was no
danger that they feared, or hardship they would not endure,
or adventure they were unprepared to undertake. Before a
common enemy they could unite and die as hero comrades on
the battlefield, but they could not live in harmony together.
Strong wills and hot tempers made clashes between equals
fierce and frequent enough, but between commander and sub-
ordinate they were the rule. All of these men professed a pas-
sionate loyalty to their King, but they chafed under every
other authority. The relations of a chief with his immediate
second were particularly difficult and delicate, and neither
Dom Rodrigo nor Jorge de Abreu stood the test.

From existing accounts it seems that Jorge de Abreu was
the more to blame. He was a man of very haughty disposition,
and he felt that as second person of the embassy due promi-
nence was not given to him.

Dom Rodrigo, for his part, made light of the dignity attach-
ing to an understudy's post. "You are second only that you
would take my place were I to die," he pointed out, to Jorge
de Abreu's indignation. The bitterness increased each time
some special attention was bestowed on the ambassador. Dom
Rodrigo should have made the Emperor understand that Jorge
de Abreu, too, was an important person who must receive
his share of every honour! The ambassador continuing oblivious of such claims, Jorge de Abreu asserted himself.

He chose the time when the court first moved and the Emperor sent to ask if the mules and slaves provided for the
strangers' journey had proved satisfactory. Dom Rodrigo replied with many thanks that beasts and men left nothing to be
desired.

Not so, then burst out Jorge de Abreu furiously and in Amharic (he had been picking up the language rapidly, it seems).

Dom Rodrigo had kept all the good mules and camels for himself. "Tell the Emperor I had only crippled mules and useless slaves!"

"That is not true!" cried Dom Rodrigo hotly. How dared Jorge de Abreu send such a message to the Emperor? A few more angry words were passed, and the colleagues fell upon each other with drawn swords, while the Abyssinians gaped in blank surprise. Their companions separated the two men before either was killed, but Dom Rodrigo had already wounded Jorge de Abreu.

Lebna Dengel heard all about it and was scandalized. Such doings in a foreign land, he said with truth, were most unseemly. He begged the parties to be reconciled. At the same time he sent some very fine mules to Jorge de Abreu, to whom he was particularly attentive after this. The fiery foreigner seems to have interested him. "He is like an unbridled horse," the Emperor is said to have remarked. Lebna Dengel was displeased with Dom Rodrigo for refusing to make peace, and looked on the embassy coldly in consequence. Nevertheless he decided at last to write his answer to Dom Manuel.

Letterwriting in Abyssinia was not undertaken in a light or frivolous spirit. "They are not in the habit of writing to one another," Padre Francisco explains. Verbal messages were the usual mode of issuing communications, the written word being reserved for momentous occasions such as this. All the most learned in the land were therefore summoned and sat down with all the books of the New Testament around to nerve them for their task.

With the help of spiritual and temporal wisdom the weighty letter was slowly evolved. As it came out, bit by bit, Saga Zaab read it aloud, Pero da Covilham translated into Portuguese, which João Escolar wrote down assisted by Father Francisco. It was particularly difficult, the chaplain says, "to render Abyssinian into Portuguese."

An Arabic translation was made out at the same time. When the triple linguistic effort was finished at last, each version was tied up in a small brocaded bag and packed into a leather-lined basket.

The Emperor sent a gold and silver crown to Dom Manuel, whom he said he regarded as a father. He gave gold and mules to the various members of the embassy, and a silver cross and crook to Father Francisco. Prayers were symbolic of the investiture of spiritual authority over Massawa, the island of Dahlak, and the other isles and islets of the Red Sea. "Pray have him made bishop of these lands," Lebna Dengel wrote to Dom Manuel. The whole of this delightful diocese was Moslem, but Francisco Alvares was graciously invited to convert all its inhabitants.

The miscellaneous Europeans at the Abyssinian court received permission to leave with the Portuguese – all but Pero da Covilham, but then it seems he did not wish to go. Two others stayed behind with him, at the Emperor's special request. The skill of Mestre João had greatly impressed the Ethiopians, who were anxious to retain his services; and the painter, Lazaro de Andrade, also consented to remain. Lebna Dengel appears to have admired the European culture and was desirous of obtaining assistance from that quarter to guide his country on the path towards progress. He begged Dom Manuel to send him skilled craftsmen of all kinds, especially printers, goldsmiths, and silversmiths.

Thus the embassy set out on the long trek to Massawa, and quarrelled as they went. The treasurer and his assistant had by that time fallen out, and one attacked the other with a lance and nearly killed him. Dom Rodrigo refused to share provisions with Jorge de Abreu, whereupon Jorge de Abreu assaulted Dom Rodrigo's quarters in the night and a free fight ensued. The Abyssinians had to intervene. Most of Jorge de Abreu's men were placed under arrest, while he and Dom Rodrigo "reviled each other with bad words before the Bahr Nagach."

And this tormented journey was for nothing after all, for no fleet came to Massawa that year. They returned to the

Abyssinian court, but Dom Rodrigo and Jorge de Abreu travelled separately.

If to enter Abyssinia was no easy task, it was even more difficult to get away. Distances were so great and communications so laborious that twice Dom Rodrigo missed the fleet when it arrived. He ought to wait nearer the sea, wrote the captain of the second squadron that failed to find the embassy within access of Massawa. All this sending of ships for nothing was a great expense.

All together, the delegation spent five years in Abyssinia. Far from waiting by the sea, they seem to have wandered everywhere during that time, but their exact itineraries are difficult to trace. We know that they resided eight months at Aksum. Sometimes they stayed at Debaroa, sometimes in the Tigré. Quite often they followed the court, at other times they travelled on their own, but always moving in two separate bands, for Dom Rodrigo and Jorge de Abreu were never reconciled. Padre Francisco appears more often in Dom Rodrigo's company, but the good-natured chaplain remained on amicable terms with everyone. The natives, too, seem to have liked him very much. He lived for eighteen months as guest in the house of a certain Abaht Ras, a man with thirty children and three wives. Perhaps Padre Francisco expounded the merits of monogamy to him, for before his visitor had left, the Ras had cut down his conjugal staff to one, the youngest and most recent wife alone being retained.

The Abyssinians did not see much harm in polygamy. No civil law proscribed it, and the Church's attitude was vague. Also there were advantages attendant on repeated marriages, for the newly wed enjoyed a month's dispensation from fasts. "Some of my friends," Padre Francisco says, "used to marry new wives on the Thursday before Lent, merely to have the privilege of eating meat."

It is not surprising if carnally minded people tried to evade the rigours of Ethiopian Lent. This was no mere abstention,

94

as in Europe, but literal starvation on bread and water for six weeks. The surrounding Moslems were so well aware of this that they always chose the Lenten fast for their incursions. During those forty days they knew that they would find their enemy too weak to put up much resistance.

It might be thought that one such fast in twelve months would satisfy the most ascetic spirit, but devout souls improved upon it. Some monks would not even eat bread, but only husks and water. Many persons carried their austerities beyond the Lenten period. Throughout the year the pious Queen Helena took her meals only on Tuesdays, Thursdays, Saturdays, and Sundays.

Mortification of the flesh did not stop at starvation. There were people who never sat down during Lent. There were men and women who spent the night up to their necks in water, and this at altitudes where "at this season are great cold and frost." Other penitents passed days and weeks in deep open graves where they could barely move. Padre Francisco visited more than one of these in their reclusion. "They have," he says, "a ledge three fingers wide on which they sit, and two on either side to take their elbows, while in the wall in front a niche has been cut to hold a book."

Such austerities, Pero da Covilham assured him, were very common in Ethiopia. As for hermits, one might be found in almost every cave. He led Francisco Alvares by desert places to where a deep gorge cut the mountains. A torrent hurling itself from dizzy heights into the dark abyss filled the air around with spray that looked like snow. Pero da Covilham pointed through the water mist to a cavern's mouth far down the rocky wall. "A monk lives there who passes for a saint," he said. Still farther down the chasm another cave was dimly visible. There, said Father Francisco's guide, a mysterious white man had done penance for twenty years. Nobody knew who he was or whence he came or when he died. One day the opening of his cavern was found to be walled up. The Emperor ordered that it should not be disturbed, and so the secret of the human tragedy that met its end behind that rock was guarded there for ever.

Though all their mountains were peopled with holy men, yet it was to the foreign priest that the Ethiopians appealed to rid the country of a plague of locusts. Padre Francisco Alvares rose to the occasion. His methods, which he has described himself, were engagingly simple: Besides appropriate prayers and processions, he wrote out a manifest, exhorting the locusts "under pain of excommunication, to move off within three hours and betake themselves to the sea, or to Moslem lands, or to wildernesses of no use to Christians. And if they failed to do this, the birds of the air and the beasts of the field, hailstones and tempests were called down upon them to destroy them. I had a number of these locusts caught, and thus admonished them in their own name and that of the absent . . . after which I let them depart in peace." This appeal to the finer feelings of the insects was not made in vain. The locusts disappeared!

On the whole, the Portuguese enjoyed their stay in Abyssinia. With the adaptability characteristic of their race they made themselves at home. But the uncertainty of when, or if, they were to get away must have been rather wearing. Until 1523 they had no news of either Portugal or India. The fleet that called at Massawa that year managed to get letters delivered to Dom Rodrigo. In these the commander, Dom Luiz de Menezes, announced that the delegation would be waited for until April 15. It was on April 15 that Dom Rodrigo received the letter, and he was at a week's journey from the coast!

This was a blow, as may be easily imagined, but the mail contained even worse news than that. The great Dom Manuel was dead. He had died over a year ago, in December 1521.

Words cannot describe the consternation carried by these tidings. In these days when royal prestige stands or falls with a prince's personality, it is difficult to understand what that man represented to his subjects' hearts. Historians fail to show us any outstanding gifts of mind or charm of character in Dom Manuel. We find in him no glaring vice, but neither do there seem to be exalted virtues. He was just Manuel the Fortunate, who reaped what his predecessors had sown and wore the laurels plucked for him by others. His personality eludes us altogether. During twenty-six years we see him raised aloft, impassive in his splendour, watching his far-called navies fade away, while the East cast glittering offerings at his feet, and heroes kissed his hand and went to die at the world's end. But he was *"El Rei, nosso Senhor"* — the serene and gorgeous symbol before whom a conquering generation bent the knee. They did not look for personality in him. Their loyal affection was obviously quite sincere, but they must have loved him after the manner that sailors can love a wooden figurehead.

His death was signalled as a national calamity. When Duarte de Menezes, then Governor of India, received the news, we are told that he emitted a wild cry and smote his own face with the baleful letter. Dom Rodrigo did not behave quite so dramatically, but he and all the embassy dissolved in tears. To exhibit their grief to all around, they shaved their heads after the custom of Ethiopian mourners. What had happened? inquired the natives sympathetically. Dom Rodrigo was too overcome by sorrow to reply, but Padre Francisco found his tongue. "The moon and stars have fallen and the sun is darkened," he told them with Oriental imagery, "for our King Dom Manuel is dead and we are orphaned."

The Emperor politely ordered three days' official mourning in the land, during which time all booths were closed and business ceased. "Who inherits the realms of the King my father?" he asked Dom Rodrigo, who had returned to court. Dom Rodrigo answered that it was the young Prince Dom João. "Such a good father is bound to have a good son," observed Lebna Dengel soothingly. "I will write him a letter."

So a new set of letters were laboriously produced, addressed to "my brother" Dom João III. "We two together can destroy the world," suggests the Negus cheerfully. "Write to me," he furthermore entreats. "Because, seeing your letters, it will appear to me as if I saw your face, and greater love exists between those who dwell apart from one another than between those who are near." Since he grasped this important truth, why was he so censorious of the European kings? "Sir Brother," he writes smugly, "I disapprove of the kings of Europe, because though they are Christian they are not of one heart, but make war upon one another all the time. Had I a Christian king for neighbour, I should never quarrel with him."

This effusion seems to have taken a month and a half to get ready, at the end of which time the Emperor gave to the delegates rich clothes and golden chains, eighty ounces of gold, and a hundred cloths for the expenses of the way, besides a mule for each one to ride, and so dismissed them with his blessing. The party, rather uselessly, journeyed to Massawa. Of course the fleet had sailed weeks before, so they returned to court.

They found the Emperor was absorbed in a new study. He had awaked to a sudden interest in the map of the world given him by the Portuguese some years ago. Would Padre Francisco explain it to him and have the names of all the countries that it showed translated into Amharic? With the assistance of Saga Zaab, each country was duly labelled, and Lebna Dengel had his first geography lesson. That was Italy, his mentor pointed out, and that was France, that one was Spain, and this, they said complacently, was Portugal.

The Emperor pondered. Was that really Portugal? said he. But it was very little! How could so small a country be expected to hold the Red Sea against the Turks? Might it not be wiser to ask the King of Spain to build a fortress at Zeila, the King of France to erect another one at Suakin, while Portugal could occupy Massawa? So disconcerting a result of "showing Prester John the roundness of the world" had not been anticipated. The Portuguese began to wish that they had been less anxious about his education.

Portugal, Dom Rodrigo declared with conviction, needed neither the King of Spain nor that of France to hold her fortresses against Egypt and Turkey. Besides, he added, patriotism rising above the fetters of scientific truth, maps were very misleading. Their designers naturally did not devote much space to a country so well known as Portugal. Look also at Venice, Jerusalem, and Rome – world-famous cities all of them – how tiny they appear upon the map! It was the obscure and unexplored portions of the earth that took up the most room, because instead of names one had to fill them up with lions and elephants and mountains. Let him observe his own Ethiopia on this map. It occupied much space merely because the land was little known. It seems that this strange explanation was accepted by the Emperor, for we hear no more of calling in the King of France.

A few days after this, Lebna Dengel announced his intention of writing to the Pope. How did one write a letter to the Pope? he asked Dom Rodrigo de Lima. Dom Rodrigo, who had never carried on a correspondence with the Holy See, seems to have been quite scared and flustered at the thought. They had not come to Abyssinia to write letters, he declared, nor would any member of his staff be equal to the task of writing to the Pope.

Padre Francisco, however, was prepared to rise to the occasion. He would word the opening paragraphs for the Imperial scribes, he said, and they would "follow up with what was in their hearts." "Bring all your books," they said, "then we can begin." Padre Francisco replied that he had no need of books, and sat down then and there and wrote out the first lines, to the wondering delight of the Ethiopians. The document was handed round respectfully. He had not looked at any book, they cried; alone he did it! After which, by the usual processes, they completed the letter.

"Padre," said Dom Rodrigo unhappily when the chaplain

returned to his tent, "I wish that I had not told them that there was no one among us who knew how to write to the Pope. They will conclude that we are rather ignorant men. I hope that you will come out strong, and do what you are able!"

"Ill or well," Father Francisco answered modestly, "it is done, as you see." So saying, he produced his letter, and Dom Rodrigo was very pleased.

To Lebna Dengel, a letter to the Pope meant no more than an exchange of compliments with the head of the Western Church. It did not imply the slightest desire on his part to adopt Latin rites. To Padre Francisco, however, it seemed a step towards reunion. He gladly agreed to be the Emperor's messenger to Rome and carry Lebna Dengel's letter to the Pope, together with a little golden cross.

Prester John resolved to send an ambassador to Portugal as well. Would Saga Zaab be a suitable person? he asked, and they assured him that the choice could not be better. "Already he understood us, and we him."

In spite of all these preparations — or perhaps because of them — another fleet was missed in 1524, but 1526 found the delegation upon the Bahr Nagach's territory in good time for the navigating season. They were quite unprepared for the next blow.

Were they waiting for the fleet? the Moslems of Massawa asked them happily. Then they would wait for a long time. There was no Portuguese fleet in all the Indian Ocean any more — there were no Portuguese in India! Both men and ships were all destroyed — wiped out — annihilated! The Crescent now reigned supreme from coast to coast.

This was appalling news. The delegation saw themselves condemned to perpetual exile. What were they to do? Return to court at once, said Dom Rodrigo de Lima; but the others had no wish to wander back inland.

Padre Francisco sat down by a stream alone and wept. But his cheerful disposition soon reasserted itself. "Now, this thing comes from God," he reflected, "and if it is His will that I should remain here, the Lord always be praised! I know this country better than any native because I go hunting, and I know the mountains and the streams, and the fertile soil that will give all that may be planted or sown." On the strength of this knowledge he would remain on this spot and take to farming. He had some good slaves and fourteen cows and rams that he could exchange for ewes. He would settle where there was water and till the soil and sow and plant. He would build a little chapel in which to say Mass, and he would live upon his own produce.

He returned, greatly cheered, to his companions and set forth his scheme. The Portuguese is rare who finds no charm in agriculture, and everybody thought the chaplain's idea excellent. All volunteered to join him. They knew the country and they knew the ropes. They would carry their fruit and vegetables to sell at neighbouring markets. For distraction they would hunt and fish. It might not be a bad life on the whole. "They all embraced me except Dom Rodrigo." Dom Rodrigo, it seems, still hankered for the court; the rest agreed to settle there and make the best of it.

Upon this atmosphere of philosophic resignation Padre Francisco's native servant, Abetai, burst in.

"The Portuguese!" he shouted. "The Portuguese are on the sea!"

"Are you sure what you are saying, Abetai?" his master exclaimed, electrified.

Abetai was. A man arriving from the coast had just gone to tell the local chief.

The Portuguese sat up all night to waylay this man, but, after all, the news he brought was vague. Shots had been heard off the island of Dahlak. That might have been anything. Perhaps the Turks!

Three days of suspense were endured, and then the whole fleet swung serenely into Massawa. The scare had been entirely without foundation. Not only had there been no defeat, there had not even been a battle. A galley had been captured by Moslems near the Gulf of Cambay. No other origin could be ascribed to the fantastic tale.

This time the delegation really got away. In the joy of departure Francisco Alvares did not forget his old patron, Duarte Galvão, who for nine years had been lying in an obscure grave at Kamaran. The faithful chaplain had marked the spot, and he found it again when the fleet halted beside the island. Sailors are superstitious folk and they considered it unlucky to embark a corpse, but Padre Francisco secretly by night unearthed the bones. "I found them all," he says, "except the teeth." These remains were enclosed in a casket and smuggled on board. Antonio Galvão, sole survivor of the dead man's sons, received them reverently in India.

On July 24, 1527 the wanderers arrived in Portugal. Some of them had been away for eight and others for twelve years. How often on sweltering days on Abyssinian plains or Red Sea beaches the travellers must have sighed for the fresh breezes of their native land! Yet, such is the irony of fate, they disembarked in Lisbon, Francisco Alvares affirms, "beneath the greatest heat that I have ever known." These wanderers seasoned to earth's hottest climates were knocked out by a European summer day! More than that. They tell us that two Red Sea Arabs of their party died of heatstroke, under a bridge at Santarem!

PART II

HOW PORTUGAL SAVED PRESTER JOHN

9

The Patriarch's Recruits

✠

The Emir Mahfuzh's trunkless head was preserved as a trophy in the royal tents of Ethiopia. On Saturdays and Sundays and all festivals the Abyssinian maidens and young men made merry with the grisly toy, while Lebna Dengel gazed upon the shrivelled features of his enemy and felt like David looking at Goliath's head.[1]

"God has granted me repose from all my enemies," he had written to Dom Manuel in 1521. "In all the confines of my lands, each time I march against the infidels they fly before my face."[2] Thus Lebna Dengel boasted in the pride of his victorious youth. God granted him this rest for five years more, and then an enemy arose who did not fly before him.

Ahmed-ibn-Ibrahim el Ghazi was the avenger's name, and he was son-in-law to the decapitated Emir. The terrible left-handed Imam Ahmed, once an obscure Somali warrior from Harrar, had risen to supremacy among the Moslem tribes. The Portuguese refer to him as King of Zeila, but this, it seems, was inexact. Whether or not Ahmed was a king, he wielded the same power. The conquering Turks of Egypt and the Red Sea were his allies. They furnished him with firearms and munitions and placed troops of janizaries at his command. With such support Granyé (the Left-handed One) became Ethiopia's scourge. Raid followed raid, and battle followed

105

battle. Fire and sword devoured villages; churches and monasteries were burned and harvests lost. During decades of misery the warfare never ceased.

Lebna Dengel was a fighter. He fought and lost and fought again. The noblest of Ethiopia were slain fighting at his side. His eldest son was killed in battle, and the second carried away captive into Arabia to the Pasha of Zebid. His beautiful Queen, Sabla Vangel, with her younger children, was a refugee for many years on the most inaccessible of Abyssinia's mountains. Vainly the enemy prowled round this eagle's nest. Granyé longed to seize the lovely woman for his own harem, but her citadel was inexpugnable, and Sabla Vangel's youth and beauty faded on the mountain-top.[3]

In all those weary years her husband never sheathed his sword. Disaster followed disaster and left him undismayed. One by one he saw his provinces laid waste. He saw himself abandoned by his chiefs, who, despairing of their country's liberty, cut their own losses by deserting to the victor. He found himself hard pressed and driven back from one mountain stronghold to another, while the iron circle of his foemen slowly closed around. Himself a shadowy ruler with the remnant of a kingdom, he saw all these things clearly, yet with a small and faithful band Lebna Dengel fought on; he still refused all humiliating terms of peace, and died in 1540 still unconquered and still fighting.

What then of his royal ally, his "brother," Dom João III?

The alliance between Portugal and Abyssinia was theoretically a splendid thing. In practice it had one serious drawback: the relative geographical position of the allies was such that regular communications were not easy to establish. The fort of Massawa was to have been the link — but the fort of Massawa had not been built. The appearance of the Portuguese beyond Bab-el-Mandeb continued to be meteoric and irregular. "Close — very securely — the doors of the Straits," had been Albuquerque's dying counsel to Don Manuel,[4] but this advice was disregarded. Long after Albuquerque's death the "doors" were open still, and the Turks had occupied most of the ports of the Red Sea. Their supremacy was challenged from time to time. Every few years a Portuguese fleet swept up to Jidda and to Tor, carrying devastation into the enemy's strongholds. But having bombarded and burned, the Christians sailed away. They made no settlement by the Red Sea, and Abyssinia remained isolated.

Dom João III at the time, unconscious of Ethiopia's plight, was more interested in the Inquisition than in Prester John. The King's ambassador at Rome was using every diplomatic wile to persuade the Pope to have the Holy Office established in Portugal. Till that boon was obtained, other matters were shelved. Poor Padre Francisco Alvares, who had travelled to Rome with Lebna Dengel's letter, was kept waiting for his answer indefinitely. The Portuguese ambassador, quite engrossed by the question of the Inquisition, would do nothing to remind the Pope of the remote affairs of Abyssinia.

In Lisbon the equally unhappy Saga Zaab marked time. He could not go home until he had the answers of both King and Pope. When years passed and he did not return, Lebna Dengel grew furious with his innocent ambassador. What was the man doing, the Emperor wondered angrily, to stay away so long? He resolved to send another envoy after him — the Patriarch himself.

Needless to say, it was not Mark. That gentle centenarian was already dead, and Alexandria had not been called upon to find him a successor. A new Abuna was recruited on the spot — how qualified it would be difficult to say, for in the freshly appointed head of the Abyssinian Church we recognize the physician Mestre João!

How the metamorphosis happened is not clear. The practice of medicine does not as a rule lead to supreme ecclesiastical honour, but Mestre João appears to have been one of those fortunate conceited people who manage to be taken at their own face value. Mestre João fancied the role of Abuna, which high function he felt that he would worthily adorn, and it seems that he got Lebna Dengel to agree with him. The lawfulness of the investiture has more than once been queried, but lawful or otherwise, it suited the Negus that his Patriarch should be a Portuguese. Thus Mestre João makes his shining reappearance on this page as Dom João Bermudez, high pontiff of the Abyssinian Church.

The ex-physician was nothing loath to visit Europe arrayed in his new glory. There Lebna Dengel dispatched him, in 1535, that he might call Saga Zaab to order and expound Abyssinia's straits to Dom João III.

Travellers to Europe from Ethiopia had two routes from which to choose: that of the sea via India and the Cape, which meant waiting at Massawa for the uncertain arrival of the Portuguese fleet, or the overland route up the Nile Valley, by which you could save time if you were lucky enough to be captured neither by the Turks in Egypt nor by pirates in the Mediterranean afterwards. Dom João Bermudez chose the shorter and more risky road. "I was caught by the Turks and nearly killed," he tells us, in spite of which he seems to have reached Europe in great form.

His mission was entirely a success — according to himself. The King received him graciously, and the Pope was delighted to do him honour. The guilty Saga Zaab, like a dog with its tail between its legs, came meekly slinking up to kiss the Patriarch's hand, whereupon "I had him loaded with chains," says Dom João Bermudez fiercely.

Dom João III — the Patriarch is our informant still — gladly conceded everything that Lebna Dengel asked. He promised to send help to Abyssinia, and arranged to have the Patriarch sail for India with the new Viceroy, Dom Garcia de Noronha, who "was happy to take me with him." But having been poisoned (he supposes) by that villain Saga Zaab, "I suddenly fell ill," and could not leave that year — which must have been a blow for Dom Garcia!

All the King's physicians were summoned to the bedside of the interesting invalid, and, thanks to their care, the Patriarch was restored to health in time to sail with the 1539 fleet for Goa, where — again we have his word for it — he was received with overwhelming honours.

The Viceroy, João Bermudez states, was most attentive to him, and prepared to lead a fleet to Massawa without delay. Thither Dom João Bermudez would have sailed that year with an imposing escort, but Dom Garcia died of dysentery at Cochin, and the privilege of carrying the Patriarch to the Red Sea was left to his successor. . . .

Dom João Bermudez's account of his own triumphs reads well. We ought to be impressed. Unfortunately, there exists a nasty little document — a letter written some years later by Dom João III to the Negus — which tells another tale. The King, it seems, had not admired the Patriarch — if Patriarch indeed he were, which fact Dom João doubts: "I do not believe him to be more than a simple priest, and of the powers that he says the Holy Father granted him, I know nothing at all." [5]

Unimpressed though he was by the messenger, it is certain that the King did not ignore the message. Existing records tell us little on the subject, except of course the narrative of Dom João Bermudez, from which we gather that the sole objective of the cruise to the Red Sea in 1541 was to carry him to Massawa, together with an expeditionary force entirely organized by him and under his supreme command. The impression given by the chronicles, however, is that the Patriarch was just an incident and not the pivot of the voyage! Nor is there any mention of a plan for sending help to Abyssinia in the two letters that the Governor's brother wrote to the King before he sailed.[6] This new Governor, Dom Estevão da Gama, who arrived in India from Malacca, found among his predecessor's papers instructions to lead a fleet up to Suez, destroying all the Turkish ports, and he at once prepared to do so.

The fleet called at Massawa to make repairs, and there they heard the latest Ethiopian news. It was not very cheerful. Lebna Dengel had died six months before, and Galawdewos (or Claudius), his son, was reigning over what was left of Abyssinia, supported by such chiefs as had not yet deserted. Galawdewos was very young and felt entirely lost. The enemy was as numerous as ever and more active. The Emperor had no firearms nor munitions to oppose their guns, and most of his subjects were traitors. No wonder that, in the words of Dom João de Castro, "he wrote letters that were more than piteous and miserable, on all of which above his signature was depicted Our Lord Jesus crucified."

Dom Estevão da Gama had no time just then to consider these heart-rending appeals, for he was in a hurry to proceed to Suez. He decided to leave the heavy ships at Massawa while he took the lighter craft up the Red Sea. Massawa was supposed to be subject to the Abyssinian Empire, but the Moslem tribes that occupied the coast had long ceased paying tribute to the Negus. An enterprising scallywag — one of Granye's chief men — had taken possession of the port and styled himself King of Massawa. When the Portuguese fleet appeared, however, the "king" had modestly withdrawn and held himself at a safe distance several leagues away. Dom Estevão sent a message after him: "Pay me twenty seraphims for the expenses of this fleet, and give me Suez pilots, if you would not have me destroy the land."

The "King of Massawa" made answer that he had no money and he had no Suez pilots, but he could offer two for Suakin — and Dom Estevão might destroy the land if he saw fit.

Dom Estevão, obliged to own that you cannot lay waste a desert, accepted such pilots as could be had. Thus he sailed, leaving his kinsman, Manuel da Gama, at Massawa in command of the larger ships.

The Patriarch, of course, also remained. He had been, he tells us, overcome with grief at Lebna Dengel's death. He would have liked to die. But the Governor and all the important people in the fleet had gathered round him to console him. "They visited me many times, so I took courage." Meanwhile, a messenger was sent to advise Galawdewos of the am-

110

bassador's return. The Emperor was requested to send somebody who would take charge of Dom João Bermudez.

The Emperor's camp was far away in the mountains of
Shoa. Weeks must elapse before the messenger returned. The
Patriarch, now reconciled to life, waited in Manuel da Gama's
ship and proved a source of trouble.

As may have been observed, João Bermudez was a man
whom dignity inflates, and that of Patriarch had swelled him
up to bursting-point. In Abyssinia, he informs us, the Patriarch
enjoys the same consideration as the Pope in Europe. He was
therefore dazzled by his own importance and he wished to
dazzle others too. The more the land of his adoption was ex-
tolled, the brighter shone his own reflected glory. Thus he
talked of Abyssinia constantly and he talked very big. Men
listened open-mouthed to his tales of the greatness and riches
of that enchanted land and the magnificence of its monarch.
Silver and gold were as little to the Negus as they had been to
his ancestor Solomon. There was nothing that he would deny
to those who fought for him. His empire was the place where
every able-bodied man could win a fortune. Abyssinia was
the land of all delights.

It was the more tantalizing that the men were actually dying at Massawa. Massawa was everything unpleasant. "The
heat of this country is unbelievable!" groans an unknown
writer who had sampled it himself. It was also unhealthful.
Manuel da Gama was soon obliged to set up a hospital ashore,
and new patients entered it daily to die "of an illness that
lasted only two days. They felt a great pain in their chests,
and after this had started they could live no longer." For those
who were not ill there was nothing to do and, worse still,
hardly anything to eat. Either through faulty organization or
owing to lack of funds, the ships' stores had given out, and
supplies had to be purchased on land. They had to buy food
out of their own pay; they were poor and it was very dear,
wherefore "besides the heat, we suffered so from hunger that
a hen was paid for in gold, and everything else in proportion.

Well might the men consider the time that they spent here as the worst in their lives." [7]

The days dragged on, Governor did not return, and Manuel da Gama was unpopular. He seems to have been as harsh a commander as the great Vasco himself, without the same gifts. "He was so difficult to live with," one writer declares, "that nobody could stand him." [8] The men began to grumble openly. Since they had been abandoned in this hole, why should they not travel to the land of plenty and take service with Prester John?

The Patriarch applauded the suggestion. It seems that the King had given him authority to raise volunteers for Prester John. Placing a broad interpretation upon this permission, Dom João Bermudez encouraged would-be deserters from the fleet. He was lavish with promises on the Emperor's behalf, and made endowments right and left — on paper. He looked forward, no doubt, to appearing before Prester John backed by a strong contingent, but he overreached himself at last. His glowing tales made men's mouths water and they could not wait. One by one they slipped ashore and disappeared. Vainly Manuel da Gama proclaimed that under pain of death no volunteers might go inland except when Dom João Bermudez went, and subject to the Governor's leave. Evasions still continued.

The Patriarch's propaganda brought about yet more serious results. Some eighty or a hundred men made up their minds to escape all together. They collected their muskets and their swords. They chose a captain — Antonio Correa [9] — and a guide was engaged ashore to lead them to the Emperor's camp. They stole a boat one night and rowed away, quite determined that nothing would turn them back.

The watchmen saw them go and sounded the alarm. Manuel da Gama with a boatload of armed men launched out in pursuit. He ordered the fugitives to be fired upon, but the gunners' sympathies were on the side of the deserters, and "as they did not shoot with a good will, all missed the mark." [10]

The adventurers landed safely on the beach and organized their little band. They had a fife and drum to enliven the way, and a pennon to carry before them. The guide was found at the appointed place, and, full of hope, they plunged into the desolate hinterland.

All night long they followed their guide across the black and burning mountains where "the sun had left such heat that it seemed to be shining still." The path was steep and rough and rocky. After scrambling for some hours over these scorched stones, breathing the fiery dryness of the desert air, the travellers were afflicted by a maddening thirst. Here was a detail that they had overlooked in their light-hearted escape. They had thought of drums and trumpets and guns, but it appears that they had brought no water, and none could be found in this stricken wilderness. As the heat and discomfort increased, "they shouted to the guide to take them where they could find water." If they had to walk on in this oven they must drink.

The guide "showed great good will and led them into some valleys between mountains, saying that there was water farther down." Gasping, but happily expectant, the adventurers plodded on. Under the paling stars of dawn they plunged into the narrow gorge — and straight into an ambush.

Then "our men understood that the guide had deceived them that they might all be slain, and so they killed him and began to fight the Moors with their guns, and the Moors with arrows and slings which showered so many stones upon them that they did not know what to do; none the less, the guns did much harm to the Moors and kept them at a distance.

"These Moors were men of the King of Zeila and the King of Massawa . . . with them were Turkish musketeers; but the worst evil [for the Portuguese] was the great thirst from which they suffered."

Antonio Correa was the first man to be killed, but another captain was appointed hastily, and the battle continued. The fugitives fought desperately, and the struggle might have

113

been prolonged if the Moslems had not devised a stratagem.
They suddenly cried out that the fighting should cease. It
had started only by mistake. They really were all Christians
and loyal vassals of Prester John! They had supposed the Portuguese were robbers at first sight — hence the attack. Now
that daylight had revealed their true identity, why not make
peace?

Hostilities were suspended at once, but some of the Portuguese remained suspicious. It would be more prudent, they
said, to go on fighting. But the majority were frantic with
thirst and could not think of anything but their longing for
water. The risen sun shone on an arid waste; they had no
guide, and if they killed these men, who could lead them to
where there was something to drink? The improvised captain
especially felt that he could endure the agony no longer. "He
was feeble," comments Gaspar Correa, who was used to commanders made of sterner stuff. This man prevailed upon his
comrades to make peace, at which the Moslems all embraced
the Portuguese like long-lost brothers. Did they want water?
asked the kindly souls; they should have some at once! So they
were led, all unsuspecting, to the King of Zeila's tent.

The terrible Granyé was sitting with his hands devoutly
clasped about a string of beads to which was hung a little
wooden cross. Reverently he handed this chaplet to the Portuguese captain. "I say my prayers with these," Granyé explained.

The fugitives were in no mood to query the sincerity of his
devotions. Could they have water? they implored their pious
host, who brought gourds full of water then and there. The
sight was too much for parched and weary men. Oblivious of
all else, they cast their weapons to the ground and drank.
They drank and drank and drank, and then loosened their
belts to drink still more.

The Moors, meanwhile, laughing and chatting pleasantly,
picked up the muskets, swords, and lances and examined
them. It all was done in such an innocent and casual manner

that the Portuguese paid no attention. They were only roused from their orgy of water-drinking when "the Moors, having taken possession of most of the weapons, attacked the Portuguese with them, killing and wounding as many as they could."

"Surrender," cried the King, "and your lives will be spared." As nearly all of them were disarmed and defenceless, this appeared the only thing to do, but fourteen valiant souls refused. "Unfortunate men!" they shouted to their comrades. "Why surrender to traitors? Die like men, for they will kill you cruelly!" So saying, they grasped what weapons they had left, and stood their ground and died. In a few minutes all was over. But one man out of the fourteen had the presence of mind, as he fell wounded to the ground, to roll over and lie still as if dead, face downward in his blood. With rigid self-control he played the corpse all day, and so he witnessed his companions' fate.

"Those that had surrendered, the Moors bound hand and foot; they stripped them naked, and shut them in a cattle-pen." Towards evening the Moors lined up outside on horse-back, with all their lances bristling in the fading light. "They ordered the pen to be opened, loosed one of the captives, and bade him come out to where the King and his captains sat on their horses by the door. As the wretched prisoner emerged, thus naked, the King thrust at him with his spear and gave him the first wound, and then the others did the same, and all tormented him." As soon as the victim fell dead, a second was called out, and so the ghastly game continued until no one was left. "And when the sun had cooled, the Moors loaded their packs and removed to another place, because of all the dead men that lay there."

The living man, alone among the dead, still dared not move for hours. It was only after stifling darkness had blotted out the scene of horror that, by a superhuman effort, he rose. The way back to the coast was long, and his wounds were severe, but the horrors that he had seen that day gave him unnatural strength. Step by step, and watching constantly, he dragged himself in the direction of the sea. All through the hours of darkness, like a hunted thing, he strained on in his halting flight, until at dawn, from a hilltop, he saw the sea that stood for his salvation. He struggled successfully across the intervening wastes, reached the shore, and followed it to Arkiko and Massawa. He finally rejoined his ship, but in what condition he arrived is not recorded.

"Sir," said the deserter to his commander-in-chief, "I present myself to you to punish as you may think fit, for all the Portuguese who went from here to seek Prester John have met with great chastisement."

They had met with no more than they deserved, said Manuel da Gama wrathfully. God executed judgment upon those who disobeyed their King and the representatives of the royal authority.

A storm of protests greeted these words. Whose fault was it, his followers demanded of the captain, if starved and desperate men escaped and so met death? They had no governor to help them and relieve their misery. What Manuel da Gama ought now to do was to lead an expeditionary force ashore in order to avenge their slaughtered comrades. "There was not a man who would not be delighted to undertake the work."

Manuel da Gama showed no wish to go. He said that he was glad those Moors were there as a chastisement for the disobedient. Mutiny and desertion in the face of hardship were against the Portuguese tradition. It seemed, he added witheringly, "that now they wished to use the treachery and evil ways of Italian soldiers — men in whom is neither truth nor law." And he reinforced his maxims by hanging five men whom he accused of having known of the deserters' plans.

In the end he did attempt a punitive raid ashore, but the Moslems disappeared into the landscape at the Portuguese approach and were nowhere to be found.

The five corpses were still hanging on the beach when the Governor returned to Massawa.[11]

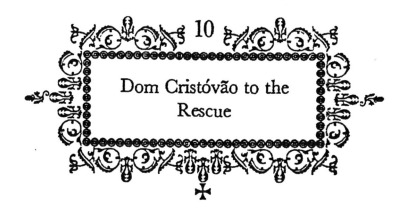

10

Dom Cristóvão to the Rescue

✠

Dom Estevão da Gama's cruise from Goa to Suez has been immortalized by Dom João de Castro. That learned hero kept a minute log of the whole voyage, from which we gather that the fleet was back at Massawa by May 22.[1]

It was a triumphant return. Dom Estevão had carried out his raid upon the Turkish ports with that brilliance and efficiency to be expected of the great admiral's son, while the prowess of the Governor's young brother, Dom Cristóvão, further maintained the family tradition.

Their arrival at Massawa was hailed with joy. Manuel da Gama, whose position had been fast growing untenable, was thankful to hand over the supreme command, while the men were happy to be delivered from Manuel da Gama. Thus harmony was automatically restored, and Dom Estevão was able to turn his attention to the Abyssinian question.

It was clear that something had to be decided about this. The Bahr Nagach had come to Massawa to fetch the Patriarch, and there the Governor found him — a woebegone and tearful Bahr Nagach. He was one of the few Abyssinian nobles who were faithful, but even his own father had deserted to the enemy. Trembling with emotion, and with eyes that "streamed like living fountains," the loyal Ethiopian pleaded his country's cause. Here was a Christian realm, he said, usurped by

117

infidels — a Christian people led into captivity. Prester John implored his royal brother, who was champion of the weak, to rescue him and to restore his lands, which really belonged to the King of Portugal and were held in his name.

Such a humble and pathetic cry for help could not fall on deaf ears. Dom Estevão assembled his captains at once and asked them for their views. The answer was unanimous. Not only did all agree that Prester John ought to be helped, but everybody volunteered to go. It was finally decided that four hundred men should be sent, and that number was easily made up. To choose a captain for them was more difficult. Every *fidalgo* in the fleet implored the Governor to appoint him, and Cristóvão da Gama, more especially, gave his brother no peace.

Dom Estevão hesitated. He had enough foresight to estimate what such an undertaking really meant. Dom Estevão was a man of nearly forty and had ceased to see the world through the enchanting glamour of first youth. To rush off in a white heat of crusading fervour to the rescue of a Christian realm might be a holy and a glorious enterprise, but how was it likely to end? Dom Estevão looked across the bay towards that terrible hinterland where thunderclouds obscured the distant mountains. Up in those fastnesses, above the coast like an inferno swept by demon hordes, the citadel of African Christianity still held. It had stood for centuries like a rock while the waves of Islam beat in vain about its base, but to-day the rejuvenated forces of the conquering Turk had loosed upon it all the fierce tribes of Somaliland and the hordes of Arabia. And this rock was already undermined. What hope was there for Abyssinia? It was a kingdom overrun and lost, doomed by its own dissensions. The young ruler, abandoned by his chiefs, clung to his dying empire, but the Christian island was about to sink into the Moslem sea. Portugal, in honour bound, had to send help, but what were four hundred men to stem that tide? It was a forlorn hope.

Dom Estevão thought of all these things before he chose a

captain for the volunteers. "It can only be my brother," he announced at last. "I can sacrifice him, but I have no right to risk the son of any other man." [2]

Dom Cristóvão da Gama was overjoyed to be the chosen victim. He was a youth of twenty-four with all his father's tireless energy and grim tenacity of purpose. He also shared the family ability. It is certain that he was a young dare-devil, but he had a good head on his shoulders and a gift for leadership. Responsibility might safely rest with him. He and his selected companions made their preparations enthusiastically. The chief names recorded of that gallant band are Manuel da Cunha, João da Fonseca, the brothers Inofre and Francisco de Abreu, Francisco Velho, Luiz Rodrigues de Carvalho, and Miguel de Castanhoso, who has told their tale.

The reverend Patriarch, of course, was of the party, though he does not figure conspicuously in any narrative except his own, from which account, however, we may gather the impression that the real commander of the expedition was himself.

The soldiers were picked men, the best in all the fleet, and very well equipped. Eight pieces of artillery were given them, a good supply of ammunition, and a hundred muskets, besides which each man carried a double set of arms. Dom Estevão presented this smart little army to the Bahr Nagach.

"I have assembled these men whom you see," the Governor said, "and I deliver them to you, together with my brother, who is prepared to serve till death, as are also all the Portuguese who go with him. . . . Sir Brother," he added, embracing Dom Cristóvão, "remember before everything the service of Our Lord. . . . And especially, I beg of you, that what you least esteem should be your life."

Dom Estevão was very loath to say good-bye to his young brother. He seemed convinced that it was a last farewell. He led him away alone by the seashore, where for a long while the two sons of Vasco da Gama were seen pacing the beach and talking to each other. Estevão wept as he embraced Cristóvão fervently before they rejoined their companions and the expedition was officially dismissed.

The Governor took a banner of white damask embroidered with a crimson satin cross and handed it to Dom Cristóvão in front of all his men. "Sir Brother," he said, "I deliver to your keeping this standard of the King, our lord, bearing the emblem of Christ, and I charge you and command you on our good father's blessing that you defend it and uphold it in every way you can, as far as in you lies, with every power you possess, and even with your life."

"Senhor Governador," replied the young man proudly, "I trust in the Passion of Our Lord that while I live I shall perform such deeds that the King our lord will greatly thank you for having placed this charge upon me. Time shall be witness."

Thus Dom Cristóvão and his four hundred men set out on the long trail while Dom Estevão went back sadly to his ship.

There was no sadness in the hearts of the young enthusiasts who turned their faces to the distant mountains. They were crusaders and knights-errant, with a throne to rescue and the Infidel to fight. They were embarking on a holy and a chivalrous adventure that, if they lived, would cover them with glory, and if they died meant certain paradise. Nothing discouraged them, meanwhile – not the long and tedious march from Massawa into the heart of Abyssinia, neither the roughness of the road, the blistering heat, nor even lack of water. Each obstacle was gaily overcome as it arose. When the fiery sunshine of June in the desert made day progress impossible, they marched at night and slept by day instead. Since the mules and camels given by the Bahr Nagach were insufficient to mount everyone, all walked and used the beasts only to bear the loads. When those vertiginous paths were reached at which the camels jibbed and would not carry their burdens any farther, Dom Cristóvão and his men relieved the animals and struggled up the mountains with the artillery upon their backs.

Dom Cristóvão to the Rescue

In this manner [writes Miguel de Castanhoso] we travelled for six days, on the last of which we climbed so high a mountain that to reach the top took us from dawn till dusk. And when we were upon the summit, we discovered wide pastures and a cool and level land where the air was very pure, and there was water clear and good.

This was the tableland of Debaroa — a paradise after the arid wilderness. But it was a ruined paradise. The Moslem scourge had passed over those fertile fields and laid them waste. All signs of human life and cultivation were wiped out, and the large church where the party rested for two days was half demolished.

They travelled on across this pleasant region, "which we enjoyed more than the hot country we had left." Here was fresh air, and water in abundance, but the scene continued to be one of smiling desolation. The villages were uninhabited and the crops left to their fate, for the villagers had fled before the Moors and hidden with their cattle in the mountains.

On the outskirts of Debaroa a melancholy procession met Dom Cristóvão. All the monks came out with crosses in their hands and, chanting dolefully, they threw themselves at the young captain's feet. They welcomed him as their deliverer. "Our Lord has brought him!" they cried. "For fourteen years the enemies of our holy faith have trodden down the land and demolished His sanctuaries." Dom Cristóvão like an apostle of God had been sent to save the people from captivity. "I do not think," observes Miguel de Castanhoso, "that any man could have been there without shedding a thousand tears."

The monks then led their champion to prayers within the ruined monastery, where elaborate carvings still remained beneath an improvised roof of straw thatch.

The Bahr Nagach advised the Portuguese to camp at Debaroa until October, when the rainy season, just beginning, would be over. Before then it would be difficult to join forces

121

with Prester John. The Emperor, it appeared, had just suffered a fresh defeat and was sheltering in high mountains some three hundred leagues away. When the dry season set in, he would no doubt march to meet his allies with what little army he had left.

The Bahr Nagach, meanwhile, had tents pitched outside Debaroa for the Portuguese, and the peasants brought them what little produce they had left from their neglected fields. These people came down from the heights and re-entered their homes when Dom Cristóvão and his men arrived. Hope had returned to Debaroa, for they felt that the white strangers could not fail to save. Had not Dom Cristóvão assured the monks that "Our Lord would shortly restore their prosperity"? And they took further comfort when he told them that he came to their land for no other purpose than to expel the Moors and to die for the Christian faith.

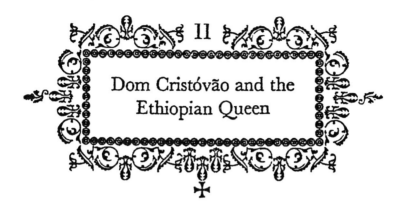

11

Dom Cristóvão and the Ethiopian Queen

Upon a platform perched above a precipice, Queen Sabla Vangel mourned her widowhood. Besides her husband she had lost two sons, and the eldest one surviving — only eighteen years old — was fighting far away. While the young Emperor carried on the losing struggle for his father's throne, it seemed that his family was doomed to end its days upon the mountain-top. At least they were removed from any danger. Above the world and out of it, Sabla Vangel with her mother, two fair daughters, and a younger son had found a certain refuge from their foes.

It was the strangest and the strongest fortress Nature ever built, which only a winged enemy might storm. A huge bare rock that tapered to a giddy height curved outward at the summit just as if the mountain wore a hat or else was balancing a tray upon its head. The plateau so formed measured a quarter of a league around and appeared inaccessible from down below. It was, in fact, inaccessible to any casual climber, for the breakneck spiral path that led up to the crest came to a sudden end against a wall of rock. The last part of the ascent could only be made in a swinging basket lowered from the guardhouse seventy feet above.

A stronghold such as this could only be surprised by treason, for hunger could not drive it to surrender. Upon this platform hung in space all cereals grew and flourished. Goats multiplied upon the rocks, hens scratched there happily, and innumerable swarms of bees provided honey. Two enormous cisterns gathered in the yearly rains, providing water sufficient for five hundred persons. Thus Sabla Vangel and her children suffered no hardship on their island in the air, which, Castanhoso observes, "appeared made by the hand of God expressly to save this lady and her people from captivity, and that a monastery of friars established up there should not be destroyed." A monastery on such a site was inevitable. The recluses of Abyssinia had the instincts of the chamois and the eagle, and any retreat so hopelessly cut off could not fail to find favour in their sight. But we should like to know how the first ascension of that mountain was achieved!

From Debaroa, which was not far off, Dom Cristóvão dispatched two men to fetch the Queen. Manuel da Cunha and Francisco Velho pitched their tents at the mountain foot and sent to announce their arrival to the guard aloft.

Sabla Vangel was thrilled. The Christian conquerors of the East were coming to deliver her! With such an escort she could safely leave her mountain. Let the messengers come up at once, she said, that she might see and speak to them, and she would prepare to come down with them next day.

The basket was let down the cliff; the two white men were hauled up one by one and welcomed by the Queen as heaven-sent guests. Sabla Vangel wept for joy. She called Dom Cristóvão and all the Portuguese her sons. She knew that she would soon be avenged of her enemies, she said, now that the Lord had sent these men to rescue Abyssinia.

Two days later a picturesque procession entered Debaroa. Sabla Vangel rode side-saddle on a beautiful grey mule, caparisoned with silks that swept the ground. A screen upheld over the royal traveller concealed her form from curious-eyed. The Bahr Nagach walked humbly at her bridle-rein. He was naked to the waist and with a lion-skin flung across his shoul-

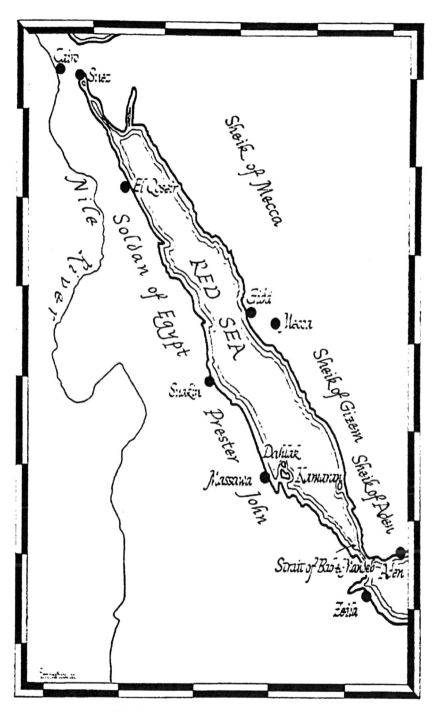

Cairo

Suez

Sheik of Mecca

El Coseir

Nile River

Soldan of Egypt

RED SEA

Gidda

Mecca

Suakin

Sheik of Gizem

Prester John

Dahlak

Kamaran

Sheik of Aden

Kassawa

Strait of Bab-Mandeb

Aden

Zeila

COASTS OF THE RED SEA IN 1513

ders, which dishabille was in accordance with the strictest court etiquette. For an Abyssinian to be seen in the Imperial presence fully dressed would be unpardonable presumption.

With blue and white pennons fluttering in the breeze, and carrying their white and crimson flag, Dom Cristóvão and all his men turned out to meet the Queen. They were wearing "their best clothes, which were very good." Sabla Vangel, too, had made a toilet equal to the occasion, as was revealed when she opened her screen. She was dressed in finest white Indian cloths, under a grey satin cloak embroidered with golden flowers. Her headdress, Castanhoso observed, was "after the Portuguese fashion," but a veil before her face hid all except her eyes. Her approach was greeted by a roar of artillery and crack of guns, while the troops lined up to form a guard of honour on each side of the bewildered Queen.

Dom Cristóvão stepped forward gallantly. His breeches and his doublet were deep purple embroidered with gold; a French cloak of black and gold hung from his shoulders, and a black cap with a gold medallion completed the colour scheme. He was a personable young man. The Queen received him graciously and raised her veil while talking to him.

Dom Cristóvão was ready with a little speech, which a kneeling interpreter translated. He told her how the Governor of India, hearing of Ethiopia's plight, had sent them to the rescue, and how they were all quite ready to die in defence of the land. Sabla Vangel listened happily. Neither she nor any prince on earth could repay them, she said, but only God.

In this manner Queen Sabla Vangel left the silent peace of limitless horizons to join the martial stir and bustle of the camp. She does not seem to have regretted the exchange. All through that rainy season at Debaroa she was the hidden and interested witness of her allies' activities. Peeping through the aperture of her tent, she admired their shining arms, she listened enthralled to their fifes and drums, and she marvelled at the elaborate military manoeuvres which Dom Cristóvão and his young sparks performed with a peculiar zest born of the consciousness that the Queen and her ladies were looking on.

There were less romantic things to do, however, than parading in front of the royal tent. Material of all kinds had to be collected for the coming campaign. Gun carriages were necessary, and woodwork for the fortification of camps. To make such things these young *fidalgos* all turned carpenters. "We cut the wood ourselves," says Castanhoso, "and sawed it too, because the natives have no skill for anything." Dom Cristóvão was the master of works, and "directed them as if he had been born and brought up to such labours." It was all part of the day's work and he was very happy. Twenty-four carts were constructed under his guidance. Animals, of course, would be required to draw the vehicles, but they, too, were obtained. "With the Queen's permission, we assaulted a few Moslem villages, where we took many mules on which we rode — for until then we all went afoot — and we also captured many cows and oxen, which we trained to draw the carts."

Working by day, and maintaining armed watch by night, they passed the winter and it was time to join forces with Prester John. Letters from him had already arrived. The Emperor was enthusiastic over the coming help. It was what might be expected, he declared, from such a great King as his brother. Besides, it had been prophesied of old that Abyssinia was to be saved by white men. As soon as weather made it possible to take the road, the Emperor would set out to meet the Portuguese.

The camp at Debaroa was raised on December 15. The Queen and her women accompanied the army, besides two hundred Abyssinian carriers.

Dom Cristóvão divided his forces into five captaincies of fifty soldiers each, while the remaining men guarded the flag. Two captains, turn and turn about, marched with the baggage wagons, the rest riding ahead. Dom Cristóvão with four men mounted on swift mules rode down the ranks twice daily

Dom Cristóvão and the Ethiopian Queen

to make sure that all was well, and Miguel de Castanhoso, bringing up the rear, was escort to the Queen.

It was a strenuous march. The transport of troops and war material over Abyssinian mountains has never been an easy matter, and in those days there were no facilities at all. "In many places where the oxen could not draw the carts," says Castanhoso, "we had to pull them up ourselves." But a stage upon the route was reached at which even this mode of traction failed. The carts stuck fast and could not be moved one way or another. In vain Dom Cristóvão scanned the rocky heights that closed in on every side. There was neither path nor trail where anything on wheels might pass. What was to happen? asked Sabla Vangel in dismay. The men might climb the mountains, but the wagons simply could not get across.

But Dom Cristóvão was determined that they should. Imperturbably, he had his carts taken to pieces, and unscrewed the various parts belonging to the artillery. He shouldered everything that he could carry, and each one of his companions did likewise. "It took us three days to climb those mountains with our loads." But the top was reached at last, and nothing left behind, to Sabla Vangel's great astonishment. There were no people like the Portuguese! she said with deep conviction.

Upon those heights, whipped by a dry and icy wind, they lingered to reassemble their carts. A little white town was perched there aloft, and on the highest peak (of course!) a hermitage. The trail that led there was better designed for goats than for the human foot, but the travellers, it seems, had still the energy to climb up and explore. Within the hermitage a strange sight met their eyes. No recluse occupied these walls, only three hundred mummies of white men "sown up in thongs of dry and worn-out leather. The bodies were almost perfect, with only nose, lips, and some fingers missing."

Nobody was able to explain the origin of these mysterious human remains, though the natives all agreed that they were centuries old. One tradition had it that they were men who had conquered the land in Roman times. Others preferred to think that these were saints, for did not sanctity preserve a corpse? They were both saints and martyrs, affirmed Dom João Bermudez, on the strength of which assertion some men prudently laid in a stock of holy relics.

Miguel de Castanhoso accepted this theory with reserve. Certainly, he says, there seems to be some mystery here. But the mere desiccation of dead bodies does not strike him as miraculous, even the living in this air risk being shrivelled up, for "I have never been in any country where it was so dry and cold."

Leaving the nameless dead to their eternal sleep, the troops resumed the march.

No Moslems had been encountered as yet, for the King of Zeila still was far away. Such few of his officials as were in the villages to levy tribute made themselves scarce when the army appeared, and everywhere the peasants offered their allegiance to the royal flag. Districts that had been conquered by the Moors at once surrendered, and now some chiefs who still were faithful dared to express their sentiments and join the Queen. But the number of Ethiopian chiefs who had unblushingly deserted astonished Castanhoso's honest soul. Prester John, he says, could never have been brought so low if his people had been as loyal as the Portuguese.

They were now approaching the first stronghold conquered by the King of Zeila from the Emperor. This was the famous Amba Sanayt, another of Abyssinia's natural fortresses. The beautiful and fertile tableland above could only be reached by one of three passes, any of which had to be climbed in full view of the garrison aloft. Two of these ways of approach were breakneck paths protected by stone walls and powerful gates, but the third required no reinforcements beyond those of Nature's making. A precipitous slope of loose stones that only a barefooted man might scale without disaster terminated in a cliff in which some footholds had been cut.

Dom Cristóvão and the Ethiopian Queen

Years ago a party of harmless-looking merchants had held a fair at the base of this mountain. The people from the high tableland came down to see their wares. They bought and sold, and took the friendly merchants home with them to set up business in the mountain villages. As soon as they were safely on the heights, the merchants threw off their disguise and showed themselves as Moslem warriors. So Amba Sanayt was taken by treason, and Granyé followed there himself and made it very strong. Five hundred men were placed on guard at every pass, and a body of horsemen was kept in readiness to conduct raids upon the villages below. This garrison became the terror of the countryside, for none knew when the band of robbers might swoop down to burn and plunder and to carry men and women off into captivity.

Queen Sabla Vangel trembled when she heard that Dom Cristóvão proposed to storm the eagle's nest. She sent for the young man and gravely remonstrated. She assured him that Amba Sanayt was impregnable. It would be easier to rout twelve thousand men upon the battlefield than penetrate that eyrie. Besides, his army was still too small to make such an attempt. Better avoid Amba Sanayt by a wide detour, and when they had joined forces with her son, see then what might be done.

Dom Cristóvão listened unmoved. He must take Amba Sanayt, he replied. It would be a military error to pass on with such an enemy stronghold behind one's back. But there was no cause for alarm, he earnestly assured her, for they were Portuguese! With God's help he hoped to take the mountain without much peril, and the Queen could set her mind at rest, because they all would die before they let her come to harm.

As it seemed to Sabla Vangel that they all would die in any case, this thought did not really console her. "Do as you think best," she said at last, finding her champion quite determined. But her heart sank as she looked up at the forbidding mountain with a church converted to a mosque perched on the top.

Leaving his trembling protégé, Dom Cristóvão studied the approaches to Amba Sanayt. He allotted one pass to Francisco Velho and Manuel da Cunha with their respective men and three pieces of artillery; João da Fonseca and Francisco de Abreu, similarly equipped, would take the second, while he himself attacked the last and most dangerous of the three with the rest of the men. He left the Bahr Nagach and all his following to guard the Queen, and a few Portuguese were detailed to stay with them.

Sabla Vangel watched everything unhappily. She nearly gave way to panic when Dom Cristóvão feigned a preliminary assault. He wished to find out how the land lay and on what lines the defence would be conducted, so while the enemy flung rocks about, he made his observations and retired. The Queen, who did not understand such a manœuvre, concluded that this was a defeat, and it required all Dom Cristóvão's eloquence to persuade her that everything was well.

"Next day at dawn," writes Castanhoso, "we commended ourselves to Our Lady and said a general confession before a crucifix which a priest held in his hands, and we were absolved by the Patriarch." So fortified, they marched up the mountain, the signal for the attack was given, and all three passes were assaulted simultaneously.

It was the artillery that won the day. The Portuguese would have been crushed beneath the boulders and stones hurled down upon them if they had not thinned the foemen's ranks by constant and well-directed fire upon the height. Covered by their artillery, they charged uphill, Dom Cristóvão leading the way. They scaled the slippery slope and negotiated the rock wall. This last was very difficult with missiles falling from above — "Twice we were thrown down when nearly at the top" — but in the end they climbed and stayed.

The other two passes were similarly stormed and a fierce battle was soon raging on the tableland. The Moslems fought bravely, but the unexpectedness of a triple assault threw them into confusion: "Those who fled from Dom Cristóvão fell in with Manuel da Cunha's men, or with those of the other captains, so all were trapped and none escaped our swords." The resistance ended in a panic. Some leapt wildly over the cliff to meet their death upon the rocks below, others took shelter in the houses of the native mountaineers, who promptly turned against their vanquished tyrants and slew them without mercy.

Dom Cristóvão made his way to the mosque. That edifice was immediately reconsecrated as "Nossa Senhora da Victoria" and Mass was celebrated there next day. There, too, the Portuguese buried their dead, who numbered only eight, though fifty wounded swelled the list of casualties.

Many captive Christian women were found in the village and released. The Moslem wives and daughters, also numerous, were presented to the Queen. Sabla Vangel might have increased her retinue of slaves, but she hardened her heart against her foewomen and put them all to death.

The Queen was amazed at Dom Cristóvão's rapid victory. Truly, she said, her allies had been sent by God, and nothing was impossible to them. Dom Cristóvão invited her to climb up and inspect the captured mountain, but she refused. The slopes were strewn with dead bodies, and though Sabla Vangel might calmly order wholesale executions, she could not bear to look upon a corpse. Dom Cristóvão had to come down to her.

The conquered territory was given to a faithful Abyssinian chief, and the Portuguese lingered there until the wounded had recovered. Another joy was shortly added to the pleasure of their victory when two compatriots turned up quite unexpectedly from Massawa with letters. The Governor, Dom Estevão, had sent five ships to the Red Sea early in 1542 to find out how the Abyssinian expedition fared. What letters meant to men who thought themselves cut off from their own kind is easy to imagine. "We all were happy to have news from India," Castanhoso says.

Dom Cristóvão was able to write to his brother of his recent victory. He also sent Francisco Velho with forty men to ask the captain of the Red Sea squadron for supplies of gunpowder and other material.

A fortnight was calculated necessary for the answer to return from Massawa. The messenger was anxiously awaited, for now at last it seemed that the enemy was near. Prester John wrote to Dom Cristóvão urging haste. Already the King of Zeila trod the warpath with a formidable host. The Emperor and his allies would have to make an effort to join forces before either met the terrible Granyé.

12

The Clash of Arms

✠

Ahmed-ibn-Ibrahim el Ghazi was an old campaigner, not to be outmanoeuvred easily by two young men. Dom Cristóvão had not been more than two days on the march when his scouts informed him that the King of Zeila held the way. It was necessary to choose between immediate battle or retreat into the mountains until the Emperor arrived. Bad for prestige was the general verdict on the latter course. Also, the Portuguese said to one another, there was the moral effect upon the natives to consider. At the slightest sign of weakness on the part of their allies the time-serving aborigines would cut off food supplies. "It would have been far worse," in the opinion of Miguel de Castanhoso, "to risk starvation and being discredited than fight the Moors, for victory rested in the hands of God."

Happy in this assurance, Dom Cristóvão decided to give battle, and so rode back to meet the Queen, who followed the rearguard. He received her with a special display of pleasure and rejoicing "because she was a woman and full of fear." Gently encouraging the trembling lady, her knights-errant led her into the middle of their camp. They left the Patriarch there to strengthen and console her, and a guard of fifty men as well. Meanwhile the Moslem host drew near and spread itself over the countryside. Poor Sabla Vangel must have repented bitterly of having left the safety of her mountain.

Left-handed Ahmed, with three hundred horsemen following, appeared in silhouette on a hilltop against the sky. Two white flags with a crescent moon and one red flag with a white crescent fluttered at his side. The Moor reined in his horse and for a long while "he stood there looking at us." Granyé gazed upon his foes until his heart grew light, and scorn welled up within it. The Portuguese had taken up a good position, but how few of them there were! While he observed, his army spread and surrounded the hill on which the Christians camped. He had them in a trap.

Dom Cristóvão concluded that he planned a night attack, so all kept vigil fully armed, with powder handy and matchlocks alight, shooting at intervals into the dark. Nothing happened, however, and when morning dawned, a herald from the King of Zeila appeared at the camp.

Granyé's message was in a lofty tone. It was plain, he said, that Dom Cristóvão must be very young since with so few men he dared to defy him, but Ahmed could not blame an inexperienced youth. The fault lay with the natives of the land and with "that woman who had deceived him." The King of Zeila added that he was sorry for Dom Cristóvão. Let him but abandon the Queen and he would be forgiven the presumption of facing Granyé — a thing that none had dared to do for fourteen years. Two courses were open to Dom Cristóvão. He could either take service with the conquering Moslem, or else depart in peace. This magnificent offer was made because the King of Zeila knew it was "that woman who misled him." Clearly the man could not forget how he had once desired "that woman" for his wife!

This message was accompanied by the presentation of a monk's cowl and a rosary. Granyé would make monks of them all, said he, if they did not obey his will.

Dom Cristóvão knew the rules of the game. He received the envoy with all the courtesy that chivalry demanded. He gave him a cap with a costly medallion, and a purple satin cloak.

He then escorted him politely from the camp, promising to send an answer in due course.

A well-dressed young man riding on a mule delivered the reply, written in Arabic. The Great Lion of the Sea, declared the letter proudly, had sent his subjects to the rescue of his brother-in-arms, the very Christian Prester John, who had been defeated and disinherited by the enemies of the Holy Catholic Faith. The small army that Granyé saw was quite sufficient to resist such evil men. The justice of the Emperor's cause alone was ample to defend it. If the Moslems had triumphed hitherto, it was because the Lord had wished to chastise the Abyssinians for their sins. Dom Cristóvão now hoped in God that the moment had arrived when their captivity was to be turned. Next day would witness what the Portuguese could do. They certainly would not take service with Moslems, nor recognize another master than the King of Portugal, whose vassals were all the kings of India, Arabia, and Persia, and most of those of Africa, and whose vassal Granyé would one day be, with the help of Our Lord!

To the taunt implied by the cowl and rosary, Dom Cristóvão retorted in what was felt to be a most becoming manner, by sending his enemy "a pair of small tweezers for plucking eyebrows and a large mirror — making of him a woman."

It seems that Granyé was annoyed, but he said that they must be brave men to wish to fight with him.

The King of Zeila had good reason to be confident. Fifteen thousand bowmen followed his flag, and one thousand five hundred horsemen, besides two hundred Turkish arquebusiers. It was to these few Turks that he owed much of his past success, for Abyssinian armies fled in terror from powder and shot. These Turks, Castanhoso affirms, were valiant warriors. "They came closer to us than any of the others, and far excelled them. They even erected little walls quite near to us, from behind which they did us harm." Manuel da Cunha and Inofre de Abreu with sixty men were needed to dislodge them. But the bulk of Granyé's army still held back. Ahmed's tactics were to draw the enemy down from his strong position, and for this he knew that it was only necessary to wait. The Portuguese were quite surrounded and unable to forage for supplies. Since Granyé did not move, Dom Cristóvão was forced to take the offensive without more delay.

At dawn upon April 4 the Christian forces advanced to meet their foes. A shout of joy that shook the earth rose from the Moslem host when they saw the little army on the march. "It seemed to them they had us in their net."

The battle raged fiercely and long. The inequality of numbers was absurd. About three hundred and fifty Portuguese (forty had not yet returned from Massawa, and eight were dead) backed by two hundred Abyssinians would inevitably have been wiped out had it not been for their few pieces of artillery. "The bombardiers acted as valiant men. They shot so fast and fearlessly that the horsemen could not reach us, for the horses took fright at the fire. None the less the Moors did us much harm, especially the Turks with arquebuses." Dom Cristóvão was shot in the leg by one of these, in spite of which, says the admiring Castanhoso, he continued to perform such deeds as "neither ancient nor modern histories record of any excellent captain."

It is problematical how such a struggle might have ended, but about midday "Our Lord was pleased to remember His own, as He always does at times of such great need, according to His mercy. Thus when it seemed to us that we were getting the worst of the battle, it looked to the King of Zeila, who was watching all, as if his men were losing." Granyé was a brave man. He plunged into the thickest of the fight to rally his army, and as he did so an arquebus shot went through his thigh, killing his horse under him. Bearing their wounded leader off the field, the Moslems gave the signal for retreat. At this, the Portuguese bore down upon them furiously and so put them to flight.

Dom Cristóvão had not enough horses to follow far in the pursuit, so he "contented himself with the victory which Our

Lord had given him that day, which was not small." It was, in fact, not far short of miraculous, and they attributed it to "the blessed Apostle Lord St. James," who had not failed to put in an appearance. Several people had seen the heavenly warrior, and "without his help," Castanhoso assures us, "and principally that of Our Lord, it would have been impossible to win this battle."

While Santiago and the Portuguese routed the foe, the Queen showed that "a woman full of fear" could also be of use. She improvised a hospital tent and there tended the wounded. She and her ladies tore their veils and headdresses into ribbons for making bandages, which they tied up themselves. The army surgeon was wounded in his right hand, and so unable to do his work, but Dom Cristóvão, when he arrived, replaced him. The resourceful young man appears to have added a knowledge of first aid to his other accomplishments. Thus he treated everybody's wounds himself, "and when he had attended to them all, he dressed his own the last."

About a week was given to the wounded to recover, but Dom Cristóvão did not venture to allow them more. The enemy was still in sight and Granyé had sent for reinforcements, which might arrive any day. It was necessary to follow up the victory by a second battle before the Moslems had time to pull themselves together.

The Sunday after Easter Dom Cristóvão led a fresh attack. Granyé had not yet recovered from his wounds, but he was borne upon a litter to the field to encourage his men — "Rather unnecessary," comments Castanhoso with a touch of irony, "they were so numerous that the mere sight of how few we were filled them with courage."

It certainly had that effect upon Grada Amar, a captain just arrived at Granyé's summons with 3,500 men. Grada Amar was bursting with the lust of battle and decidedly above himself. How was it possible, said he, for such a handful to resist the Moslem power? "They are only a few hens!" he cried, and charged in fury, urging his men to massacre the lot. If all his troops had followed his example, the Christian lines would have been broken, but fear of the Portuguese artillery made some hold back. Regardless of hesitation in the rear, the captain never stayed his headlong course. He and "four or five valiant Moors' threw themselves on our lances and died like brave men."

The rest of the Moslem cavalry charged after this, but encountered a stubborn resistance. The Portuguese stood their ground and fought desperately, but the weight of the impact was tremendous and the Moslems had begun to break into the camp when, on this day again, a lucky accident occurred. Some gunpowder caught fire with great spectacular effect. Two Portuguese were killed in the explosion and eight were badly burned, but all the same "it caused our victory." The panic-stricken Moslem horses bolted, carrying their riders far away. Confusion was thus borne into the enemy's ranks, and though the Turks still rallied and returned, the first fury of the onslaught was broken.

The minute that Dom Cristóvão felt them slacken, he sounded the charge. "We rushed at them with such impetus that we drove them before us on the field till they were put to flight." Again shortage of horses curtailed the pursuit, but the foemen's camp was entered and despoiled. The King of Zeila fled far off and all his army followed him.

It was two days after this that Francisco Velho, with his forty men, returned from Massawa. They were "unbelievably sad" at having missed the battles, the more so that they had failed to find the ships at Massawa. The Bahr Nagach, however, had brought back with him forty horsemen and five hundred foot soldiers — a useful reinforcement. All were received with open arms, and Dom Cristóvão, with his army doubled, resolved to follow the pursuit.

Fourteen wounded men were unable to march, but the Governor of Tigré took charge of these. He had them carried on litters across the mountains to his home, where "it is truly impossible to say what kindness and honour we received from

him and from his wife. We could not have been better cared
for and provided for in our own fathers' house — I emphasize
this point," says Castanhoso, "because I was present all the
time, being myself one of the wounded."

Struggling through mud and rain, meanwhile, the Moslems
fled and the Christians toiled after. The King of Zeila climbed
a mountain and there fortified his camp. Dom Cristóvão en-
trenched himself upon another mountain opposite. There, at
the southern borders of Tigré, the hostile armies glowered at
each other while floods poured from the skies. There it seemed
that they would have to stay until the rains had ceased.

Dom Cristóvão dispatched a mulatto called Aires Dias to
announce their victories to the Emperor and urge him to make
haste. They had expected he would join them earlier. Awaiting him, the peasants built straw shacks for their allies on
the mountain and kept them well supplied with food.

Granyé was in worse case. It was against the Abyssinians'
principles to back a loser, even if he were of their own faith
and race. A vanquished Moslem, therefore, had no hope of
support. The King of Zeila could get no provisions except at
the point of the sword. He sent a desperate message to the
Pasha of Zebid: Unless the Turks came to his rescue, he was
lost, and all the country he had conquered for the Sultan
would return to Christian hands. Especially he must have artillery. This cry for help was made the more appealing by a
rich present of gold, silver, and jewels.

It moved the Pasha, who acted at once. He picked a thousand Turkish arquebusiers, and produced ten bombards, complete with gunners. He called a host of Arabs from their tents,
and by way of embellishment he mounted thirty Turkish
horsemen upon iron-shod steeds with golden stirrups. When
the October rains had spent their fury on the mountains, these
soldiers of the Crescent left their deserts for the King of
Zeila's camp.

Meanwhile Dom Cristóvão had been conferring with an
Abyssinian Jew. South-west of the River Tacazé stretched

the wild peaks and fertile valleys of the Simen Mountains, which were the Falashas' home. These mysterious Ethiopian Jews, whose origin is lost in speculation and obscurity, had found upon these heights a paradise as fair as their forefathers' promised land. The rich, well-watered soil could produce any crop; all flocks and herds grew fat and flourished there, and literally this region flowed with honey, which might be found dripping from every rock. The man who spoke to Dom Cristóvão had been captain of this country at the time that Prester John had been defeated and escaped over the Simen heights. Galawdewos would have to pass that way again to join his allies, but — the mountains had since been taken by the Moors. They had left few men, however, to defend their conquest. If Dom Cristóvão were agreeable, the Jewish captain could lead him up by hidden ways, and the stronghold might be taken by surprise. There was not a hope that Prester John himself could do this as he passed. Upon this point the Jew was positive. The Emperor had insufficient men to fight the garrison.

This startled Dom Cristóvão. He had always understood that Galawdewos had an army. If the Emperor had not even the force to achieve what was made out to be a very easy conquest, the future prospects were not rosy. Dom Cristóvão went to ask the Queen for the whole truth, and Sabla Vangel confirmed what the Jew had said. Her son had no real army left! Dom Cristóvão hid his consternation and decided that he must clear the path for Prester John. Besides, the Jew had told him there were horses to be captured and there was nothing that the Portuguese needed so urgently.

He could not raise his camp nor move his army, or the Moslems would occupy his mountain while he was away. Dom Cristóvão therefore departed secretly by night with Manuel da Cunha, João da Fonseca, and one hundred men.

The whole thing was not quite so simple as the Jew made out. The River Tacazé, to start with, was in flood, but that did not deter them. The strongest swimmers swam across while the others passed over with their powder and guns on rafts

140

made of inflated hides and wood. The garrison upon the mountain, represented as negligible, turned out to be over three thousand men. The raid could easily have ended in disaster, but the amazing luck that had accompanied Dom Cristóvão so far continued to hold good.

In their first furious charge the two commanders tilted straight into each other, and the Moslem was overthrown and slain by Dom Cristóvão. It seems that the former had no understudy and his troops lost nerve. Quite probably they thought it was a vanguard action and that a large army was following behind. "They had nobody to shame them or to order them," says Castanhoso, so when, to add to their confusion, the Jews arose with wild cries at their back, they simply turned and ran away, and the natives of the mountain killed them as they ran.

Such a simple and spectacular success amazed the Jewish captain. It was obvious, he said, that God fought for the Christians, and he demanded then and there to be baptized. His twelve brothers, we are told, were all converted too, and Dom Cristóvão, at their request, stood sponsor to the lot.

To the joy of this spiritual fruit of victory was added that of material profit. Much spoil was looted from the deserted Moslem camp, besides which they collected a whole herd of fat cattle, three hundred mules, and — best of all — eighty splendid horses.

Dom Cristóvão left his godson once more captain of the Simen Mountains and ordered him to send a message to the Emperor that the way was clear. Thirty Portuguese remained behind to bring the horses slowly over the rough mountain paths, while Dom Cristóvão with the other seventy men travelled at full speed night and day to get back to their camp.

The evening of his return some cannon-balls, shot from the darkness, fell behind the Christians' lines.

The King of Zeila's Turks had just arrived.

13

Granyé's Revenge

✠

If Dom Cristóvão had been an older warrior, observes Diogo do Couto with the wisdom that comes to most of us after events, those two brilliant battles with Granyé would never have been fought. Regardless of what the natives might think, he should have withdrawn to the mountains and waited for the Emperor there, harrying the Moslems from above. "But, being a proud young man, and very knightly, though inexperienced in the art of war, he was guided by the inclination of his heart and spirit, which was to fear nothing at all, rather than by the rules of military science such as prudence and circumspection." No self-respecting writer of the Renaissance can make a statement without classical support, so the examples of Nestor and Fabius Cunctator are duly cited here to illustrate the case in hand.

Diogo do Couto writes serenely of what had happened half a century back, but Miguel de Castanhoso, who lived through it all, attempts no criticism. Perhaps he had not heard about Fabius the Temporizer.

Whatever that canny Roman might have done in Dom Cristóvão's place on past occasions, this time there was no choice except to fight. Dom Cristóvão found the King of Zeila camping within gunshot of the Portuguese, quite ready to attack without delay. Instead of resting after their breathless

142

march across the mountains, the conquerors of the Falasha country had to spend the night in watching, fully armed. An Abyssinian runner was immediately dispatched to meet the men bringing the horses and to urge them to make haste. All hoped that the battle might be postponed until they arrived. Without mentioning the badly needed horses, thirty men more or less meant a great deal to such a small army. Until these absent comrades joined them, the Portuguese would number less than 340 men. It is true that there were the Bahr Nagach's troops — some 800 perhaps — but the sight of the Turkish artillery had quite shattered their nerve. It did not appear that one could hope for much support from them.

Granyé knew better than to give his enemy a day or two. Dawn of August 28, 1542 saw his mighty army marching in battle array, with a vanguard of a thousand Turks, and all the artillery in front. With a dissonant clash of instruments and emitting blood-curdling cries, the desert warriors closed around the Christian camp. As daylight spread across the hills, fire was opened on either side.

The duel lasted several hours. The Portuguese guns did great execution, but this time the Turks could give back what they got. And Turks were valiant men. Regardless of arquebus shot or cannon-ball, they charged up to the barricades that fortified the camp, and with Granyé's host pressing behind, it seemed that they must soon break through.

Dom Cristóvão saw that his only hope to hold them back lay in a succession of furious sorties, led from different sides by each captain in turn, for, states Castanhoso soberly, "they could never stand against a Portuguese charge." The history of Oriental wars for the last forty years had served to demonstrate that fact.

On this occasion it again proved true. The whole of that long day each captain in his turn led out his men to hurl themselves upon the foe, and every time the Moslems were borne back. But it was a deadly game for a handful to play against a multitude. Each sortie cost the lives of several men, and even

143

from the first all returned wounded. Dom Cristóvão, shot by
an arquebus in the leg, continued to encourage all and show
a cheerful face, while seeming to be everywhere at once. "It
is on such days," says Castanhoso, "that captains show what
they are made of. I know of no words to describe his courage,
nor do they exist." It does not occur to this hero-worshipper
that much the same might have been said about himself or
his companions. Not one hung back though they all knew it
was a desperate situation. They had no reserves from which
to replace anybody who fell, whereas each time the Moslem
ranks were broken, fresh men stepped forth to fill the gap.
With all their efforts, the Portuguese could hardly keep the
enemy outside their camp. It was like a hunted animal at bay
attempting to hold off the hounds.

Bullets and cannon-balls already fell right into the Queen's
tent. Sabla Vangel, weeping bitterly, still played a worthy
part. She and her ladies worked hard all day long, attending
to the wounded, and while they tied up bandages two women
were hit.

The captains, with fewer men each time, charged farther
and more furiously. Francisco de Abreu, in his turn, was killed.
Inofre de Abreu rushed forward to seize his brother's corpse
and was himself shot down. "Thus both remained upon the
field."

Dom Cristóvão gathered his men and led them out once
more. "Truly if we had had those horses," Castanhoso thinks,
"the victory would have been ours. . . . Every time we
charged the enemy, we drove them like sheep. But we were
already so exhausted that we could not keep it up." The number of horses that they had available were only eight. If the
eighty captured in the Simen Mountains had arrived in time, it
would have made a difference.

Dom Cristóvão returned from his last charge with his right
arm shattered and nearly all his men wounded or slain, for
"you cannot make war without shedding blood." João da Fonseca and Francisco Velho, who sallied forth successively, each

from a different side, each in his turn was killed. Of Dom Cristóvão's five captains one only survived.

The long day was declining. A few crippled and wounded men still gathered at the barricades and tried to keep the enemy from entering the camp. "Twice we threw them out," but such a defence could not be sustained. Even the least wounded were so exhausted that they could hardly lift their arms, and it would be impossible to lead another charge.

"The Patriarch, when he saw this, mounted a mule and rode off to the mountain range behind." Gaspar Correa puts it more unkindly, for he says: "The Patriarch ran away." Dom João Bermudez was no coward, but he was intensely practical. Retreat into the mountains was the sole solution to the situation, and, having decided that, he did not feel called upon to wait until Dom Cristóvão had made up his mind.

Dom Cristóvão was not easy to convince. A veteran warrior may see no shame in retreat before an overwhelming force, after a heroic resistance, but to Dom Cristóvão's youth it seemed disgraceful to abandon one's position to the enemy. He wanted to die fighting on the barricades, wielding his sword in his left hand.

His companions reasoned with him. If he would insist on staying, then naturally they would stay too, and die with him, but, after all, what was the use? There was nobody who could fight any more; it would amount to suicide. Far better to reassemble and recover in the mountains and be ready then to carry on the war and to repair the damage done. To these arguments Sabla Vangel added her tears. She, for one, was going, and she begged that they would go with her.

Dom Cristóvão, almost by force, was led away upon a mule, for by this time he could hardly have walked. But he felt that he was humiliated for all time. The Moslems did not interfere with their departure. The Turks were already entering the camp, but their minds were wholly centred upon loot.

In the darkness, on the mountain paths, it was not possible to keep together. Each man stumbled along as best he could.

The battle had left nobody unscathed, so "though some could get on better than the others, it was very hard for all."

Miguel de Castanhoso, wounded in several places and with his left arm smashed by an arquebus discharge, took up his post beside the Queen. "She had always been my special charge," he explains simply, "and I would not leave her at a moment of such peril, though I could not be of much use." With about thirty other men, they trailed away into the night. Dom Cristóvão would make no haste to reach the mountains. He did not much care what became of him. So many of his brave comrades were dead, but he had not had the luck to die with them! And he had lost his flag — the flag that his brother had so earnestly committed to his care. He had been told to die in its defence, and it was gone, and he was still alive. His honour was tarnished for ever, and his father's glorious name dragged in the dust. He never could return to Portugal again. In vain his friends argued with him. He was in no mood to appreciate their arguments. It is difficult to keep a right sense of proportion when, after a day of desperate effort without food or rest, preceded by a sleepless night after a strenuous march, one has a bullet in the leg and a shattered right arm hanging useless at one's side. Dom Cristóvão could not be made to see that he was not disgraced.

All night long Dom Cristóvão and his thirteen companions wandered blindly on the mountain-side. Towards morning they reached a deep-wooded gorge, at the bottom of which there flowed a little water. As all were more or less worn out, they decided to rest here awhile and to bind up one another's wounds. They had no healing ointments to apply and so they killed the mule on which Dom Cristóvão rode, and used the creature's fat.

That night the Moslems revelled in the abandoned Christian camp. The plunder had proved rather disappointing. There were indeed two chests of Dom Cristóvão's clothes, but the King of Zeila kept these for himself. His subordinates, exploring the Queen's tent, discovered several barrels of gunpowder there, and forty entirely helpless wounded men. The victorious Moslems were pleased with this last find. After a battle Turks and Arabs liked to have a little relaxation, and captives usually provided that. It was great fun to torture wounded men, and all the warriors joined the game with zest.

One of their victims, awaiting his turn, lay watching with a ghastly smile. It had just occurred to him that he might add his contribution to the sport. He could see a lighted fusee on the ground. Laboriously he dragged himself along until he reached it. One more effort, and the fire was flung straight into the gunpowder. A deafening noise then rent the night as, in the twinkling of an eye, captors and captives all were swallowed up in flame.

While their companions plundered and tormented and went up in smoke, twelve Turks and twenty Arabs beat the countryside in search of Dom Cristóvão. They had almost given up the hunt when, in the uncertain light of dawn, an old black woman crept out of the bush and crossed their path. The Moslems made for her at once, thinking that she might give them information, but like a frightened animal she scuttled off and disappeared into the scrub. The Turks tracked the elusive creature in and out, from bush to bush, until she came into the open and began to run. She plunged into the ravine where Dom Cristóvão and his friends were resting, and her pursuers followed in full cry. "That old woman," says Castanhoso with conviction, "was the Devil!"

The Prophet had sent his messenger, declared the Moslems, especially to be their guide, for the black phantom vanished from their sight within the valley — but there was Dom Cristóvão! They seized on him with shouts of joy and captured his companions, all but one, who, being only lightly wounded, managed to escape. Much elated, the Turks and Arabs turned back to the camp, enlivening the way by plucking Dom Cristóvão's beard and spitting in his eyes.

Granvé, in occupation of his foeman's tent, was happily collecting heads of Portuguese. He paid well for each one that was brought him, and more than eighty were already gathered in. These he proudly exhibited to his prisoner. "With such heads you meant to take my kingdom from me," he sneered. "For your boldness I will do you great honour!"

The King of Zeila then proceeded to enjoy himself. He had Dom Cristóvão stripped naked, with his hands tied behind from a rope round his neck. The captive first was cruelly flogged, then Granyé ordered his black slaves to take off their sandals and beat Dom Cristóvão's face with them. The next game was making wax candles out of his beard and setting them alight. At last, with a sinister smile, Granyé produced the tweezers which Dom Cristóvão had sent him the year before. "We don't use these," he observed pleasantly, "but I kept them for you." The young man's eyebrows and eyelashes then were plucked out hair by hair, which process his tormentors varied by tweaking out small bits of flesh. Dom Cristóvão, his face streaming with blood, made no protest. However painful this might be, he preferred it to the mental agony he had endured before. Now he knew that he would not return to Portugal dishonoured. To be tortured to death by the Moors would mean a martyr's crown, so, after all, his family was not disgraced. "He thanked God," we are told, "for bringing him to this."

When Granyé had made merry to his heart's content, he considered that his captains ought to have their turn. The patient victim was led from tent to tent, tormented and abused in every one. To jerk the cord which bound his hands to his neck behind, so making him fall down, was the delight of every humorous Turk. They would beat him then until he rose. This show had to be repeated many times before it palled.

They did get tired of him at last, and so restored him to Granyé, who ordered that he should be dressed in filthy rags.

"If you will fight for me and send for your comrades to join you, you shall be pardoned and granted your life," the King of Zeila said, "and I will treat you well."

"Moor," answered his captive proudly, "if you knew the Portuguese you would not speak vain words. You can do what you like with me, for I am in your power, but know for certain that if you gave me half your kingdom I would not bring a single Portuguese to you. The Portuguese will not live with Moors, who are vile and enemies to the holy faith of Christ, my Lord."

Granyé, beside himself, whipped out his sword for sole reply and smote off Dom Cristóvão's head.

They buried him under a heap of stones, with a dead dog by his side.

Why had Granyé slain the captain of the Portuguese? the Turks demanded wrathfully. They had meant to take him living as a gift for the Grand Turk. There was nothing that the Sultan would have prized so much. They departed in high dudgeon for Arabia, bearing Dom Cristóvão's head with them, and all the prisoners but one, who had escaped. It was this man who told the tale of Dom Cristóvão's fate. His twelve companions, carried off to nameless prisons in the desert, have never been heard of from that day to this.

Just over fourteen months had passed since Dom Cristóvão had led his men inland from Massawa. In that time he had reconquered a hundred leagues of territory for Prester John. He had come as a deliverer to a people without hope, and shown them that their enemy was not invincible. Twice the King of Zeila's mighty host had fled before his face, and he had wrested from the Moslems those strongholds that barred the Emperor's path. When Galawdewos returned to the fight, he no longer had to face the morale of an undefeated foe.

Dom Cristóvão had died, and half of his comrades were dead, but they had cleared the way.

14

Ethiopia Delivered

✠

Sabla Vangel with her women rode ahead, weeping, upon her mule. Her weary escort struggled on behind, and at the tail of the whole sad procession followed ten or twelve wounded men who could only just walk. Two friends named Fernam Cardoso and Lopo de Almança, having had the good luck to be only lightly hurt, had constituted themselves guardians of these crippled ones and were helping them along.

Progress was necessarily slow, and already the fierce morning sun shone high over the hills when, looking round, they saw they were pursued by a band of Moslems led by two Arabs on horseback.

Fernam Cardoso and Lopo de Almança were determined that their charges must be saved at any cost. "Go ahead," they told them, "and hide if possible. We shall stay and defend you till we die."

Grasping their shields and lances, the two brave men turned back to meet the Moors.

The riders curveted up to the spot, and were perhaps somewhat surprised to find only two men when from afar it had appeared to be a party on the move. They must have suspected an ambush, for they reined in their horses at a little distance and from thence they summoned the companions to surrender.

Fernam Cardoso and Lopo de Almança took rapid stock of the situation. The horsemen were only two, but they had a detachment of infantry fast coming on behind. "Even before arriving within range of lance or sword, the Moors could destroy them by stones and arrows." The wounded comrades, happily, were out of sight and possibly had not been seen at all. It seemed that the best way to protect them would be to surrender, for then the Moslems would most likely turn back with their prisoners and, "even if the Moors put them to torture, they would not confess that there were other Portuguese ahead."

Lopo de Almança knew a little Arabic. He shouted to the horsemen to approach and take their arms.

Then a strange thing happened. Castanhoso is quite convinced that "Our Lady inspired them."

They must have recollected suddenly the fate of other prisoners on past occasions, for it appears that both exclaimed in the same breath: "Santa Maria! With our own weapons they will kill us!" Saying these words, they charged the men on horseback who were near, and overthrew them both — one dead, the other wounded in the arm. "When their riders fell, the horses stood stock still, and the foot soldiers, though numerous, began to run away, which clearly seemed to be a miracle."

Fernam Cardoso and Lopo de Almança did not remain to wonder at it. Each leaped into an empty saddle and, seeing the enemy turn tail, they also turned about and galloped after their companions, who had despaired of seeing them again. Hoisting the weakest ones onto their horses' backs, our paladins related their exploit, which, if not exactly in accordance with the rules of chivalrous warfare, was, in the circumstances, not unpardonable.

Their tale was heard with joy and wonder, and all came to the same conclusion that "Our Lady, seeing their good intention, had come to their aid. . . ."

"Thus these two men saved their companions and all those

who went ahead, for if the Moors had followed after, all would have been killed, none having weapons to defend themselves."

The broken remains of Dom Cristóvão's army gathered together on the mountain-side. The thirty men with the horses from the Falasha country met them there — too late — and heard about the tragedy that their arrival possibly might have averted. Meanwhile the Queen sent scouts to comb the ranges and find out news of Dom Cristóvão. To have no idea of his fate "is what we minded most, the more so that we knew he was severely wounded."

This suspense was not prolonged. The man who had escaped from the Turks in the valley soon appeared, and was followed shortly by the fugitive who had witnessed Dom Cristóvão's death. "At which news we felt all that may be imagined."

Sabla Vangel mourned for her young champion as if for a son, but she did not forget the survivors who had fought so well. "She sent for all of us and made a speech, consoling us for our great loss and our contrary fortune, and this in very discreet and virtuous words."

At wearing a brave face in adversity her listeners were not to be outdone. "We asked the Patriarch to answer her for us and to encourage her. . . . She was pleased, and said that the resolution of the Portuguese was very great."

It was about a hundred of them who now rallied around the Queen. Another fifty were reported to have wandered with Manuel da Cunha into the mountains of the Bahr Nagach. Of the 400 Portuguese who had left Massawa in 1541, no more survived.

Sabla Vangel, with her allies, decided to await the Emperor in the Simen Mountains. There they realized the value of the last conquest that Dom Cristóvão had achieved before he died. These mountains over which the Emperor had to pass were natural fortresses enclosing fertile valleys where an army could recover and refit, supplied by the friendly Falashas with all that they might need. Prester John himself arrived there ten days later, but he brought "so few men with him that if Dom Cristóvão had not conquered these mountains it would have been impossible for us to join him, nor would there have been any means of restoring the realm."

Galawdewos was inconsolable upon hearing of Dom Cristóvão's death. He could not have shown more grief, we are told, for his own son and heir, but as the Emperor was six years younger than Dom Cristóvão, the simile might have been more aptly chosen.

Galawdewos was a grateful soul and felt that he could not do enough for the allies who had fought so heroically for him. They must never count themselves as strangers in his land, he said. Let them consider everything as theirs, and the kingdom as belonging to the King of Portugal, his brother. He distributed mules to everyone and clothed them all in silk.

Though the Portuguese were now so few in number, their presence at the Emperor's side had an astonishing effect upon native morale. Galawdewos by himself had been almost abandoned. Now that he had joined forces with a hundred Portuguese, the mercurial aborigines came flocking to his flag. The Portuguese watched them arrive with increasing excitement, and "when we saw all those men assembled, we went to Prester John and begged him to help us to avenge the death of Dom Cristóvão."

But Prester John still had a wholesome fear of his old enemy. He thought that the army was not yet strong enough to beard Granyé. He was, however, persuaded to try his fortune, provided that the Portuguese who had gone with the Bahr Nagach could be summoned in time. "Fifty Portuguese in that country," remarks Castanhoso complacently, "are a better reinforcement than a thousand natives."

A messenger was therefore sent to search for Manuel da Cunha's party, and at the same time to fetch a good supply of extra weapons left by Dom Cristóvão in Sabla Vangel's citadel near Debaroa. While waiting, everyone turned to and made gunpowder. Sulphur and saltpetre abounded in the Simen

Mountains, and happily the specialist who understood the manufacture of explosives had survived.

Prester John was in the end obliged to take the field without Manuel da Cunha and his fifty men. They were found to be no longer with the Bahr Nagach. Believing all their comrades to be dead, they had gone down to Massawa, there to await the fleet. It was supposed that they had sailed for India.

The Emperor raised his camp on February 6. He took with him 8,000 bowmen and 500 horse. In front of the whole army marched the 100 Portuguese. They refused to have a captain chosen from among their number. After the one that they had lost, they said, they could appoint no other. The Emperor could command them if he liked, and the flag of Our Lady of Mercy would be borne ahead to lead them on. Thus they departed full of enthusiasm, nor would the lame and crippled stay behind. All swore to be avenged upon the enemy or die in the attempt. The Emperor, on his side, offered his sister's hand in marriage to any Abyssinian who would bring him Granyé's head, or if it were a Portuguese, a rich reward.

All this time Granyé, quite happy and carefree, was with his wives and children on the east shores of Lake Tana. He knew that he had wiped the floor with Galawdewos the last time that they met, so he looked for no further trouble from that quarter. The Portuguese he was quite sure he had annihilated. Who, then, was left to challenge his supremacy?

At harmony with life, therefore, Ahmed-ibn-Ibrahim el Ghazi enjoyed the pleasures of his harem and his home until one day, over the mountain crest, an army hove in sight and camped before him. It was no other than the Emperor, he was informed — the Emperor and the Portuguese! As Ahmed had supposed there were no Portuguese in Abyssinia by this time, to see them reappear was something of a shock. He and his men prepared themselves for battle, "for they could see that we were bent upon revenge."

Prester John still hankered after those fifty men from Massawa. The latest news was that they had not sailed, and even now were travelling inland to join him. Galawdewos resolved to postpone action until they arrived. Meanwhile the armies gazed at each other and skirmished every day. The result was interesting to amateurs of feats of arms, but weakening to the forces of both sides.

A celebrated Arab captain who commanded two hundred horse had daily passages with sixty mounted Portuguese. In the end he was killed at the game, "which was great loss for them."

The Abyssinian cavalry was also in high fettle and anxious to show off to their allies. Especially their captain, Azmache Cafilom, "did marvels with his horsemen."

Unhappily the gallant Azmache Cafilom had to do with an unsporting enemy. Granyé's Turks hoisted the white flag one day and said they had a message for the Abyssinian commander. As he rode to the trysting-place, Azmache Cafilom saw only two Moslems advancing to meet him. Like a gentleman he bade his followers hang back and went forward himself with only two. While the fictitious messengers held him in conversation, some hidden arquebusiers shot him down. The Turks had horses ready and galloped away before the startled Abyssinians could pick up their dead commander. There were wails and lamentations in the Emperor's camp, for Azmache Cafilom was married to Galawdewos's own cousin.

Abyssinian troops appear to have been very temperamental. They could show great bravery on the battlefield when all was going well, but the courage that will die for a lost cause was seldom theirs. They were so dismayed on this occasion by their captain's death that many resolved to slip away, "for victory seemed impossible to them."

This jerked the Emperor into action. He sent for the Portuguese and asked them to prepare for battle the next day. It was no good waiting any longer for Manuel da Cunha. Galawdewos knew that if the fight were long deferred his army would dissolve and fade away.

The Portuguese were ready. Dawn found them praying before the flag of the Santa Misericordia, "asking God to have mercy on us, and to grant us vengeance and victory over our foes." A general confession was said and absolution pronounced by a priest, and so they placed themselves in the front line of the vanguard. Two hundred and fifty Abyssinian horsemen went with them, and 3,500 foot soldiers followed. According to Castanhoso, the Ethiopian army numbered all together 8,500 men.

"The soldiers of Galawdewos were few, like those of Gideon," says the more poetic Ethiopian chronicle. As for the King of Zeila's army, "They were like multitudes of locusts, and even exceeded them, for their number was thousands of thousands, and millions of millions, all ready for the fight, as strong as lions and swift as eagles. . . ." The Moslems were from twelve to fourteen thousand men, the Portuguese records inform us with the colder realism of the European.

In the King of Zeila's vanguard marched 6,000 infantry, 600 horse, and the famous 200 Turkish arquebusiers. The Pasha of Zebid was obliged by treaty to keep his corps up to that strength, but the other Turks who had fought in the previous battle, as we have seen, were angry with Granyé for killing Dom Cristóvão, and so had left him and did not return.

The sight of those 200 Turks made the Portuguese see red. Led by their sixty horsemen, they hurled themselves like tigers upon these arquebusiers and made great devastation in their ranks. The Abyssinians, easily inflamed if easily cast down, followed with enthusiasm, and the Moslem vanguard was getting the worst of it when Granyé rode up accompanied by his small son. "How many years have I persecuted them?" he cried to those around. "And shall they stand before my face today?"

The tough old warrior exposed his person recklessly and soon was recognized. Every Portuguese arquebusier took aim at once, and Granyé fell across his saddle-bow, shot through the chest. Mortally wounded, he was borne away upon his

Uerdadera informaçam das terras do Preſte
Joam, ſegundo vío τ eſcreueo bo padre Francíſco Aluarez capellã del Rey noſſo
ſenbor. Agoza nouaméte impzeſſo poz mandado do dﬔo ſenbor em caſa deﬔuíſ
Rodrigues Nureíro deſua alteza.

FRONTISPIECE OF THE FIRST EDITION OF FATHER
FRANCISCO ALVARES'S BOOK ON ETHIOPIA

panic-stricken horse while a young Ethiopian galloped wildly after.

The Moslems, seeing their leader fall, lost nerve and fled — except the Turks, whose captain especially "fought like a valiant knight." With his sleeves rolled up and brandishing a great axe in hand, he held all enemies at bay, hewing a wide space all around him. Five Abyssinian horsemen vainly set on him at once. They could neither kill him nor make him surrender. He snatched the lance from one of them and slashed through the legs of another's horse "so that they did not dare approach him."

A Portuguese, João Fernandez, charged him with a lance. The Turk, though wounded by the thrust, caught the lance in his hand and held it in a grip of iron, while with his axe he cut the sinews of João Fernandez's leg. João Fernandez drew his sword and killed the Turk, but remained lame for life.

Meanwhile the King of Zeila's army fled, hotly pursued "principally by the Portuguese, who could not be sated in avenging Dom Cristóvão's death." It was the Turks who paid the heaviest toll. Of the 200 who had marched to the battle, Castanhoso tells us grimly that only forty survived.

Granyé's wife, with 300 horsemen, fled from his camp, bearing away the treasure that her husband had once taken from the Emperor. Nobody noticed her departure, for all were bent on putting Moslems to the sword. Only the women and children were spared, and these were carried off into captivity. Many Christian women were discovered among their number, "which caused the greatest joy." Some Ethiopians found their long-lost sisters, some their daughters or their wives, and "such was their delight that they came to kiss our feet and gave us all the credit of the victory, saying that it was thanks to us that they had regained their freedom."

Amid all these rejoicings a youth on horseback galloped up. A gory head was swinging by its hair held fast between the rider's teeth. This was the young man who had followed after

Granyé. He had overtaken him and dealt the final blow, and now he brought the head and claimed the Emperor's sister for his bride.

The Emperor examined the trophy with a searching eye. "There is only one ear!" said he suspiciously. "Where is the other ear?" At this a Portuguese stepped forward and produced the missing organ from his pocket.

They tried it on the head, and lo! they found that it fitted the place. "The King," says the Ethiopian chronicle, "then ordered that lying man of Ethiopia to hand over Granyé's adornments to the Frank."

Castanhoso makes no mention of this ghoulish little incident of the severed ear. He says that Galawdewos would not recognize the claim of the youth who had brought him Granyé's head. The King of Zeila, he declared, already was wounded to death when the Ethiopian had launched in pursuit. He could not pretend that he had slain him, and the mere removal of the Moslem captain's head did not deserve the hand of an Imperial princess! The true author of Granyé's death could only be a Portuguese, for Abyssinians did not handle arquebuses, but as nobody could tell for certain who had aimed the fatal shot, no one could have the prize.

Granyé's head, impaled upon a lance, was carried to rejoice the heart of Queen Sabla Vangel. Thence it was borne in triumph all around the realm that people might believe their enemy was dead. It was a happy day for Abyssinia.

The war ended with Granyé's death, for the heterogeneous host that followed him had no cohesion. In the words of the Ethiopian chronicle, the moment that their leader was no more, "his troops dispersed like smoke and like the cinders of an oven."

The Emperor's army did exactly the reverse. In a few weeks its number had increased to 26,000 men. All the deserters who had followed Granyé in his victorious days now coolly returned to their old allegiance, quite ready with "the poor excuses of a disloyal people," says Castanhoso scornfully.

Galawdewos cut off a few heads. but pardoned most of the traitors. He could not very well do otherwise. "for if he had put all to death, he would have had no men left."

The Bahr Nagach's father blandly presented himself. This simple soul had adhered to the King of Zeila "because it seemed to him that the realm would never be restored." He had won the favour of Granyé, who appointed him as preceptor to his son. Now that, contrary to all expectations, the Abyssinian Empire was restored, the elderly opportunist was not dismayed. He calmly sent to beg the Emperor's pardon and offered to hand over his young charge.

Galawdewos hesitated, but the Bahr Nagach pleaded for his old scalawag of a parent. In recognition of the son's loyal services the father was eventually forgiven and he cheerfully delivered Granyé's son into captivity.

There was one renegade captain who did not fare so well. The Portuguese discovered that he was one of those who had captured Dom Cristóvão, and they protested loudly against his pardon. Galawdewos was distressed. Had he known of this, he said, he would not have granted the man his life. Having once done so, however, he could not break his word — but, he added significantly, he would like to see that man torn to pieces by a lion!

The Portuguese did not require a broader hint. Without discussing the matter further, they sought the tent of the renegade and promptly stabbed him. His death, we are informed, "did not grieve Prester John."

Easter was passed beside Lake Tana, where Castanhoso for the first time in his life saw hippopotamuses. This beast, in retrospect, loomed large in his imagination. "They are the size of horses," he writes, "and the shape and colour of elephants. They have excessively large heads and a very wide mouth with many teeth above and below like those of serpents. On the lower jaw they have two great pointed teeth. When this animal opens its mouth, it is astonishing, for truly an average-sized man standing upon the lower jaw would not reach the upper with his head, and two men together could go into its mouth."

By this far inland lake Europeans and Africans joined happily together for the Easter celebrations. A very effective procession was organized in which the Portuguese walked fully armed, firing off their arquebuses and the captured Turkish artillery, as well as other gunpowder devices made for the occasion. The Emperor was delighted with the lovely noise.

On the anniversary of Dom Cristóvão's death, a great memorial service was held for him and all the Portuguese who had laid down their lives for Abyssinia. Masses were said with many candles, and six thousand poor were fed and clothed that day.

During the whole of 1543 the Portuguese travelled about with the Emperor. They taught him the European style of riding, and he adopted many European customs, we are told.

As they followed Prester John across his realm from end to end, the Portuguese saw and heard a number of strange things. What appears to have struck Castanhoso most were the rock-hewn churches of Lalibela. Each one was cut out of a single rock "with two very lofty naves, pillars, and domes, all carved from the same stone without a join, and the high altar and other altars were also cut out of the rock. . . . Each church is about the size of São Francisco of Evora in Portugal . . . and I measured the smallest . . . and found it to be fifty paces wide."

Long ago — so local tradition ran — a saintly white King came from foreign lands and caused these sanctuaries to be hewn out of stone. Every day an ell of rock was broken by the workmen's pickaxes, and every morning it was found that in the night the Lord had done three more. Thus the churches took shape and grew out of the mountain-side, and when the last one was completed, then the strange King died a holy death. "They showed us where he lay buried, and all took earth out of the sepulchre to keep as relics." The visitors were also shown some torn and ancient parchments covered with an unknown script almost effaced by age. "They thought that we could read them," Castanhoso says.

The monks living there, moreover, told the tale of how the King of Zeila would have turned these churches into mosques, but when two Moors on horseback attempted to enter one, their horses fell down dead.

Leaving these holy heights nimbed with an aureole of miracle and legend, the Emperor descended to the plains of Fatagar. He had re-established his authority in all the country that Granyé had conquered, and the tour ended here, among the Moslem tribes that formerly were subject to the Abyssinian crown. Galawdewos accepted their submission to his rule again and took the customary tribute.

After that, says Castanhoso, there was nothing more to do. He, for one, began to think about getting away. His wounded arm had never ceased giving trouble. It would not heal, and no surgeon was available in Abyssinia. He begged for leave to go to Massawa and there await the fleet.

Prester John was much perturbed. Not only was he loath to part with any of the Portuguese who had helped him so loyally, but as the King of Zeila had deprived him of his treasure, he was in no position to bestow rewards. "He was king of nothing except much land and many provisions. . . . He often told me not to leave until he could reward me, because it was slighting him to go before, and he was greatly grieved at my departure."

Castanhoso insisted. He said that he probably would die of his old wound if something was not done about it. He could not obtain treatment in Abyssinia, so he must go to India.

In the circumstances Galawdewos could not decently detain him any more. Reluctantly he gave him leave to go, and fifty other Portuguese decided to depart at the same time.

Then the Emperor sent for all the gold and silver in the churches of the land, and added to it all the jewels and bracelets of his womenfolk. He apologized for having nothing more to give. He assured the Portuguese that he would make their fortunes if they would only wait. There was a province on the confines of his realm to which Negroes came from far away in caravans with sacks of gold which they bartered for linen cloths. He suggested that the Portuguese should go with him and conquer these gold-mines.

But they refused the concrete gold and silver that he pressed upon them, nor were they tempted by the distant El Dorado depicted by him. They had not come into this land in search of any gain, they said, only to serve God and their King.

And so they left, empty-handed as they had arrived, with the flag of Holy Mercy still leading the way.

At Massawa, just one small foist appeared, commanded by a Diogo do Reinoso. He had been sent to find out news of the Abyssinian expedition, but in India it was believed that all were dead. The little ship was full of soldiers and could not take on fifty more men. As few could go, it was decided that they all should stay except Miguel de Castanhoso, whose need was the most urgent. He promised to entreat the Governor to send a ship for them, and if the Governor failed to do so, he would apply to the King.

"Next day, at dawn, on Sunday, February 16, 1544, I embarked, leaving my companions greatly desirous of doing likewise. After saying good-bye very sadly, they remained praying before a crucifix they bore upon the flag, after which, with many tears, they mounted their mules and rode away inland. . . .

"And we set sail for India, where by Our Lord God's will we arrived safely on April 19.

"May it please Our Lord to remember me and bring them back in peace to Portugal."

But most of them died in exile.

PART III

THE PARTING OF THE WAYS

15

Heresy and Schism

✠

I entreat you for the sake of Our Lord Jesus Christ's death and Passion, and by the great mercy of Our Lady, His blessed mother, that you will not let me die in your realm." So wrote the unhappy Saga Zaab to Dom João III, on July 12, 1536. He expected to die soon, he added mournfully, for he was "ill and very sad."

At the same time Padre Francisco Alvares was begging not to be allowed to die at Rome. But the powers upon the throne and at the Vatican continued to keep both envoys hanging on. Francisco Alvares, it seems, actually died in Italy, but Saga Zaab must have set sail in 1539 with Dom João Bermudez.

Poor Saga Zaab had been a solitary figure at the court of Portugal. Neglected by the King, badgered by theologians who were anxious to test his orthodoxy, and desperately homesick, he remained in Europe for twelve years that must have seemed like an eternity to him. But at least he made one friendship which does him great credit — that of the humanist Damião de Gois. The brilliant scholar, a pupil of Erasmus, steeped in the culture of the classics, and newly returned from Europe's chief centres of learning, appears to have formed a genuine esteem and attachment for the black monk educated in the isolated mountains of Ethiopia.

Damião de Gois was one of those wide-open, inquiring intellects which the Renaissance produced before the Inquisition had had time to clip their wings. Regardless of the host of troubles that he was laying up for his old age, his youth was wholly spent in tracking knowledge down whatever paths the quest might lead. The same spirit of universalism which had already brought him into friendly intercourse with Luther and Melancthon as his brother intellectuals now induced him to investigate the tenets of the Abyssinian Church with great curiosity.

Damião de Gois's interest in the land of Prester John was of long standing. It must have dated from the year 1514 when, as a twelve-year-old page at Dom Manuel's court, he had witnessed Matthew's arrival from India. The boy cannot fail to have heard how the envoy's religion had been examined by the doctors of the Church before the King. When, seventeen years later, he found at the house of a Portuguese at Antwerp a copy of the Armenian's replies, Damião de Gois had seized upon the document with great interest. He translated it into Latin then and there and published it in 1532. On meeting Saga Zaab in Lisbon shortly after, he showed him this work and asked for further information.

Saga Zaab studied his predecessor's declarations critically. It was clear, he said, that Matthew was no theologian. The Church's doctrines were imperfectly defined by him. This was, however, what might be expected of a layman and a foreigner. The better instructed Saga Zaab would write a correct exposition for his friend.

Damião de Gois left for Italy before the work was finished, but the Abyssinian did not forget his promise. He wrote out a detailed profession of his faith and sent it on to Padua.

Damião de Gois was delighted with the treatise, nor did its heterodoxy shock him in the least. That broad-minded tolerance which had enabled him, a Roman Catholic, to feel no horror in the company of German heresiarchs permitted him to read, without turning a hair, of circumcision practised in the Abyssinian Church, the sanctifying of Saturday, and other rites which smacked of Judaism. He found it all extremely interesting; he translated it into Latin under the title of *Fides, religio, moresque Æthiopum,* and he gaily published the treatise.

It appeared in 1540 at Louvain — the first authoritative exposition of the teaching of the Abyssinian Church. It is true that Saga Zaab had set them forth in slightly attenuated form. Deliberately, or unconsciously, he had skated over definitions of the Trinity, and no Eutychian doctrines are presented in his work. It has been suggested that Saga Zaab, isolated as he was, would have been careful to avoid any dangerous stone of dissension, but what he said was quite enough to scandalize the Grand Inquisitor. Many rites and ceremonies discountenanced by the Latin Church, but practised from time immemorial in Abyssinia, were not only described but defended by him.

The Cardinal Infante Dom Henrique, Grand Inquisitor of Portugal, would never have agreed with Padre Francisco Alvares that "God was willing to be served in different ways." He shook his head in disapproval over the *Fides, religio, moresque Æthicpum* and placed a ban upon the work. He wrote to Damião de Gois to say that he had done so, much to that learned man's surprise. What harm was there in publishing the treatise? asked the puzzled intellectual. He could not see how anyone would be the worse for being told about religious customs in Ethiopia.

The Cardinal thought that such an attitude was risky. He wrote back kindly but very firmly. He had not ceased, said he, to regard Damião de Gois "as a good man and a good Christian," but in view of the fact that the Holy Inquisition was newly established in Portugal, one could not be too careful. It was necessary to guard against any laxity in these bad times, with so much heresy abroad. Thus *Fides, religio, moresque* was suppressed, after having been subjected to the lynxlike scrutiny of the greatest theologians in the land.

The Land of Prester John

The curious part is that for over twenty years no one had troubled much about the difference between the Latin and the Abyssinian Churches. It is doubtful whether laymen left to themselves would even have been seriously disturbed by it. Pero da Covilham, the men of Dom Rodrigo de Lima's embassy, Dom Cristóvão da Gama and his companions, all seem to have accepted the Ethiopians as their brothers in the faith. However different externals might appear, the fundamental truths appeared the same. Their Holy Scriptures were identical, as was their belief in the fall of man and subsequent redemption by Our Lord. The two Churches kept many of the same feasts, professed the same devotion to the Virgin, reverenced the same saints; and both worshipped Three Persons in One God. As for their different definition of the Second Person of the Trinity, it does not seem that anybody noticed it. The average layman does not probe very deeply into the mysteries expounded in the Athanasian Creed, and it is improbable that it would have occurred to Dom Cristóvão's soldiers or to their Ethiopian colleagues to discuss together the dual nature of Our Lord. Each saw the other bow before Him as the world's Redeemer, and they were quite satisfied with that. Castanhoso, Castanheda, and Gaspar Correa all describe curious religious rites and ceremonies practised by Ethiopians, but none of these writers ever call them heretics.

Neither does Father Francisco Alvares, a priest, apply that term. He was the best of friends with the Abuna and did not hesitate to worship in the Abyssinian Church. Though certainly he disapproved of some things that he saw, he seldom seems to have been really shocked. He accepts the Abyssinians as true members of the Christian Church, and if their way of celebrating Mass seems strange to him, he consoles himself with the reflection that as all was done to the glory of God, all must be well.

But times had changed since those far-off days when the men of Diogo Lopes de Sequeira's fleet and the black monks

168

of Bizan had wept in one another's arms at Massawa, "joined in ties of spiritual brotherhood by the sign of the cross, which filled them with faith and love and charity." The Europe to which Francisco Alvares returned was animated by a very different spirit. Faith flourished certainly, but love and charity were not in evidence. Christendom had become a seething cauldron of religious polemics. Inkpots were being emptied in controversy, while each rival theologian demolished the others' doctrines. While some countries shook off allegiance to the Church of Rome, in others that same Church was in full hue and cry pursuing Jews and Protestants. Everywhere truth and error were being bitterly discussed, and heresy-hunting was the order of the day.

Into the midst of all these burning questions was flung that of the Abyssinian Church. The most learned theologians had cross-questioned Saga Zaab, and they were not satisfied with his replies. They multiplied their conferences with him and concluded that he was unsound. Father Francisco's narrative, published in 1540, threw further discredit upon Abyssinian orthodoxy, and *Fides, religio, moresque* came to confirm the gravest fears. A list of errors was drawn up from the two books, and the damning total numbered forty-one.

So the hideous truth gradually dawned. That Prester John's church was schismatic all had been aware. The distance and difficulty of communications had been blamed for that. Overcome the one, and facilitate the second, and it was assumed that Prester John would be quite happy to make submission to the Church of Rome.

But the case was found to be far worse than a mere schism. There was heresy to be eradicated too. There was no getting away from it. Prester John, the supposed bulwark of the Christian faith, the upholder of the Gospel torch amid the night of Islam, the ally of whom Portugal had expected so much — Prester John was a heretic! Thenceforward it would be necessary to face this painful fact.

The result was the Jesuit mission.

16

The Bishop Takes a Hand

✠

As Patriarch of Abyssinia, João Bermudez was not a success. Very shortly after joining each other, he and the Emperor had already fallen out. We only have João Bermudez's version of the quarrel.

He says that he urged Galawdewos to make submission to the Pope as his father Lebna Dengel had done before. The young Emperor answered that his parent had done nothing of the kind, and the discussion that ensued was lively.

"You are not our Abuna, nor prelate of ours," the Emperor said to Dom João Bermudez, "only Patriarch of the Franks and," he added with a fine confusion of theology, "you are an Arian who has four gods."

"And I told him that he lied. I was not Arian, and I had not four gods; but since he would not obey the Holy Father, I considered him as a cursed excommunicate."

"You are the excommunicate, not I," retorted the young man, and they parted in anger.

It was not a promising beginning, and though that first tiff was made up, relations between the Emperor and the Patriarch stiffened from day to day.

Galawdewos was an intelligent young man with a passion for religious controversy, and it did not take him long to plumb João Bermudez's depths. "He has no learning at all," is the verdict of an anonymous Portuguese contemporary, "and he chants the divine service with great difficulty, because he knows no better." He never preaches, we are further told, "because he does not know how." In twelve years that he was with the Portuguese he neither said Mass nor yet confessed himself. In spite of this "he excommunicates and absolves very easily owing to his great lack of prudence." The Emperor kept him prisoner on an island for nearly a year because he was exasperated by his ignorance. The Patriarch, it would appear, took the sacrament after the Abyssinian fashion, which, rather surprisingly, annoyed Galawdewos: "Since he had come to teach them," said the Emperor, "why should he use the native ceremonies?"

It seems, however, that there were worse sins than those of ignorance to be laid at Dom João Bermudez's door. "He is," the same informant tells us, "a man covetous of temporal possessions and extortionate of what is given for his maintenance."

When Castanhoso left for Portugal he carried a letter from Galawdewos to Dom João III complaining of the so-called Abuna's conduct.

The King knew Dom João Bermudez, and his sympathy was for his royal colleague. "I am very displeased," he writes on March 13, 1546, "with the doings of João Bermudez, whom your father sent me as ambassador." The King promises to send to the Emperor a new Patriarch next year. This one would be a "person of such zeal and exemplary life that in all things he will serve Our Lord and give you satisfaction. You will be able to discuss together the affair of João Bermudez and come to what decision you think fit concerning him." Dom João is quite willing that the culprit should be punished "according to his errors." The King only recommends that the man's life should be spared out of regard for "that dignity of Patriarch which he had chosen to assume, though no one gave it to him." Otherwise great discredit might be brought on Christendom.

Having thus washed his hands of Dom João Bermudez, the King wrote to the Pope and to Ignatius Loyola, requesting them to take charge of the spiritual welfare of Abyssinia.

Ignatius Loyola would have loved to go himself had he been able to do so. He had to be content with selecting some of his best men, and composing an entirely tactful letter to the Emperor in which he explained at great length the unity of the Christian Church under the Roman See. "Your Highness," he points out, "should give Our Lord infinite thanks, that in the days of your fortunate reign He should have sent your devout people true pastors of souls, who are dependent upon the chief shepherd."

But His Highness was serenely unaware that either he or his devout subjects might need pastors from Rome or Portugal. He had already sent to Alexandria for a new Abuna, and banished Dom João Bermudez from his court.

The discredited Patriarch wandered about the realm, cursing the villages through which he passed. After several years of travel and adventure he came to Debaroa, waiting for an opportunity to sail for India. There, in 1555, he met a Jesuit priest, Father Gonçalo Rodrigues, who told him that another Patriarch was on the way. Between the Abuna from Alexandria, already installed in Abyssinia, and the Patriarch from Portugal, João Nunes Barreto, who had reached India by that time, there was no room for Dom João Bermudez. He sailed for India and thence to Portugal, where he arrived in 1559. He lived near Lisbon in retirement for eleven years, finding solace in the composition of his more or less veracious memoirs. He enjoyed the favour of the boy King Sebastião, to whom he must have had some thrilling tales to tell, and Diogo do Couto says that he died a very holy death.

The Jesuits, meanwhile, were doing what they could for Abyssinia, but the good fathers found it uphill work.

Padre Mestre Gonçalo Rodrigues, referred to above, had been the first one to arrive. He was a zealous and learned young man, who had been sent from Goa with a brother of the Company to announce the coming of a Patriarch next year.

When the Emperor received this news he looked a little blank. How good of his brother Dom João, he murmured politely, to take so much trouble over these things! Galawdewos felt deeply grateful to the King of Portugal and was entirely at his service. The conversation fizzled out in empty compliments, and before Padre Gonçalo could get in another audience, the Emperor was seized with an urge to visit his grandmother. She lived a week's journey away, and a month went by before her dutiful grandson could tear himself away from the old lady. But Padre Gonçalo Rodrigues wasted no time. He stayed in the house of one of Dom Cristóvão's late companions and there composed a treatise on "The Errors of Ethiopia and the Truth of Our Holy Faith."

When Galawdewos was presented with this work, we are told that "he was filled with ire." Ethiopia had no errors, said he wrathfully.

"Your Highness has none," Padre Gonçalo answered with some tact, "but your subjects have."

This Galawdewos refused to admit. How was it, he demanded, that though their faith was of such ancient standing, no one had ever come before to say that they erred?

"I replied," writes Father Gonçalo, "that owing to man's sin Our Lord sometimes permits such things, but he ought to give thanks to God for having allowed him to be shown the evangelical truth."

Galawdewos, however, was quite satisfied with evangelical truth as expounded by the Church of his forefathers. When asked if he would make submission to the Pope, he said emphatically that he would not. As for the "learned and religious men" that his brother of Portugal proposed to send him, what was the use? said he. He had learned and religious men in his own realm and so needed no others. Could the

Portuguese Patriarch not come to Abyssinia, then? Of course he could come if he wished, was the polite reply. The Emperor would be very pleased to see him.

Padre Gonçalo Rodrigues felt that the situation was highly unsatisfactory. It seemed that Prester John would give more trouble than had been anticipated. At any rate the treatise on truth and error enjoyed some success. In spite of the indignation it had first aroused in him, Galawdewos studied it with great interest and showed it to his family. He even had a quarrel with his own Abuna, it appears, for forbidding him to study the pamphlet. The Emperor was obviously a man of independent views and not to be coerced by anyone.

Father Gonçalo also tried his dialectics on the Abyssinian monks, not wholly without fruit. On one occasion when, backed by the Scriptures, he had been demolishing all monophysite definition of the Trinity and pulverizing minor errors, one of his listeners at least was quite impressed. "He came and whispered in my ear, so that the other monks who were idiots should not hear him, saying that I spoke the truth, and he would keep it in his heart."

Except for such slender encouragement, Gonçalo Rodrigues had not a favourable report to give to his superiors at Goa upon the Abyssinian attitude towards religious truth. "Prester John is such a heretic," he said, "that he considers we are so, and that *they* are good Christians."

The Viceroy and Council decided that the Patriarch himself ought not to go until the Emperor was in a more receptive frame of mind. His understudy in the mission, the newly consecrated Bishop of Hierapolis, would first try his hand, and when the ground had been prepared the Patriarch could follow.

The Bishop's name was Dom André de Oviedo. He was a Castilian by birth, tall, thin, learned, saintly, and ascetic. He was the first of Ignatius Loyola's Company to wear a mitre, which dignity the Pope had specially bestowed on him in order to add lustre to the Abyssinian mission.

The Bishop Takes a Hand

Dom André left India in 1557, with two fathers and three brothers of the Company. They reached Debaroa on March 25 and were received with open arms by the survivors of Dom Cristóvão da Gama's army. With the exception of Miguel de Castanhoso and one or two others, none of these men had been able to get away. Far from sending a ship to fetch them, as Castanhoso states that they requested, the King had ordered them to remain in the land of Prester John. They seem to have accepted their exile with resignation, and with true Portuguese adaptability they made the best of it. The Emperor helped to reconcile them to their lot, for Galawdewos was by nature both generous and grateful. He gave them the best of everything he had, and those who turned out to greet the Bishop on his arrival were a splendid sight. They quite outshone the Abyssinians, says the chronicler, by the diversity and richness of their dress, while the retinue of servants, horses, mules, and tents that followed them made them appear as the lords of the land.

One, João Gonçalves, brought his wife, a high-born Abyssinian lady, to introduce to the Bishop. She rode upon a handsome mule all draped with brocade trappings. She was elegantly dressed in a rich tunic over a black velvet robe. She had silk Turkish trousers drooping to her feet, adorned by golden buttons; massive gold bracelets hung upon her arms, and on her head was a tall velvet hat. Her husband was also bedecked in costly clothes, though his slashed cap with golden points is described as old-fashioned.

Beside this ornamental couple rode another Portuguese whose following of thirty lackeys all were armed with swords, lances, and guns. More and more resplendent figures joined the party, all eager to present their wives and exhibit their children. And the Bishop "praised God to see the Portuguese thus married, rich, and happy in this land, all full of zeal to receive and to serve their prelate."

Dom André de Oviedo and his five priestly companions were entertained by one after another. They were taken to the

175

beautiful *quintas* and pleasances owned by the Portuguese and "banqueted splendidly" in every one.

Amid all this feasting and rejoicing the fathers found much work to do. There were innumerable confessions to be heard, some of them years in arrears — like Pero da Covilham, these exiles seem to have been shy of unbosoming themselves to Abyssinian priests — and we gather that there were also a number of unsanctified unions to bless. The Jesuit fathers married and confirmed, confessed, and administered the sacraments with unfailing delight. They found this part of their mission wholly satisfactory.

The Emperor proved a harder case, though he received the Bishop "with humanity and love" and made him sit down by his side on a leather cushion upon a rich carpet. Galawdewos was reclining on a couch, dressed in a tunic over a Moorish shirt, and long trousers of Persian cotton. He was "a broad black man, with large eyes and an imposing presence." They found him "noble and discreet and friendly to the Portuguese," but the Bishop's eloquence might as well have been expended on a rock. Not that the Emperor did not listen to Dom André's words. On the contrary. Galawdewos, like his father, Lebna Dengel, had a passion for theology and could have argued with the Bishop all day long. They got down to it almost at once, closeted alone together. What passed between them is not known, but the Bishop emerged visibly upset. "That man," said he in agitated tones to his colleagues, "is a great heretic!"

Galawdewos had, no doubt, enjoyed a most interesting talk, the first of many discussions, oral and in writing. The Emperor and the Bishop argued — sometimes with heat — each time they met, and bombarded each other with the theological treatises that either composed. The Bishop's hair was made to stand on end by the heresies which the Emperor coolly enunciated in defence of circumcision, the observance of the Jewish Sabbath, and similar abominations. Such practices, the Bishop told the Emperor roundly, would certainly take him to hell!

Although Galawdewos appears to have found pleasure in shocking the Bishop, he is to be commended for his patience none the less. It cannot be agreeable for a monarch to be told before his court that he is heading for eternal flames. Nor can it be less trying to have a foreign priest upbraiding him "in public and in private" on the error of his ways. When, beyond all this, we read that the Bishop tried to persuade the Portuguese that it was wrong to serve so obstinate a heretic, we are moved to admiration of the Emperor's restraint. "He was always very courteous to the Bishop," writes the Superior of the mission, Father Manuel Fernandes, in his report to headquarters at home, "and treated him in such a manner that, while he lived, no one ventured to show him disrespect, and he provided for us very liberally, for he was by nature generous and open-handed, especially towards those connected with the King of Portugal. to whom he realized that he owed much . . . he was so friendly to the Bishop that in spite of all his pertinacity we always hoped that some good might result."

All the same, there seem to have been one or two occasions when this friendly intercourse came near to breaking down. A couple of monks from a monastery, won over by the Bishop's eloquence, announced their intention to embrace Catholicism "and save their souls." The abbot demanded their return, and persuaded the Emperor to intervene. The Bishop, as might have been expected, refused to hand over his converts, and Galawdewos lost his temper. "No?" said he, pacing the floor in agitation, and turning, made as if he would attack the Bishop. Dom André expected to be killed. He threw off his cloak, and waited upon his knees for the blow. The Emperor gazed at him and clapped his hands together with exasperation. But Galawdewos had a saving sense of humour.

"You think that you will die a martyr at my hands?" said

he. "I will not give you that glory! Go, and take your monks. Give them eggs on Friday, and you can be Bishop of two monks." Then turning to the Portuguese who were present: "You see," said he, "the man that my brother the King of Portugal has sent me! Had he no Portuguese available?"

Castilian though he was, Dom André had been sent by the King of Portugal, and so continued to enjoy the Imperial protection. It seems, moreover, that in spite of all their differences Galawdewos esteemed the genuine goodness of the man. But the Emperor feared that his successor might not be so tolerant or so bound by gratitude. "Poor Bishop!" he remarked when marching to repulse a Moslem raid. "If I die, what will become of him?"

The Emperor did die, as it happened, fighting like a hero after his army had fled, and nearly all the Portuguese who went with him were cut down at his side. The Moslem chieftain Nur ibn Mudi Ali Guazil sacked the Emperor's camp, took prisoners, and slew and then departed. In this manner Granyé was avenged by Galawdewos's death — a judgment on the Emperor, the Jesuits said, for refusing to embrace the Catholic faith! Adamas, his brother and successor, on the other hand, viewed Galawdewos's end as a divine chastisement for suffering the Church of Rome to flourish in Ethiopia.

Adamas was a violent man who looked askance on foreigners and newfangled ideas. The Portuguese soon found that they had fallen from their high estate of trusted allies and honored guests to that of alien undesirables. Even their children, Ethiopian by birth, were viewed with disfavour as being Catholics. The charge of heresy is one that may easily be flung back at the accuser's face, and the dart shot by Europe into Abyssinia recoiled upon the Europeans settled there. The Emperor issued a decree forbidding Abyssinian wives of Portuguese from following the religion of their husbands, and he confiscated right and left the lands that his brother had bestowed upon Dom Cristóvão's companions. As for the Jesuits, he announced his intention of burning them all alive, and he imprisoned the Bishop. He told Dom André that he would cut off his head unless he left off preaching. The Bishop replied that if he had many heads and were to lose them all, he still would preach the holy faith as long as he had breath. The enraged Emperor seized the Bishop and would have killed him there with his own hands if the Queen had not restrained her angry husband. Dom André de Oviedo was banished into the wilderness with one companion.

It might have fared worse with the foreigners if Adamas had not soon alienated his own subjects. It seems that he was something of a tyrant, and before his reign was two years old, the nobles rose in rebellion, headed by the Bahr Nagach, and crowned Adamas's young nephew Tascaro. The Emperor defeated the rebels in one battle, took his nephew prisoner, and subsequently hurled him down a precipice. The Bahr Nagach, however, found another princeling to crown and made alliance with the Turks.

Such a dangerous situation appears to have cured the Emperor's xenophobia. He felt obliged to make friends with the Portuguese, for they were the best fighters in the land. As the Ethiopian chronicle describes them: "They were valorous and constant men, athirst for battle like the wolf, and hungry for combat like the lion." We do not know how many of Dom Cristóvão's army still survived after twenty years, but of these at least thirty, including their captain, Gaspar de Sousa, had gone over to the Bahr Nagach. The majority refrained, however; on principle they disapproved of subjects taking arms against their lawful sovereign. Insubordination to captains or governors was comprehensible, not to say inevitable, at times. A subject might defy a subject if he chose. But to rebel against one's king was the act of a traitor. Most of the Portuguese, therefore, condemned the Bahr Nagach and looked askance on their compatriots who were supporting him.

About this time we find them all at court again, and seemingly in favour. The Bishop and his fellow missionaries were also there, though not apparently enjoying similar esteem.

They were "very afflicted and oppressed," writes Padre Manuel Fernandes. If, however, as Diogo do Couto says, they were intriguing with the Emperor's enemies, we can hardly blame Adamas for viewing them with coldness and suspicion.

It was the foreigners who kept up the Emperor's drooping spirits. Adamas was a superstitious man. He had been consulting auguries and oracles and found them all unfavourable, and hence was sunk in gloom. He could not fight, he told the Portuguese to their disgust.

They chose a strange method to excite his martial ardour. One evening after supper seven of them seized their swords and shields and loaded guns and proceeded to the royal tent, beating a drum and shaking tambourines. As they drew near, they all began to dance, singing at the top of their voices:

> "*Viva o Rei de Preste João*
> *Que para of Turcos é um leão!*"
>
> (Long live the King Prester John
> Who is a lion against the Turks!)

The din that they made was tremendous. The Emperor, the Queen, and her ladies turned out with thirty torches to see what was the matter, and stood there watching while the Portuguese cut capers. When the dance was over, the dancers all fired off their guns, shouting to the Emperor to raise his tents and march against the Turks. Declaring their willingness to die for him, they drew their swords and began to fence with great agility. The Queen and her ladies were delighted. "These are angels and not men!" they said ecstatically. The noisy serenade roused the whole camp. All the other Portuguese, waving their swords, rushed up to join the fun, and the Emperor, infected by the warlike fury, expressed his readiness to do or die.

In the dispassionate light of day his pessimism revived. He felt quite certain that he would come to grief, and he told the

Portuguese that he was sorry for them. "With you," he declared sentimentally, "I am like a hen that gathers her chickens under her wings at the appearance of the hawk," and "I am your only friend," he added, forgetting that he had not always qualified for such a title.

The Emperor Adamas met his rebel subjects and their Turkish allies on April 20, 1562. The Portuguese on either side avoided one another and went for the Abyssinians or the Turks. All might have been well with Adamas if his Ethiopians had not been incurably gun-shy. When they heard the Turkish cannon roar, they all turned tail and fled, and Adamas was killed. The Emperor's camp was sacked and the Jesuits were taken prisoner, but delivered by the Portuguese who had been fighting in the rebels' ranks.

There is no clear record of the subsequent history of Dom Cristóvão's old companions, nor of the part they took in the wars of the next reign. The Jesuits are better documented, and we know that they made their headquarters at Fremona, near the modern Adowa.

They were not persecuted by the new Emperor — merely ignored. Malac Segued, we are told, regarded them as holy men although doctrinally unsound. Adamas's son did not share the family passion for religious controversy, and the Jesuits were never given a chance of expounding their views to him. He left them to do what they liked at Fremona.

It was a hand-to-mouth existence that they led. Deprived of the Imperial patronage, and cut off from the outer world, there was no one to provide them with the necessaries of life. The Bishop lived in a straw native hut. His food was black and sour bread, linseed and cabbages — which vegetables, says the shocked chronicler, he had to cultivate himself "with his pontifical hands." He was so short of everything that when he wished to write a letter he had to tear out the blank leaves of his breviary, and after those were gone to cut the margins of its pages.

Dom André de Oviedo was a saintly soul. He endured all

this misery with cheerful resignation, and whenever he had anything to give away he promptly parted with it. He visited the sick throughout the neighbourhood, acting as both doctor and nurse, regardless whether the invalid were "freeman or slave, Catholic or heretic."

The Christian virtues that the Bishop displayed had more effect on those around him than all his former polemics and learned treatises. Many Abyssinians, it appears, turned Catholic out of pure admiration for the man. Such a holy life, they reasoned, could not be founded on erroneous doctrine. Thus the Bishop had the joy of making some converts at last.

In this manner Dom André de Oviedo lived, happy in spite of poverty and persecution, until, struck down by fever in 1557, he still more gladly died.

The whole reign of Adamas and that of his son, Malac Segued, is a blood-stained record of revolution and civil war. To the devastation of internal struggles was added that of Turkish raids. "This realm," the Bishop wrote in 1567, "will never know peace and order until the coming of the Portuguese." He hoped to see five or six hundred Portuguese soldiers from India sent to clear up the Abyssinian mess. With their arrival "all Ethiopia would be converted," he declared, in the sure conviction of his generation that forcible conversions were better than none.

In India, however, not very much was known of what was going on in Abyssinia, for news filtered through rarely and by devious ways. In 1557 the Turks had captured Massawa and every other port that gave the mountain empire access to the sea. It was long since the Portuguese had sailed in force beyond Bab-el-Mandeb, for the great days in the East were almost over and the power of Portugal had begun to decline. Persistently for more than half a century her finest manhood had been shipped in annual batches to die overseas, and the inevitable exhaustion was already manifest. There still were twenty years to go before the final tragedy, but absorbed between what has been called "the slaughterhouse of Asia" on the one side, and the limitless Brazilian forests on the other, the nation's lifeblood was ebbing away.

Meanwhile the Portuguese in India and in Abyssinia attempted to communicate, mostly without success. At Goa the Jesuit Patriarch was waiting still, desperate at being unable to reach his post and wondering what had happened to the Bishop. He begged the viceroy to give him a ship and land him anywhere upon the Red Sea beach — he was quite willing to risk whatever followed. But the Viceroy refused. Dom João Nunes Barreto, he said, was too high a dignitary to expose to such danger. Brother Fulgencio Freire. an old soldier and a less important person, might try his luck and carry letters to the Bishop. as well as other useful things.

Brother Fulgencio Freire embarked, but neither reached Abyssinia nor returned to India. The ship on which he sailed came up against the Turks. The captain might have avoided battle, but would not. With fifteen men he chose to take on fifty, and so the ship was lost. Brother Fulgencio was carried off to Cairo by the Turks. The Viceroy refused to send another ship that way, and the Patriarch died of despair in 1562.

From the other side attempts were also made to break the iron ring. Father André Gualdames, escorted by a Portuguese named Marco Fernandes, tried to pass the Turkish lines and sailed for India in disguise.

They got as far as Massawa, and there they were betrayed. The Turks drew out their scimitars and hewed them into slices.

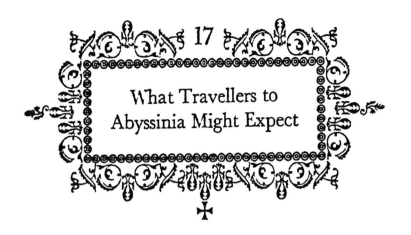

17

What Travellers to Abyssinia Might Expect

✠

An Armenian walking through the streets of Diu attracted the attention of the schoolboys of that town. Armenians dressed not very differently from Moslems in those parts, and the urchins did not know one from the other. "Mohammed!" they all howled at the stranger passing by, for young Diu was fanatically Christian as became the grandsons of Moslems.

The Armenian took no notice but went on his way. When he entered the fort, however, the sentinel beside the gate did not behave more decently than the schoolboys. "Ah, Moor!" he cried, drawing his sword. "How dare you come into a Christian fort?" A comrade pointed out that it was an Armenian not a Moor, and so the man was suffered to proceed. Anybody who had cared to dog his steps might have seen him joined at some time by an older man who was dressed in the same fashion, and whoever listened to their conversation would have heard the two Armenians talking Spanish. The pair were, in fact, the Castilian Father Pero Paes and his Catalan colleague Father Antonio de Monserrate, both Jesuit priests who had left their headquarters at Goa on February 3, 1588, and were hoping to reach Abyssinia with the help of the Lord.

The travelling joys to which they might look forward had already been experienced by the Fathers André Gualdames and Fulgencio Freire. Facilities had not increased since the

Turks had cut up Father André at Massawa; on the contrary. only profoundest secrecy and deep disguise could get a traveller past the danger zone. Yet when the Provincial at Goa received orders to send more Jesuits to Abyssinia, we are told that all the fathers were anxious to go.

The Provincial made careful selection among the men of various nationality at his command. He picked out Father Antonio de Monserrate, a veteran missionary from the court of the Great Mogul, and Pero Paes, a young man fresh from his studies and newly arrived in India. Father Antonio, though richly experienced, was rather old to send on such a journey, but the choice of Pero Paes could not have been improved upon. He had all the earnestness of his compatriot Dom André de Oviedo, tempered by infinitely more tact. Pero Paes was, moreover, cheerful, intelligent, adaptable, resourceful, quick at languages, and what today would be called "a good mixer," for he was able to get on well with all sorts and conditions of men.

The adventurous pair disguised themselves and sailed for Diu to study there the problem of how to cross the Moslem lands. A real Armenian from Aleppo offered his assistance in the matter. He said that they could travel with him to his country via Basra, and he would put them on the way to Cairo. At Cairo they were sure to meet some caravan bound for Ethiopia which they might join.

A very complicated route! commented Belchior Calaça, captain of Muscat, where the ship bearing the Jesuits and their Armenian friend put in for water. Instead of trailing up the Persian Gulf and right across the desert, why not take ship direct to Zeila or some port of the Red Sea? An Arab pilot who was a good friend of his and often sailed that way might easily be persuaded to take the priests as passengers.

It did appear a simpler plan. The companions left their Armenian to continue his journey without them and waited until the Arab was ready to sail. Thus it came about that the end of December 1588 saw the two missionaries, with a young

Syrian interpreter, on board a little ship that vainly tried to fight its way up the Arabian coast against a strong head wind.

The weather grew worse as they went along; to make progress in such a storm was quite impossible, but neither could they put back to Muscat. There was nothing but to run for the nearest land.

Detached fragments of the desert cast into the sea, the Kuria Muria Islands raise their forsaken rocks off the Arabian coast. These isolated dots upon the map, known to history only in records of shipwreck, had for inhabitants the poorest fishermen, who lived in seaweed-covered huts and fed on sun-dried fish, uncooked for want of fuel. Their boats, it seems, were better than their houses, and the Arab pilot managed to hire one in which he hoped to sail as far as Zeila, for the ship in which he had left Muscat was no longer seaworthy. A week was spent at Kuria Muria, equipping the new vessel for the voyage, which delay was long enough to seal the Jesuits' fate.

Belchior Calaça's friend the pilot was no doubt a worthy man. The only trouble was that he, too, had a friend to whom he could not refrain telling important bits of news. That two Franks were travelling to Zeila on his ship was sufficiently novel to be worth talking about, and so he passed it on. The friend listened to the secret with interest, and immediately wrote to inform a friend of his, living at Dofar beyond the Kuria Muria Islands: a ship carrying two Portuguese (all Europeans were Portuguese to Orientals of that time) was sailing up the coast. If a sharp look-out were kept, some useful prisoners might be caught for ransom!

The men of Dofar took the hint, and the delay at Kuria Muria played the game into their hands. A flotilla patrolled the coast until the travellers had set sail once more, when the ship was waylaid and the two Jesuits with their interpreter were carried off.

The captain of Dofar eyed the foreigners suspiciously. What were they doing on that ship? he wished to know. They told the truth, that they were Christian priests bound for Ethiopia to join the Portuguese already living there, but the captain thought it was not a convincing story. The prisoners were divested of most of their clothes and consigned to a dilapidated building which Dofar ambitiously referred to as the fort. Antonio de Monserrate and Pero Paes spent a few days within its ramshackle walls, half-starved and eaten up by fleas "and similar nocturnal guests – a common produce of those countries," the chronicler says tersely.

The captain later sent for them again. The question of their belongings troubled him. Little had been found beyond the clothes they wore, and as he had to dispatch the prisoners to his King, he feared that he would be suspected of holding something back. He therefore had them questioned before witnesses, and after thus establishing his innocence he shipped the three captives on a coasting dhow. Five days later they were landed on an arid shore and, turning their backs upon the sea whence lay a Christian captive's only hope of rescue, their jailers led them off into the desert land.

It was a long and weary journey into the unknown. Day after day the camels padded their way across the sand through the great emptiness, their drivers guiding themselves by the sun and stars as men do in mid-ocean. At first the prisoners were expected to run barefoot beside the camels, but finding that the unfortunate wretches could not keep pace, they were allowed to ride among the baggage.

No food was offered them but roasted locusts. Antonio de Monserrate and Pero Paes were both ascetic men, but they did not succeed in emulating John the Baptist. They found it quite impossible to swallow the insects, so their captors made them some very little loaves out of the flour that had been confiscated from the prisoners' own stores.

After ten blazing days they reached Tarim, in the heart of Hadhramaut. The dwellers in those lost towns of the desert had not often the chance to see a foreign face; the whole of Tarim therefore turned out to gape at the strange sight. Were these men followers of the Prophet? was the first question asked. On hearing that they were not, all Tarim scowled and burst into a torrent of abuse. When words failed to express their pious rage, they spat in the prisoners' faces. By degrees the faithful worked themselves up into such a frenzy that the Christians would have been torn to pieces if their custodians had not hurried them into a house. Pero Paes and Antonio de Monserrate were smuggled out of the town at early dawn before the fierce fanatics were abroad.

The next village was better. A brother of the King received the captives pleasantly. He plied them with refreshing drinks and asked them many questions. He also sounded their religious views, but "These men never will turn Moslem" was the conclusion which he reached as a result, and he sent them on to his brother, King Omar, at Henan.

The inhabitants of Henan were less fanatical than the men of Tarim. They made no attempt to stone the prisoners, but they spent a happy two days staring at them in the turret where they were confined. Never in their lives had Pero Paes and Antonio de Monserrate been the objects of such embarrassing publicity. The people came in relays and they came in batches. Each time one man had gazed his fill, his place was taken by another. All through the stifling day the foreigners were surrounded by groups of swarthy Arabs whose carefully curled locks were caked with dust and soaked in rancid butter.

The townsmen had not ceased to feast their eyes upon the strangers when King Omar desired his turn and sent for them. The scanty clothes that had been left the captives at Dofar were much the worse for desert travel and not considered seemly to appear at court. The confiscated garments were therefore restored before the two priests entered the royal presence.

King Omar, a personable man aged about forty, was seated on a dais spread with brocade. He was festively attired in very fine green cloth and wore a gold-embroidered turban.

He greeted the prisoners graciously and told them to sit down. Waving aside the Syrian interpreter, he summoned an old Peguan woman out of the harem. The King addressed her in Arabic, which she translated into reasonably good Portuguese: "The King tells you not to be distressed, for God has led you here — but," she added in an aside, "I say that for your sins you have been brought among such evil men."

The afternoon was spent in question and in answer, for King Omar was curious and had many things to ask. In the end the priests begged that they might have their breviaries returned to them, to which the King agreed. He sent the books back the next day, "which was no small consolation."

There was not much else to console the prisoners during the long empty days they passed in that forsaken town, wondering what their fate would be.

The Peguan woman came to visit them at last and explained the position. King Omar, it appears, would have liked to keep the prisoners until they were ransomed, but dared not for fear of his overlords, the Turkish conquerors of Yemen. The Pasha had decreed that Portuguese prisoners were his by right, and no doubt would demand them.

The Jesuits asked the woman to tell them her story and how she came to be in this Arab town. She told them that she used to be a Christian and embarked many years ago upon a ship sailing from Chaul to Ormuz. A tempest threw them onto the Arabian coast, where the eight Portuguese with whom she was had been enticed ashore and captured. She and they were taken to Omar's father, then the reigning King. The woman, no doubt young and attractive at the time, was sent to the harem, but the men endured a cruel captivity. The King tried to persecute them into turning Moslem, which all eight steadily refused to do.

One of them, whose name was Preto, said the woman, thought that he had made a friend. This Arab, who sailed to Melindi every year, agreed to carry a letter to the Portuguese stationed there. Preto therefore wrote to his compatriots, im-

ploring them to send a ship to the Arabian coast and capture
a few natives there in order to exchange them for the prisoners in Hadhramaut.

Somebody in Henan must have been able to read Portuguese, for the gist of the letter was repeated to the King. He
sent for Preto in a fury. "Is this your letter?" he demanded,
and the prisoner said it was. "Then," cried the King with rising
anger, "you shall turn Moslem here and now, or else die at
my hands!"

"I am not a man to turn Moslem," said Preto sturdily, whereupon the King had his head smitten off and his body flung
out of the window. His seven companions, though they stuck
to their faith, did not meet with such a violent end. Worn out
by hard treatment and illness, one by one they died, and so
the woman alone remained.

And would she not return to the Christian fold? pleaded
the captive priests, but, weeping, she refused. She had not
the courage, she sobbed, to confess Christ before Moslems,
and their preaching drew from her nothing but tears.

Antonio de Monserrate had spent four months in Henan
before the Pasha of Yemen heard about their existence. He
sent word to Omar that these prisoners were his and he must
have them.

The Arab kinglet hastened to obey. The captives were dispatched at once, together with a present of four horses — not
a love gift, but an offering prompted by fear in order to placate
the Turkish tyrant.

On June 27 the last fortress of Omar's kingdom was left
behind, and the pathless desert engulfed the caravan. Four
days and nights the camels ploughed the wastes before they
reached and rested by an oasis. The next day they passed
through Melkis, a town left in the desert long ago, for centuries abandoned to the sun and sand. Here ruins of great
buildings raised by a forgotten race bore inscriptions that no
Arab could decipher. The Queen of Sheba, so the local legend
ran, had ruled over this city in her time. This appeared to the

Jesuits to be likely enough, and they gazed upon the ancient stones with keen interest.

The capital of Yemen, on the Arabian plateau, concealed its fruitful orchards and its palmy gardens behind a powerful encircling wall. Here was the Pasha's residence, and his Governor rode out of the city gates to meet the prisoners with trumpets sounding. He made a spectacular return into the town with the captives walking before his horse as in a Roman triumph. Having undergone the customary cross-questioning at the Pasha's palace, the two Jesuits were led away to an evil-smelling dungeon — in every way as bad, the chronicler affirms, as the prisons of Tetuan.

Father Antonio de Monserrate struck his jailers as being too old and weak to put in irons, but Pero Paes was young and able-bodied; heavy chains were therefore clamped on his ankles, and in these fetters he was daily led out to work.

The two Jesuits were not alone in their foul prison. They found twenty-six Portuguese and five Indian Christians there, who had been captured off the Malindi coast. It would be edifying to be able to say that these companions in misfortune were like one big family, but the melancholy truth is that they were at daggers drawn, and on the point of murdering one another. Close confinement makes men sick of their comrades' faces — especially men whose tempers are short. The two priests found good work cut out for themselves.

Their mission was successful. Such was the effect of precept and example that before long even the Turks could hardly recognize their fiery prisoners. And it seems that virtue brought its own reward, for soon after the captives' reformation they found their lot greatly improved.

It happened that the Pasha was a keen horticulturist. He had begun life in a humble way as gardener to the Grand Turk. Though he had risen to greatness, he did not blush to own his lowly origin. On the contrary, he gloried in it. The hoe with which he once had tilled the Sultan's garden at Constantinople hung like a trophy in the palace hall. His own gardens were the finest in Yemen, and now the idea occurred to him to employ his Christian captives in cultivating them.

The Portuguese seem to have been delighted, for the love of gardening is deeply rooted in that flower-loving race. They applied themselves to their new work with enthusiasm and, we may gather, with considerable success. At Easter time the chapel which the Jesuits had improvised in their prison was transformed by the gardeners into one bright mass of flowers.

The prisoners' quarters were no longer in the dismal cellar where they were first confined. In this respect also conditions had improved. The Christians had been allowed to move up to the airy and spacious first floor of the building, where they seem to have had the whole place to themselves and divided up the accommodation as they chose. The priests were allotted two large apartments, in one of which they fitted up their little chapel, "very well arranged," we are informed. Not only was it beautified at Easter time, but at Christmas it was bright with many candles made with wax which the gardeners obtained from the Turks in exchange for fruit and flowers. The fathers also managed to make and put together one of those *presepios* (Christmas cribs) which are still popular in Portugal today. The Turks were fascinated by this one and flocked to gaze upon it. They must have been far less fanatical than the Arabs of Hadhramaut. Christians would never have been allowed such latitude at Tarim or Henan.

In this manner two years went by, not without consolations. From time to time money arrived from Christian centres (the ransom of captives was a favourite charity in that age, and the object of pious legacies), and one prisoner or another obtained his liberty. But the Pasha expected a higher sum to be paid for the two priests.

The young Syrian interpreter who was their travelling companion had been more fortunate than they. The Governor of the town took a fancy to this lad and made him his house slave. Like Joseph, the young man won favour by his excellent conduct, and his master made him caterer for the household. The youth handled money so faithfully and was so exact in returning the change that his lord was often moved to give him handsome tips, which he always handed over to the two priests, who often lacked the necessaries of life. This little help was soon cut off, however, for the Syrian had a further stroke of luck. He met a Turk hailing from his own country. This man had influence with the Pasha and obtained the boy's freedom from him. The Syrian set off joyfully for his native land, but promised the Jesuits not to stay there long. He would return to India overland via Ormuz and report to headquarters about the missionaries' captivity and have them ransomed.

One day it seemed that they might not have to wait till then, for they, too, were in luck. The Pasha had a wife of Christian origin, who greatly wished to see the two Jesuits. Her curiosity went no further than this – she knew that she could not speak to a man. A pretext was found in the person of her small son, aged seven. The lady sent word that she would like to show this prodigy to the stranger priests. A time and place accordingly were fixed. The gardeners gave the Jesuits a jar of their rose water to present to the child. Thus they visited the Pasha's son, while the Pasha's wife, hidden behind a shuttered window, feasted her eyes upon the foreigners unseen by them.

Antonio de Monserrate and Pero Paes must have adopted the right manner towards the little boy, for they clearly made the conquest of his mother. She told her son to beg his father for their freedom and to send them to Jerusalem. The Pasha was a fond father and listened to his child. He promised to give the priests their liberty and would actually have done so, but his treasurer protested. It was madness, this Turk declared, to let the Jesuits go. Did the Pasha not understand that 5,000 cruzados could be extorted for their ransom? Did he feel like sacrificing such a sum?

That certainly would be a pity, the Pasha concluded on

second thoughts. He had given his word, but what of that? Sentiment ought not to weigh when 5,000 cruzados were at stake.

He appears to have awakened to new interest in the two Jesuits' ransom. Since they were worth so much money, he told the treasurer, better take steps to squeeze it out. The treasurer hastened to put on the screw, and life became very grim for Pero Paes and Antonio de Monserrate. The Turk, hoping that starvation would have the desired result, reduced their ration to one loaf a day, of husks rather than flour. The reason for this rigour was duly explained, but, in accordance with the rules of sound bargaining as recognized throughout the East, since 5,000 cruzados were the price that had been fixed, the Turks demanded 20,000.

During a wretched eighteen months the only consolation in the captives' life was Mullah Ali. This rather intriguing personage was a Turk from Argel, son of a Christian slave. He was deeply learned in all the holy books of Islam, and his frequent pilgrimages to Mecca had invested him with an aura of sanctity. Devout Moslem though Mullah Ali was, he does not appear to have been bigoted. He remembered that his mother had been a Christian woman, and he could meet Franks without prejudice. He moreover revelled in theological discussions, to which of course the Jesuits had been highly trained. Mullah Ali therefore enjoyed talking to Pero Paes and Antonio de Monserrate, and, happily for them, he liked such conversation during meals. The starving prisoners were invited to "copious dinners," and while partaking of earthly refreshment they discoursed with their host of heavenly things.

At these banquets they were often joined by Ali Pasha, a native of Seville, who had been captured by the Turks when he was eight years old. He had been educated in the faith of Islam, and risen to high honour in their midst, but he never had borne arms against Christians, he told the priests.

These intellectual parties were only an interlude. Mullah

Ali and Ali Pasha both went away, and so, the chronicler says sadly, "that was the end of the good dinners."

A very savage Turk appeared upon the scene about this time. By way of speculation, he offered to buy the captive Jesuits from the Pasha of Yemen. They could not agree about the price, however. He would not offer above 3,000 cruzados, and the Pasha hoped to do better than that, so the deal was off. It was a lucky escape for Antonio de Monserrate and Pero Paes, for this Turk seems to have been a dangerous lunatic. The Pasha, for reasons of his own, seized some of his luggage and refused to restore it; whereupon we are told that this man, "full of an infernal impatience," slashed himself open in his rage and, pulling out his own entrails, proceeded to cut them into little bits until he died! When his son tried to stop him at this ghastly operation, the ruthless suicide turned the knife upon the young man and stabbed him to death.

Meanwhile the Pasha's treasurer had informed the captives that 5,000 cruzados was the lowest sum that his master could think of accepting. The Jesuits replied that much as they desired their freedom, they could not promise what they did not possess, so they were once more cast into chains. This time they were relegated to a tiny dungeon where three people might just have squeezed, sitting with their heads touching the ceiling. They would have died there very soon, but not wishing to incur financial loss, their jailers took them out in time. They were dispatched to Mocha, by the shores of the Red Sea. It would be easier to negotiate their ransom from this port, where merchants' ships from India came and went.

Thus the priests were sent upon their third journey across Arabia. They travelled via Taiz to the coast, a very trying trek. Father Antonio de Monserrate was fast wearing out and did not feel safe perched on a camel. Having fallen off once, he begged to be allowed to ride a donkey, but as it happened, this made matters worse. A camel knocked the little donkey down with Father Antonio underneath. The poor old man was badly bruised and shaken and had to be supported for the rest of the way by Pero Paes and a kindly Brahman who followed the caravan.

What about those 5,000 cruzados? was the remark with which they were greeted at Mocha by the Pasha's minion who took charge of the prisoners. They were incarcerated in a dark and stifling warehouse, filled with bales of pepper, cinnamon, and cloves, the scent of which, brought out by the terrific heat, came near to asphyxiating them.

It was a scorching day, hot even for the southern shores of the Red Sea, and everyone was gasping. The Pasha's officer upstairs was having water sprinkled on him by his Abyssinian slave, who seems to have been a good-hearted lad. "Sir," he exclaimed, "if even up here we are roasting in this fiery heat, what will happen to those wretches down below among the bales of spices? Let me go and fetch them out before they die." His master consented — the prisoners after all were worth money — and the boy rescued them just in time to save their lives.

The Pasha's deputy later on sent for Pero Paes.

"My master orders me," he said, "to chain you foot and neck. I shall put the collar on you, but not the fetters, for you will have to run before my horse, with my sword pricking from behind to goad you on."

"And you can kill us with it," answered Pero Paes serenely, "if those are your orders. There is nothing that would make us happier than to die for our holy faith."

"Since you so ardently desire it," sneered the Turk, "you soon will meet with death — when you are flayed alive."

These, however, were only threats. So long as there was any hope of ransom, no attempt would be made on the prisoners' lives. The Turk did not flay them alive, but sent them to the galleys.

The lot of galley-slaves was bad at best, and these two tasted it in its worst form. The master of their galley had himself been a slave chained to the bench, and he took special joy in avenging upon other wretches what he had once endured.

One would have thought that in their captors' own interest the oarsmen should have been well fed, but they were starved. A very small ration of red millet was issued every day, which chicken-feed they had to grind without a mill and which there was no wood to cook with.

Pero Paes was resourceful. He managed to find two stones between which by superhuman efforts he could crush the corn. The broken fragments he put in a jar, and dropped sparks on them. The result was partly burnt and partly raw, but such as it was, they had to eat it or starve.

If the days were bad, the nights were even worse. In the fiery heat of the Red Sea the cramped and filthy space below the galley deck was humming with mosquitoes and crawling with fleas. The prisoners could hardly snatch a wink of sleep, but spent the hours brushing away the myriad insects that settled on their faces, "some singing and others biting." It is a marvel that these men did not go mad.

Antonio de Monserrate was an old man and at the end of his tether. His son fell very ill. Even so the Turks would have kept him chained to his bench if his companion had not remonstrated with the captain. The Pasha would doubtless hold him responsible, said Pero Paes, if that captive were to die. This made their tormentor thoughtful. After all, the Pasha would not like to lose his money. Antonio de Monserrate was given leave to go ashore, with Pero Paes in charge of him, but from the moment that they left the galley, their meagre ration was cut off.

A kindly merchant took pity on them in these straits. He gave them rice and butter of his own, and lent two cruzados for their maintenance until some help from India should arrive.

With such resources Pero Paes nursed his invalid and fed him upon rice. The old man must have had a splendid constitution, for in spite of every disadvantage he recovered and resumed his seat upon the galley bench.

It was only for a short time. Their ransom really came at
last — thanks to the faithful Syrian. He had kept his promise
and returned to India via the Persian Gulf and told the story
of the priests' captivity. The Viceroy took immediate action
and so one day a ship arrived at Mocha from Diu with joy-
ful news. An Indian native had been sent with letters and
the ransom!

Negotiations were opened at once. The Viceroy's orders
were to ransom the missionaries at any cost, but the pair saw
to it that the demand was not excessive. An Oriental may be
past master in the art of bargaining, but a southern European
is not very far behind. Antonio de Monserrate and Pero Paes
shrugged their shoulders and displayed such complete, such
convincing indifference to their liberty that instead of the
5,000 cruzados for which they had clamoured, the Turks were
soon agreeing to accept 1,000! Even then the prisoners raised
loud protests. What was the use, they asked the Viceroy's messenger, of wasting so much money? They were accustomed to
their captivity — keep the ransom for others! But the Indian
was quite satisfied that he would not get better terms and
counted out the sum.

The two priests were just about to leave Mocha, free men
at last. Already the anchor was weighed, the sails unfurled,
when the captain of the Turkish galley appeared on board,
deeply aggrieved. Where did he come in? said he. He had received no compensation for the time he had permitted them
to stay ashore. A hundred cruzados, he felt, would be necessary to meet the case, and if they did not propose to pay, he
would drag them back to his galley forthwith.

There was no time to appeal to the Pasha against this highly
unjustified extortion, and the Turk if he chose had power to
carry out his threat. The ruffian was given his hundred cruzados, and the captives really got away.

After seven years' captivity in the Arabian desert Antonio
de Monserrate and Pero Paes reached India once again. After
the dungeons of Yemen, and benches of the Red Sea galleys,

the austere monastic life of their brethren at Goa seemed luxury and rest. Antonio de Monserrate did not live to enjoy it long. He died at Goa shortly after their return, as might have been expected.

A few years later Pero Paes set out again for Abyssinia.

18

Success

There came to our country a man from Jerusalem named Moallim Petros. . . . His beard was red as flames of fire . . . he spoke Geez and knew all our books better than our own wise men. . . ."

This fiery-bearded stranger moving through Ethiopian legend has been identified with Father Pero Paes. He did reach Abyssinia in the end, and was followed there by two colleagues, Father Antonio Fernandes of Lisbon and the Neapolitan Father Francisco Antonio de Angelis.

Pero Paes arrived in 1602, when for many years no white man had reached Abyssinia. The most recent attempt had been that of the Maronite Jesuit Father Abraham de Georgiis, who was beheaded by the Turks in 1595. In 1597 the last of the five priests who came with Dom André de Oviedo had died at Fremona, and the Catholics in Abyssinia felt themselves very much cut off.

These "Portuguese," as the descendants of Dom Cristóvão's army persisted in calling themselves, were no longer recognizable as such. The Jesuit chronicler Baltasar Teles tells us that a few of the original heroes survived, but they must have been over eighty years old. Their sons and grandsons by Ethiopian mothers could not claim to be white men any more. Yet, Ethiopian though they were in birth, custom, and colour, their heart's loyalty was still for the far-off ancestral home. Their exiled fathers had taught them to feel in some measure like exiles themselves, and the little kingdom by the Western Ocean had been painted to them as a lost paradise. Thus these half-castes fostered their sentiment of nationality and clung to the religion of their fathers as part of the birthright that marked them for a race apart. The last Jesuit's death was like the severing of a link with a beloved past; the successive arrivals of Pero Paes and his companions were therefore greeted with joy.

Pero Paes had forced the Turkish barrier thanks to a pious fraud by means of which, Baltasar Teles says, he had "deceived the Devil." It was the good man's Arabic, perfected during seven years' captivity, that made it possible to foil the Evil One, with the assistance of a histrionic gift. Pero Paes personated an Armenian so successfully this time that no one found him out, and he struck up a warm friendship with a Turk from Suakin whom he met at Diu. This amiable Ottoman offered to repatriate him, and the supposed Armenian jumped at the idea. Fraternizing happily with a crew of miscellaneous Orientals, Father Pero Paes sailed into the Red Sea. At Massawa he said that he must go ashore to fetch some things of his that had remained there, and so he disembarked and walked away. He had managed to find a messenger at Massawa to go ahead and tell the Portuguese of his arrival. They sent at once to meet him on the way, and he was guided safely to Fremona, in spite of robbers that walked the hills by day, and "a large and fearsome lion" that strolled around the tent by night.

Ethiopia was in the throes of its habitual dynastic struggles. Each one of Lebna Dengel's grandsons and great-grandsons appears to have made his bid for the Imperial throne. Constant upheavals were the result while these princes murdered and exiled one another, and fought the savage Galla tribes by way of interlude.

Pero Paes did not at once proceed to court. He remained at

Fremona, where he catechized the so-called Portuguese and taught young Abyssinians. He also devoted himself to the study of Geez and Amharic, both of which languages he picked up in an amazingly short time. While so engaged he translated into the vernacular a "holy little book" by the Jesuit Father Doctor Marcos Jorge. This was a form of brighter catechism in which the Church's doctrines were expounded painlessly in a series of dialogues. The most promising of Padre Pero Paes's little pupils were made to learn these dialogues by heart and repeat them before selected audiences.

The result was an unqualified success. It filled their listeners with joy to hear these infants hold forth fluently upon "the height of divine mysteries," and the youthful theologians were in constant demand to go through their performance at the houses of local magnates.

Pero Paes's fame as an educationalist soon reached the temporary Emperor, Za Danguil. This monarch is described as "very affable, and at the same time very curious." He sent for Pero Paes and received him graciously, inquiring politely after the health of the Pope and the King.

The Emperor moreover heard the Jesuit say Mass and listened while he preached. Father Pero Paes no doubt had plenty to say, but, in order not to weary anyone, he considerately cut down his sermon to "only one hour's duration. . . . Generally speaking," reflects Baltasar Teles, "if a preacher continues over an hour, his listeners are bored."

The missionaries had great hopes of Za Danguil. Though he did not actually pronounce himself, he strongly inclined towards the Church of Rome. He composed a letter to the Pope, and also to the King of Portugal, Dom Felipe — the second of those four "intruder kings" who reigned over both Spain and a disgusted Portugal.

"Peace to Your Majesty!" Za Danguil wrote, and "How are you?" He told of the arrival of Pero Paes, and referred to the past victories of the Portuguese. "Now we have some enemies called the Gallas," the Emperor further explains, "who lay waste our land . . . wherefore we beg Your Majesty to send us warriors, and at the same time your daughter to marry our son that our friendship may be firm, and we may have one body and one heart. Our son is seven years old, and we hear that your daughter is three. Let us bring them up together with the milk of wisdom, and teach them the Holy Scriptures."

Dom Felipe, however, was not called upon to invent an excuse for not sending the future wife of Louis XIII to drink the milk of wisdom with the small Ethiopian prince. A certain Za Selassie rose in revolt against Za Danguil and slew him with his own hand. Abyssinia only calmed down again when Susenyos took command.

Susenyos was a prepossessing person. His face was long, his forehead broad, his brown eyes pleasant and vivacious. He had a pointed nose, thin lips, and a thick black beard adorned his chin; his stature was above the average, and he was powerfully built. But for his dark complexion, we are told, he might have been a European.

Susenyos and the Jesuits became friends at once. Since Pero Paes's arrival in 1603, several colleagues had succeeded in joining him, and the Emperor gave them some "very good lands" in Dembea, and permission to build a church at Gorgorra, near Lake Tsana. His favour went even further than that — he actually invited them to dine!

This was an almost unheard-of distinction. The Emperor always ate in solitary glory, his greatest condescension being to invite a favoured and exalted few to finish what was left over from his repast after he had withdrawn. The Jesuits, however, were to enjoy the unique honour of dining while the Emperor dined, at a table beside his own, divided from him only by a curtain.

"Table" is not quite the correct word to use for the circular boards or trays placed on the floor on which the Abyssinians laid their meals. Neither in this nor in any other way had the amenities of dining made progress since the Ras of Angot entertained Father Francisco Alvares, almost a century earlier.

There were, declares Baltasar Teles, "neither fork nor spoon, nor napkin, cruet, cinnamon-sifter, sugar-basin, salt-cellar, nor pepper-pot, neither dish, nor carvers, nor anything else." Trenchers of bread did duty both as napkins and for plates till they were eaten, and of course there was no tablecloth.

Throughout the meal the curtain veiling the Emperor from his guests was never lifted – which our chronicler suggests was just as well, for to see His Imperial Highness eat was not a pretty sight. In Ethiopia the great and noble considered it beneath their dignity to feed themselves; the Emperor therefore sat impassive while his pages rammed balls of food into his mouth. These balls, made up of bread rolled and well kneaded by hand and dipped in sauce, were of such size that the pages could hardly poke them between the monarch's open jaws, "but still they go on putting them, not to say stuffing them, in, one after another, in the manner in which here in Portugal we fatten ducks for a feast."

Susenyos's favour to the Jesuits was not a passing fancy. He gave them audience every day, and all their conversation with him, it appears, was on religious matters. Their words of wisdom deeply impressed the Emperor, and he granted them full liberty to teach and preach throughout the land.

In spite of protection from the throne theirs was no easy mission. It was not the difference between the Roman and the Abyssinian Churches that caused the stumbling-block – it was their similarity. The Western priests had no new Gospel to preach to Christians of the East, and the great schism which had divided the Churches was over abstruse theological definitions such as most laymen are content to leave to doctors of divinity. Beyond this was the observance of sundry ancient rites dear to the people's heart, and the question of obedience to the Pope, who was a vague and almost mythical figure to the Abyssinians, a year's journey away.

In the circumstances the missionaries' best chance of success depended on their personality, and, as it happened, this was their strong point. It is certain that they compared favourably with the average Abyssinian priest. They were men of blameless lives and rigid morals, whereas the standards prevalent in Ethiopia were very low. Also, coming as they did from centres of a higher civilization, the European priests were intellectually superior to their ignorant African colleagues. There is no denying that the Jesuits were a power for progress in the land. During the whole of Susenyos's reign their efforts were untiring for the moral and material welfare of the people among whom they had cast their lot. They opened schools and taught both in Amharic and in Portuguese; they set up a printing press and made new translations of the Gospels into Amharic, and rendered European commentaries on the Scriptures into Geez. They traced roads and they built bridges, some of which have been in use till modern times; they erected a number of churches, and they taught the Abyssinians to build two-storeyed houses in stone and cement.

The Jesuit mission also contributed to the general store of human knowledge. They studied all the Geez and Amharic records, and gave the world some detailed histories of the ancient African Empire. They took notes of the customs of its people, and described the geographical features of the land, which they explored from end to end. Father Pero Paes visited the sources of the Nile. Father Manuel Barradas wrote a full description of the Kingdom of Tigré, and Father Antonio Fernandes, searching for a safe route from Ethiopia to Malindi, penetrated into the almost unknown lands of Enarea and Janjeiro.

The most powerful factor in the success of the mission was, undoubtedly, the personal magnetism of Pero Paes. That man possessed to an astonishing degree the indefinable something that we lamely describe by saying that "he had a way with him." Padre Pero Paes was everybody's friend, and the Emperor simply could not do without him. Susenyos had never seen such a man: "I have everything in him," he said, "teacher, counsellor, and general handyman."

Without ever having learned, it seems that the versatile

Pero Paes could take a hand as painter, locksmith, architect, mason, or carpenter, and he designed a palace for the Emperor, training the workmen himself and teaching them to make their tools. The result was impressive, and still stands today. "It could quite well have served as country house for a European prince," was the white man's verdict upon the new palace, and to the Abyssinians it seemed one of the wonders of the world. They had never seen a two-storeyed building before, and they called it "a house above a house." Many came to the conclusion that these very knowing foreigners must also be worth listening to upon religious matters, and so they joined the Church of Rome.

And Pero Paes converted the Emperor! His brother, Seela Krestos, had already become a fervent Catholic when, in 1615, Susenyos convened all the doctors of the Abyssinian Church to defend their beliefs while the Jesuits expounded theirs.

An epic debate then took place, which continued for days. As might have been expected, the learned foreigners had very much the best of it. "These heretics," explains Baltasar Teles, "had never studied logic, nor were they versed in syllogisms, enthymemas, and modes of argument, nor had they any knowledge of the subtleties of scholastic theology." Not for nothing had the European divines made a fine art of polemics! When they turned their batteries upon the simple Ethiopian, he could no more stand up to them than to the foreign cannon.

Annihilated though they were by syllogisms, enthymemas, and the like, the Abyssinian priesthood remained unconvinced. Not so the Emperor. He issued a decree ordering his subjects forthwith to believe in the two natures Human and Divine, each distinct from the other, united in the Person of Our Lord.

The Abuna Simon had not been present at the debate. He came rushing to the spot with loud protests, and the whole discussion was renewed. The result was identical. The Abuna, like his fellows, was silenced but not persuaded, while the Emperor, more convinced than ever, reissued his proclamation — this time announcing death to be the penalty for those refusing to agree with his religious views.

The priests of Abyssinia were all filled with horror and dismay. Wailing, they threw themselves at their Emperor's feet, imploring him not to depart from the faith of his ancestors. Susenyos refused to withdraw his proclamation, and sixty monks of Damot threw themselves off a rock rather than violate their conscience.

Abyssinia was shaken to its foundations. As always happens when religious disputes rend a nation, beside the true faith that makes martyrs political opportunism did not fail to appear. Yolyos, the Governor of Ogara, having quarrelled with the Emperor, gathered round him a whole army of malcontents who, blessed by the Abuna, swore to kill Susenyos. The rebels were defeated, however. Yolyos and the Abuna both were slain, and their heads displayed triumphantly on a cushion in the Imperial tent.

On the strength of this victory the Emperor further scandalized his subjects by ordering them to work upon the Jewish Sabbath day. "I have not changed my religion," he explained to his court, "I have only improved it. I do not hold my faith because it is that of the Portuguese, nor because it is the faith of Rome, but because it is the true faith. And do not deceive yourselves — for this faith I am prepared to die if necessary, but," he added darkly, "all those who contradict it will die first."

Here was a trumpet with no uncertain sound. Pero Paes could be proud of his convert's zeal. The orthodoxy of Susenyos was beyond reproach, but, the chronicler observes regretfully, "he was readier to defend it by the sword than to follow it in his life." It was a sore trial to his spiritual father that the pious Emperor was a polygamist.

Even in this respect, however, Pero Paes got his way at last. In 1622 Susenyos sent for the priest, made a general confession of his whole life, and gave up all his wives except the first. "Then," we are told, "Padre Pero Paes felt that his seven years'

207

captivity in Arabia and the nineteen years that he had devoted to this mission had not been spent in vain." And the veteran missionary died happy a few months after that.

Susenyos's letter to the Provincial at Goa reads like a lament:

The virtuous Reverend Padre Pero Paes was father of our soul, bright sun of faith lighting the darkness of Ethiopia. Since our sun has been eclipsed and set, our joy is turned to sadness, and our happiness to mourning. If this paper were wide as the sky, and the ink like the sea, it still would not suffice to write his virtues and his teaching. The flowers that are scattered may not be picked again, nor can we cause the passed day to return, nor gather up the water that has been split.

19

The Alternative Route

✝

Padre Antonio Fernandes of Lisbon was a good man. He was so good, Baltasar Teles says, that the Devil felt particularly bitter about him. Finding it impossible to blacken Father Antonio's white soul, the foul fiend, in a fit of childish rage, vented his spleen by flinging black splotches all over the wall of the father's cell in the College of Jesuits at Goa.

The marks were so dark and ugly and ineffaceable as to leave no doubt of their infernal origin, but Father Antonio did not allow the Evil One to triumph. Those blots, the priest declared, were symbolic of the sin still marring his soul, and as such would be useful reminders of his need for spiritual improvement. The Devil, furious to find himself hoist with his own petard, appeared to Father Antonio one day and gave him a sound thrashing.

If Father Antonio's piety exposed him to the malice of the powers below, it also won for him the favour of his guardian angel, who delivered him miraculously from at least one predicament. As the good man journeyed through Ethiopia he came one day to a deep river. He could not wade across without undressing, but – Father Antonio was not alone, and his natural modesty recoiled at the idea of appearing indecent to the eyes of his companions. Yet he needed to cross that river.

On the horns of this dilemma Father Antonio appealed to

his guardian angel, who quite understood. Modesty, Baltasar Teles would have us know, is a quality that angels appreciate. Father Antonio was wafted suddenly across the water without the embarrassing necessity of taking off his clothes! We are not told if his companions enjoyed the same facility of transport, or if they had to put the angel to the blush.

Father Antonio Fernandes was a thoroughgoing ascetic. His clothes were entirely made up of patches, his hat was battered, and his shoes were worn. He was a little man of frail physique, so emaciated by the rigours of his fasts that he appeared to have no body left. He had been an ornament to the Company of Jesuits since he was seventeen, and he sailed for India in 1600, when he was thirty-one. Three years later he followed Pero Paes into Ethiopia and there he lived and laboured for nearly thirty years, preaching, teaching, and writing, correcting and translating books of theology.

This was the man who volunteered to blaze a trail across the unknown lands that stretched between Ethiopia and Malindi and proceed thence to India and to Rome, bearing letters from the Emperor to the Pope.

When Susenyos first resolved to join the Roman Church, he wrote to tell the Holy Father the glad news, and he also wished to send his own ambassador to Rome. One Tecu Egzy, "a serious person of great prudence and valour," was selected for the post, and a Jesuit priest was asked to go with him and be his guide in European lands.

The only obstacles barring this pious purpose were the inconvenient Turks of the Red Sea. Could not some other route be found by which safer communications might be established? We find this problem recurring at intervals throughout the history of relations between Portugal and Prester John. This time someone suggested Malindi as a possible way.

It was not a new idea. As far back as 1507 Tristão da Cunha had landed João Gomes at Malindi as a starting-point from which to travel to the land of Prester John. João Gomes had failed to find the route, but now it was attempted from the other end.

Everybody must have realized that the unknown dangers of such a trial trip were likely to be quite as great as the very well-known peril of the Turks, yet all the Jesuits volunteered to take the Emperor's message — partly, we are told, "because they held it to be a holy errand, and also for the many perils involved." These would be new perils, that was the attraction! The spirit of devotion was no doubt the dominating motive in the good fathers' lives, but we fancy that the spirit of adventure came in somewhere too.

All therefore volunteered, but the great-hearted little Padre Antonio Fernandes was the chosen man. He tied the precious letters underneath his arm and, accompanied by ten Abyssinian Portuguese who wanted to go too, he set out with the ambassador in March 1613. The Viceroy of Gojam, the Emperor's brother Ras Seela Krestos, provided them with Galla guides and sent them on their way cheered by as edifying and pious a farewell speech as might have been delivered by their own Father Provincial. Seela Krestos seems to have been the leading light among the converts of the Jesuit mission.

Encouraged by this satisfactory pupil, Father Antonio travelled with Tecu Egzy towards the wild and vaguely defined outlying provinces of the Empire. They crossed the Blue Nile where it bends towards the north, on rafts of hides guided by native swimmers — it took a whole day to get over with their luggage — and then they journeyed fifty leagues due south.

Enarea today is in the middle of Ethiopia, but at that time it was a borderland. South of this realm the Emperor's rule was felt no more, and to the east it vaguely trailed away across the nominally vassal states of Janjeiro and Kambata until it ceased to be in the wild welter of Moslem and heathen tribes of Harrar and Somaliland.

The inhabitants of Enarea, black and handsome, poured out of their huts when the strangers appeared. They brandished weapons in their hands and clamoured for a gift. Fortunately they had not large ideas — a few blocks of rock salt and sundry caps made them quite happy, and before they could call their friends to join the fun, a providential shower of rain caused them to scatter while the travellers hurried on.

The King of Enarea was polite but cold, though he, too, thawed a little on receiving presents. The vicar of the local church, however, scowled. He knew of Susenyos's leanings towards Catholicism and fancied that Father Antonio had come to relieve the vicar of Enarea of his functions. A tactful visit, aided by a mellowing gift, caused him to view the situation with more optimism, and he ceased from making trouble with the King.

None the less the King of Enarea disapproved of the embassy. As a tributary king he could say nothing, but he objected to his suzerain's coquetting with foreign powers and with a foreign church. He told Father Antonio that he must on no account leave Enarea except in an easterly direction. Via Kambata and Bali was the right way.

Father Antonio knew quite well that this was wrong. It would mean heading straight for Guardafui and never to Malindi, but still he was resolved to reach the coast, and if one direction was closed to him, then he would take another.

He expressed his willingness to travel via Bali, much to the King's delight. The embassy was so unlikely to get anywhere that the King grew kind and helpful all at once. He speeded Father Antonio on his way, and gave him fifty cruzados for travelling expenses, with profuse apologies for having no more to give.

The outskirts of the neighbouring realm of Janjeiro were haunted by savage Galla tribes, the constant terror of more civilized Ethiopia. Torrential rain on this occasion kept the enemy from venturing out, while the travellers, soaked to the skin, stepped briskly through the night across a dripping forest. They rested at midnight under the shelter of gigantic trees and ate a little of their scanty store of roasted barley before plunging down the mountain-side to a deep gorge. There a long and narrow plank spanned the abyss above a swirling torrent that foamed and boiled hundreds of feet below. The frail bridge bent under the slightest weight, and creaked and quivered like a willow wand, but from the peril of the savages behind there was no other path to safety. The travellers passed over one by one, but had to leave their mules.

The jet-black King of Janjeiro sat perched upon a platform sixteen feet high. Every morning he rose before the sun, for, said the men of Janjeiro, there could not be two suns above the horizon. If his opposite number in the sky should steal a march upon him, then the King of Janjeiro could not appear that day.

The sombre *Roi Soleil* kept the envoys waiting a week, for at the time that they arrived he was engaged in magic rites. It was only when he had finished casting his spells that they were granted an audience. He climbed down from his lofty perch to take the Emperor's letter with proper respect, but he conversed with Father Antonio at a distance, and from above. It was a long and solemn interview, for each time a phrase fell from the royal lips, the interpreter kissed his own fingertips and then the ground before translating it.

His Majesty, although aloof, was gracious. He gave the party various things that they required, and he also gave Father Antonio a nasty shock by making him the present of a fair slave girl. Father Antonio, much dismayed, explained that such a present would not do for him, whereupon the King good-naturedly exchanged her for a boy slave and a mule. Father Antonio promptly baptized the one and rode the other, so everyone was happy.

After a pitched battle with armed robbers on the way, the party reached the Kingdom of Kambata, and here it is that first appears upon the scene the evil genius of the embassy, the Abyssinian Manquer. The King of Kambata would have let the travellers proceed if Manquer had not come and whispered in his ear. Did the King suppose it was the Emperor who had sent these men? Manquer knew better. They had left Abyssinia secretly with a nefarious purpose. They were going to send for the Portuguese to come from India with great force, bringing bombards — those terrible engines of destruction that killed from afar. Then Susenyos would lose his throne, and all men would be obliged to change their faith.

The King of Kambata took fright and wrote to ask the Emperor what to do. Manquer arranged to have the messengers detained for months upon the way and sent back to Kambata. A second set of messengers were in due course dispatched, but endless time had been wasted before the Emperor's answer came.

Susenyos, although annoyed at the obstructions, could not usefully threaten a vassal who lived so far away. He therefore sent him gifts, urging him to help the travellers on their way. The King of Kambata, mollified, allowed the envoys to proceed, and wrote to recommend them to the Moslem chieftain Alico, who ruled the neighbouring land of Alaba. This was really outside the Abyssinian Empire.

At this point half the Ethiopians of the embassy announced that they were going home. They would never have started on this journey had they known what it would be like. They had endured enough already, and the future would be worse. Kambata was the last Christian land upon the way; after that all was Moslem and heathen to the shores of the Indian Ocean. If they had faced death so many times within the Empire, what would it be beyond?

But the prudent and valorous Tecu Egzy was not so easily deterred, and Father Antonio was not Portuguese for nothing. His native tenacity alone was quite enough to hold him on, besides which he felt that he was bound upon a holy errand. That it was likely to prove a hopeless quest he already suspected, now that he had sampled the sort of countries that he would have to pass through. Like every Portuguese of his generation, he had heard many true tales of shipwrecked men on savage shores, and their struggles to cut across African wilderness to civilization. How many bones had whitened in the forest between Natal and Moçambique? His own mission might well be swallowed up in the wastes of Somaliland. But he would only turn back if he were forced to do so. Lost in the immensity of unknown Africa, with nothing but barbarous lands before him eastward to the sea, and southward to the Cape, Father Antonio said that he felt "like an ant crossing a wide and crowded field; and regardless of what is around, intent only upon her duty, the little ant pursues her way, bearing her load to carry to her larder." So this little ant went on with the precious burden of the Emperor's letters, into the land of Alaba, where ruled the Moslem Alico.

Father Antonio and Tecu Egzy had been recommended to Alico and brought him presents — but Manquer had written first. Alico was pleased to take the gifts, but arrested the givers. Most of their goods were confiscated, and their horses and mules, while their luggage was searched for any compromising letters.

Father Antonio had his letters safe under his arm, but he knew that their discovery would raise a hornets' nest. It is true that they did not suggest exactly what Manquer insinuated, but Susenyos did say that an armed force of Portuguese would be very useful to him, both to help him against his enemies and contribute to the conversion of his subjects. To Moslems such as Alico it was all one whether the Ethiopians were Catholics or Copts, but they did not wish to see armed Portuguese about.

Father Antonio decided that his message would have to be delivered orally, if he ever had occasion to deliver it at all. He might be searched again at any time, so the letters must disappear. He had no kindling stone, so he pretended that he wished to smoke, and asked his captors for a light — not that Father Antonio ever really smoked, Baltasar Teles hastens to assure any reader who might be shocked, nor was the habit widespread in Europe at the time.

The natives of Alaba, however, all smoked heavily, it seems, and they sympathetically supplied the prisoner with what he asked for. Father Antonio withdrew, ostensibly to enjoy a quiet smoke, instead of which he burned the letters.

He never missed them. After toying with the idea for ten days, Alico decided not to kill the travellers after all if they would agree to discontinue their voyage. Nor would Alico allow them to return the way they came, for fear that the friendly Governor of Kambata might let them out of his country from the other side.

Thus Father Antonio and Tecu Egzy were brought to a standstill half-way between the Nile and Guardafui. They travelled back through wild and desolate lands infested by Gallas. Happily for them, one of their party had a friend who was a chief among these savages, and they happened to meet this man. For a consideration he agreed to take the party under his protection, which just saved their lives, for the next group of Gallas that they ran into proposed to kill them all and sacrifice them to the gods.

After many such alarms among Moslems and heathen, they reached a mountain stronghold – an amba – to the safety of which they gladly withdrew. Father Antonio wrote to Susenyos for instructions and was summoned back to court. More than fourteen months had been expended in this search for a way out of Abyssinia that did not exist.

The slippery Manquer also presented himself at court, smiling and brisk. To his surprise he found the Emperor bent on putting him to death. Manquer would have had short shrift if Father Antonio, who was a gentle soul, had not begged for his life. With "copious tears" Manquer was banished from the land and went to join the Gallas, and so met his fate. In his first raid in their company he broke his leg, and seeing him helpless, the Gallas put him out of his pain according to their custom. As they had no knowledge of surgery, it was perhaps the kindest thing to do.

We hear no more of the Malindi route. There was no getting around the Turks and the Red Sea.

20

Rome versus Alexandria

Camel-drivers are Mohammed's colleagues, and that is why he has bequeathed his wickedness to them. Such is the opinion of Dom Afonso Mendes, Patriarch of Abyssinia.

Dom Afonso Mendes writes with feeling, after being bullied systematically the whole way from the Red Sea coast into Ethiopia. The fiendish camel-drivers would not start at all without receiving their pay in advance, and then demanded gifts at intervals along the way. "The more good that we did to them, the worse they treated us. They made us supply them with food, and be their cooks as well, insisting always that their saucepan should be first on the fire, and if ever it was late, they avenged themselves by refusing to go on that day. We had to endure it all, not to risk having our baggage abandoned in the desert."

That desert in itself was bad enough without the camel-drivers. "Where the way was not over loose sand, it was across mountains of iron ore, the stones of which were like the cinders of an oven, and so sharp that they wear out a pair of shoes in one day." As there were not sufficient camels for all the party to ride, they had to walk by turns, and when the shoes were all worn out, to put on native sandals, which rubbed the skin off unaccustomed feet, leaving them raw and bleeding. The heat was such that it melted the sealing-wax the travellers carried in their writing-cases. The only shade was that of thorn bushes, "which pricked more than refreshed." There was nothing but hard earth to sleep upon and "brackish water that smelt very bad" to drink, and even that failed during a hideous eighteen hours.

The last lap was over a salt desert that could only be crossed by night "because by day the heat is enough to asphyxiate both travellers and their mounts, and shoe-leather is blistered as if it had been cast upon live coals." No wonder that, upon emerging from this inferno, the Patriarch exclaimed to his companions: "Let us thank God that we are in Ethiopia!"

As may be seen, there was not much to choose between this route and Father Antonio's projected way out through Malindi. It had the advantage, however, that it really was a route and not a blind alley. Dom Afonso Mendes and his companions had disembarked without much trouble, not at Massawa but at Beilul, about two degrees farther south. The ruler of this region, although Moslem, was at the time on terms of peace and friendship with the Emperor of Ethiopia, and so made no attempt to cut off heads.

The travellers' arrival was awaited impatiently by a number of people. Ever since his profession of faith, the Emperor had been asking for a Patriarch consecrated by Rome, and the Jesuits had insisted on the necessity in every letter. "All is finished on our part for the good of this Empire," wrote Francisco de Angelis in 1622, shortly before his death. "We only ask for a Patriarch — all cry out for a Patriarch, and if we do not get one soon, our labour will be wasted!"

In consequence of such appeals, Father Afonso Mendes, Doctor of Theology and Professor of Latin at Evora and Coimbra, was consecrated at the age of forty-three for what would be a very different field of labour.

The Patriarch's arrival at Fremona was a triumph, and Dom Afonso was delighted with the place. "This is not the Ethiopia that we imagined," he wrote to his brethren at home,

"but a land as fresh and good as Portugal, if not better!"
If the people were only more industrious, he goes on to say,
"they need lack nothing of the necessities, or even the lux-
uries, of life."

If the climate and the country pleased the Patriarch, so also
did his flock. The Emperor received him with respectful joy;
so did, of course, that Catholic champion Ras Seela Krestos,
and other great ones imitated them. On February 17, 1626,
before the highest in the land, and all his court assembled,
Susenyos swore allegiance to the Church of Rome. All the
Imperial princes, the viceroys and lords, ecclesiastics, monks
and priests were made to repeat the same vow, while the
Patriarch fulminated excommunications against all those who
should break it. All the priests of the Abyssinian Church were
ordered to cease officiating until they had been presented to
the Patriarch, and as Ethiopian forms of ordination were a
little haphazard and vague, Dom Afonso Mendes proceeded
to reordain a number of the native clergy.

On his side the Emperor issued the usual proclamation
ordaining all his subjects to conform to the new ritual under
pain of death. "These solemn proclamations," says Baltasar
Teles, "drew the hearts of all Ethiopia to our holy faith."

To the Jesuits this seemed like the battle won. The Emperor and his brothers had adhered to the Church of Rome,
and men of that age had no conception of a state that did
not follow the religion of its rulers. In every country at that
time we find the attitude the same. The government decided
what was sound religious truth, and coercive legislation drew
the subjects' hearts in the right way. It would be unfair to
judge the Jesuits or the Emperor severely for the persecutions
that they instigated or the rebellions which subsequently
devastated the land. Religious liberty was an ideal that the
seventeenth century did not understand, and most people
would have thought it was a dangerous thing. Susenyos and
the directors of his conscience sincerely felt that they were
fighting for the truth and for the nation's good.

But they had pitted their forces against something far too strong. The missionaries' learning, their earnestness and devotion, their moral example influenced individuals with whom they came into direct contact, but the heart of the people was untouched. The Abyssinian Church was deeply rooted in the past, and her traditions had been part of the nation's life more than a thousand years. To talk about the Pope's authority seemed to the Abyssinians pure impertinence, their hierarchy had flourished independently in him during so many centuries. That foreign priests should propose in his name to reordain her clergy and to rebaptize her sons filled Ethiopia with bitterness and indignation. The whole thing puzzled them the more that the two religions were essentially the same. "We are all Christians," Baltasar Teles says they argued, "both those of Rome and those of Alexandria. We believe in Christ, and Christ will save us all. There is not much difference between the two faiths, both have their advantages and their drawbacks. Separating the wheat from the tares, we have chosen the best, and by this way we also shall be saved."

It is not to be wondered at if the well-intentioned efforts of the Emperor and the Jesuits to Westernize the Abyssinian Church resulted in confusion. There were a number of conversions — some genuine and some feigned — but discontent grew daily.

Much trouble might have been avoided if the Patriarch had had experience of the country to which he had been called. As Father Antonio Fernandes wrote: "Experience of this land is necessary, for if one would proceed without it, it is to be feared that all may be turned inside out, and occasion given for revolts and risings."[1] A newcomer, he goes on to say, "is certain to think that he can shape things his own way — as it appeared to us when first we came!"

These lines were penned before the Patriarch's arrival, and the writer was not thinking about him, but his case proved the truth. Dom Afonso Mendes, new to the country and full

220

of zeal, did expect "to shape things his own way," and all at once. A number of small concessions, involving no dogmatic compromise, might have made the change less painful for the people, but during his first years in Abyssinia the Patriarch was for wholesale reform. The feasts and fasts and rites all had to be in strict accordance with the Latin Church. It was only when he saw the hornets' nest that he was raising that Dom Afonso Mendes realized that he had gone too fast. He then agreed to the Emperor's request for restoring some of the ancient customs "that were not against the substance of faith."

The Patriarch's concessions, however, were made too late. The country was already in a ferment. Rebellions had always been common in Ethiopia, and apart from the number of consciences that were sincerely outraged, the religious question placed a powerful tool in the hands of every disaffected chief. The Emperor spent his days in quashing revolts throughout the land. Matters reached a climax when the mountaineers of Lasta slew the Viceroy of Tigré, who was a fervent Catholic. Susenyos marched against them with a mighty army and put them all to flight. The bloodshed was terrible, and though the Catholic party won the day, the price of victory was their own undoing. On every side the Emperor heard his weeping subjects make the same complaint. "Look, Sire," they said, "such thousands killed! They are neither Moors nor heathen, but your vassals, our flesh and blood, our kinsmen! How many will you put to death? They cannot understand this faith of Rome. Leave them, Sire, to the faith of their forefathers!"

Such an appeal would melt a heart of stone, and Susenyos was not a monster. He was only a sincere man who had done what he thought was right, and the result perplexed him. Since his people did not take kindly to the Church of Rome, was he therefore to see his empire soaked in blood and torn asunder? "Give us back the faith of our ancestors!" was the cry that filled his ears, till he decided that he must give way. It was reluctantly that he came to such a conclusion, and he

was not happy about it. His own conversion to Rome appears
to have been genuine, and he felt that he was betraying the
truth.

"What is a sin against God cannot be for the good of the
kingdom," Father Manuel de Almeida gravely pointed out
to him. The greatest concession that the Emperor could make
conscientiously would be not to insist upon new conversions
for the time being. But, in the case of those who had already
joined the Roman Church — "to these Your Highness cannot
say: 'I restore to you the faith of your forefathers.' To do so
would be a grievous sin, and I should sin were I to suffer or
advise it. Besides," he added, "if a foreigner may be allowed
to express an opinion on the government of a strange country,
it seems to me that for Your Highness to grant such liberty
would be the certain ruin of your realms. It would be a cause
of division and civil war — you for Rome, I for Alexandria!
What can result except strife, wounds, and death? That is
obvious — Abuna for one, Patriarch for the other — in fact
two kingdoms and two kings!" Thus spoke the voice of sev-
enteenth-century Europe, where unity of religion was felt to
be essential to an ordered state.

The poor Emperor listened with drooping head and melancholy eyes. "What can I do?" he answered. "I have no kingdom left!" He was thoroughly discouraged and depressed.
On June 24, 1632 the following proclamation was read to
the exulting mob:

Hear, Oh hear!
We first gave you this faith which we held to be good, but num-
berless people have died. . . . We therefore give you back your
fathers' faith. Let the former priests re-enter their churches and replace their Tabots. Let them say Masses, and all of you rejoice! "

This last injunction was quite unnecessary. The "sacrilegious proclamation," as Baltasar Teles calls it, "which could
only have been forged in the depths of the workshops of hell,"
was received with a display of frenzied joy. Men, women,

soldiers, priests, and monks behaved, the same writer says bitterly, "like wild beasts let out of prison." To the Ethiopians the boot was on the other leg:

> The sheep of Ethiopia have escaped
> From the hyenas of the West!

was the refrain that blithely rose from every field and village. A general circumcision was performed, followed by a universal baptism according to their ancient custom. Thus the people purified themselves from the errors of Rome, amid which devotional exercises some of the baser sort were heard to say: "In future we can marry and dissolve our marriages as often as we choose," which speaks volumes for the mixed motives of human nature!

Though the people cheered the Emperor that day, Susenyos was a broken man, regarded as a turncoat by both Catholic and Copt. What he had done was against his conscience and weighed on his mind. Shortly after, he fell ill of a low wasting fever, caused by poison some people said, and the Jesuits deemed it was the chastisement of God.

"Your Highness is nearing your end," the Emperor's confessor, Father Diogo de Matos, informed him. "Remember your soul and your eternal salvation, and declare the faith in which you die."

"I die in the faith of Rome," Susenyos said in a clear voice. "And so I told my son."

The Emperor felt a little better presently, and his servants tried to tempt his appetite with a dish of raw tripe. They succeeded too well. The invalid ate so heartily that in the night he nearly died. A Galla physician, summoned to his side, administered pills made of chalk dissolved in wine. "These formed a ball in his stomach," writes Padre Manuel de Almeida, "and caused him such pain that he died in a few days."

Susenyos's death was the beginning of the end for the Jesuit mission in Abyssinia. The late Emperor's son, Fasiladas, was

an ardent supporter of the national Church, and on his accession the pendulum of persecution swung the other way. The
Emperor's uncle, Ras Seela Krestos, an ardent Catholic, was
one of the first to feel the change. It must be owned that he
had asked for trouble. When, in Susenyos's lifetime, the Abyssinian nobles had sworn allegiance to Fasiladas as heir, Ras
Seela Krestos had expressed his oath in unambiguous terms:
"I swear the Prince to be his father's heir, and to obey him as
a loyal vassal so long as he may hold by, defend, and favour
the Catholic faith; should he do otherwise, I shall be his first
and greatest enemy."

Fasiladas had not forgotten this, and so began his reign by
confiscating his uncle's property and banishing him to a distant province. There the pious Seela Krestos had to stay for
twenty years in very straitened circumstances, which none
the less were not without some compensation. In his days of
affluence, it would appear, Ras Seela Krestos had been crippled with gout, whereas in the lean days of his later life his
health greatly improved!

The Jesuits, naturally, did not come off any better than Ras
Seela Krestos. They had established themselves in small com-
munities about the land, surrounded by the little groups of
their disciples. Imperial orders soon came to dislodge them,
beginning at Gorgorra, in Dembea, by Lake Tsana. This was
one of the most important of their centres, and the church
they had erected there was the pride of Ethiopia. "No one
had ever seen anything like that church," says the Abyssinian
chronicler. For fear that it might be profaned, the Jesuits sadly
dismantled it before they left. "Two things filled my eyes
with tears," writes Father Manuel de Almeida. "The first was
to help despoil the altars, and to leave such a beautiful and
sumptuous temple to be desecrated by the enemies of the
faith; and the second was to see the multitude of poor Portuguese who came to bid us good-bye, especially the widows
and orphans who got some help from our protection, and

now with tears and cries that rose to heaven bewailed their desolation."

For several years the Jesuits found themselves ordered from pillar to post. From Gorgorra they had to withdraw to Ganeta Jesu, to Colleta, into Tigré, until finally the intimation came that they must leave the country altogether. The Patriarch at first refused to go, but in the end he was obliged to yield. Several letters were exchanged between him and the Emperor over all this—perfectly polite and dignified on either side.

"I entreat Your Highness," wrote Dom Afonso Mendes, "for God's sake, and for the truth, that Your Highness and your noblemen should inform me in writing the reason why you uproot and banish me. Is it for preaching a false doctrine? or else for scandalous sins in my life? Is it for failing to fulfil the duties of my pastoral office, for being proud and harsh in punishment, or too careless and lax? Or is it for some other cause?"

Fasiladas answered with equal restraint. He pointed out that it was not he but his father who had sent for the Patriarch. He had acted throughout as an obedient son though disagreeing with his parent's views. Fasiladas further recapitulates the Ethiopians' several objections to the Church of Rome, and assures the Patriarch that now that they have reverted to the rites of their forefathers, nothing could induce them to change a second time. "How could they return to what they left and hated, having tasted once more of their first faith?"

It is natural that the Jesuit historian should see "abominable blindness" in this letter, but where any "horrible malice" comes in is not apparent.

A more acid note creeps into the correspondence at the last. Fasiladas did not mind rubbing in unpleasant truths. "What does Your Lordship mean by saying: 'I have vowed not to leave Ethiopia'?" asks the Emperor cuttingly. "Your Lordship

is not leaving Ethiopia — it is she who has left Your Lordship!
Your Lordship does not fly from her, she has fled from you,
as the coward flies from the sight of the battlefield." Earlier
in the same letter the Emperor refers to the expedition of
Dom Cristóvão. "They did not preach nor teach the destruction of our ancient faith, handed down by the fathers and
Apostles. They did not oblige us to observe any religion
other than our own, which they defended and delivered from
the assassins and robbers which were the armies of the Moors.
They are worthy of great praise!"

This roused the Patriarch's wrath. "With what pen and ink
was such falseness written?" he exclaims. "Would the blessed
martyr Dom Cristóvão have shed his blood upon the fields
of Ofla for the people of Ethiopia to keep the faith of Alexandria, which they had at first? Who could think of anything
so absurd?"

Dom Afonso Mendes wrote this on June 19, 1634, from
Massawa, where he and several colleagues were waiting until
the Turks permitted them to get away. The Patriarch had
lived and worked in Abyssinia for eleven years, and some of
the Jesuits had been there twice that time. All were heart-
broken to leave the country and see the fruit of their labours
come to nothing.

We go [the Patriarch says], since we cannot do otherwise, but
as a mother cannot forget her child, nor a maid her attire, neither
can we forget the many sons that we have begotten to Christ, and
we know that if they could tear out their eyes and hearts to give
to us, they would!

We shall not cease by day or night to seek the welfare of their
souls, and pray the Father of all light to illumine the understanding of Your Highness, to show you the truth and strengthen your
heart to follow it, that you may not be cast into the outer darkness,
and counted among the emperors who have persecuted the Catholic, Apostolic, and Roman faith.

Fasiladas, as it happened, had no objection to being
counted among these. A long series of executions followed

the expulsion of the Patriarch. The Emperor's brother Claudius was one of the victims. Whether he really was a Catholic is not quite certain, and it seems that he and Fasiladas had fallen out on other matters besides the religious question, which is no doubt why he liked to enrage the Emperor by praising the Jesuits to the skies. Ah, these were men! said he. Where could priests be found such as they — "continent, learned, prudent, careful, and always working for the good of souls"? He waxed lyrical about the Patriarch — "so chaste and pure, a spiritual doctor, a honeycomb, a queen bee!" Fasiladas grew tired of hearing the Patriarch described in such language and silenced his brother in the end by cutting off his head.

The late Emperor's secretary and chronicler, Azaje Tino, fared even worse, for he was stoned to death. This little man (Tino means small) made a stout-hearted martyr. "Who lacks stones?" he cried, stooping to pick up some of those that fell in showers around him. "Here is a stone, brother!" and he handed them back to his executioners.

Ethiopians seem to have been wholehearted partisans whichever side they took. A blind beggar who was a pillar of the Catholic Church was much concerned for the salvation of a local magnate's wife who was an equally ardent Alexandrian. The blind man "took it upon himself to convert her, and persuade her to good works." With this altruistic end in view he did not fail to beg from her when she passed by. The lady glanced suspiciously at his rosary. "Are you of the communion of Alexandria," she asked, "or that of the Portuguese?" The beggar told her frankly which was his religion. He also told her, quite as frankly, what he thought about hers. "All the devils are coming upon you!" he concluded graphically.

"Then you are one of them!" the good woman retorted, and she and her servants assaulted him and smashed his beads. Such reaction to his missionary efforts did not damp the blind man's interest in her spiritual welfare. He continued to call regularly at her house. "I am going to that devil," he told people pleasantly, "to see if I can do good to her soul."

"Here comes the blind devil!" the lady would cry out each time that he appeared, and the two earnest Christians would call each other names.

How it ended we do not know. The Father Francisco Rodrigues, who told the anecdote, did not live to relate what happened next. He and about five other Jesuits had managed to remain in Abyssinia. In constant hiding, these brave men led hunted lives for several years, ministering secretly to what was still left of their flock. One after another, each in turn was caught and hanged, and so the Jesuit mission ended.

Not many of the missionaries survived, for of those who left the country some fell victims to the Turks at Massawa or Suakin. The Patriarch appeared likely to meet with such a fate, but after a long and trying detention at Suakin he was at last released and did return to India, where he lived at Goa to an advanced old age.

One Jesuit was dispatched to Europe and to Rome, where he reported how the mission had collapsed. It was clear, several people said, that the Abyssinians did not like the Portuguese. Send preachers of some other nationality who would handle them with greater tact, and Ethiopia would be converted.

Six French Capuchins started for Abyssinia on the strength of this assumption. Two died on the way, and two turned back. The last two entered Abyssinia and were stoned to death.

"Which plainly shows," observes Baltasar Teles, "that the persecution of the Abyssinians is against the Catholic religion, and not against the Portuguese."

This was no doubt the truth.

21

The End of a Dream

✠

So Portugal and Prester John parted for ever. The curtain lifted for a season dropped again; Abyssinia wrapped herself once more in isolation and obscurity. As a sleeper wakened in the night resumes his sleep, so the mysterious mountain empire sank back into oblivion for nearly three hundred years.

It seems that when Ethiopia did awake at last, it was too late. The world had been going on too long without her. A more formidable foe than Ahmed Granyé was at her gates, and there was no young hero like Dom Cristóvão to save her. This survival of an earlier age was therefore swept away, and the last to occupy the throne of Judah had to shoot his lions.[1]

If the Jesuits had succeeded in their mission, Abyssinia might have been Europeanized several centuries ago and the history of the last few years might have been different. Yet that they should have been expelled was inevitable and natural, nor were the Abyssinians in the least to blame for it. Neither are the Jesuits to be reproached, except for that intolerance which they shared with all their generation. They gave the country of their best, only that best was not what the Ethiopians needed or desired.

This quest for Prester John is one of the blind alleys of history, for it does not seem to have led anywhere. Yet what enthusiasm had gone into it! For a hundred years Portugal sought Prester John. She saved him from the Turks after she found him, and for nearly another hundred years tried to convert her protégé. What was the net result of so much effort?

The first five messengers died or disappeared. Four hundred of the nation's finest manhood were lost for ever, and a band of earnest missionaries threw away their lives upon a work that had no continuity. We well may ask to what purpose this waste. The nation gained absolutely nothing by it, and to individuals the quest brought perpetual exile, wounds, or death.

Yet we must remember that none of these pioneers went to seek material profit. This is a strangely disinterested chapter in the story of mankind. Neither Afonso de Paiva, who died alone in Moslem lands, nor Pero da Covilham, who left his home for ever, nor Duarte Galvão, dying on the island of Kamaran while gazing longingly across the burning waves of the Red Sea towards the land of Prester John, nor Dom Cristóvão and his gay young volunteers, marching, as their elders guessed, to certain death, nor the Jesuit fathers who faced the Turkish scimitars and horrible captivity in nameless dungeons — one of these men were striving after earthly treasure. They were pursuing an ideal, a will-o'-the-wisp-like thing that always ran before them.

When all is said and considered, in spite of the absurdities and the mistakes that go with every human enterprise, this age-long quest after the land of Prester John had something in it of man's search for the Kingdom of Heaven. That was really how it had begun in the mysticism of the early Middle Ages, and the myth went through the various stages that youthful illusions do go through before they die.

The realm of Prester John at first was earthly paradise, and then it had no geographical boundaries. At a later date, when the kingdom was localized and recognized to be no more than human, its ruler was supposed to be the champion of harassed

Christendom — the St. George who would slay the Moslem dragon. The seekers went a little further and learned that it was they who had to save St. George or he would be devoured by the dragon! And when they rescued Prester John only to find that he was not what they imagined, they simply set to work once more and tried to make him what they thought he ought to be. It seemed they had succeeded in the end, when — will-o'-the-wisp-like to the last — the dream faded away.

So the quest of Prester John vanished into the limbo of the world's lost causes. Yet perhaps because it was a movement born of an ideal and the spirit, and in spite of all mutual misunderstanding, it left vague memories in the legends of the land as of a good thing that once came there from afar.

In 1860, travelling through the mountains of south-western Abyssinia, two Italian Capuchins were told about a sacred flag. This object of local veneration was carried in solemn procession once a year. It was a banner brought by the ancestor of the tribal chief, who had been a stranger Christian from beyond the sea. One of the travellers managed to see the precious relic. It was a flag of old Portugal — the standard of the *quinas*.

Some twenty-five years later the Viennese Dr. Philip Paulitschke found the wild Galla tribes of Harrar worshipping a sword. It once belonged to a great hero, he was told, who came into the country long ago. The Austrian obtained possession of the sacred weapon and found it was a sixteenth-century Portuguese sword.

In this manner Dom Cristóvão's men and their descendants, lost to their country, lost to the world, and lost to history, live in the vague traditions of an alien race.

As for the Jesuits, Moallim Petros of the flaming beard personifies them all. The Abyssinian people cast them off, but the legend that remained is not unsympathetic. It has been said that a legend is the spirit of history without the letter, and this one suggests that beyond the barrier of misunderstanding that human imperfection raises between man and man, the Western priests had left behind a spark of something that the people recognized and understood.

Moallim Petros [the strange story runs] cited authorities to confirm every statement that he made. The monks and priests, being unable to confound him, rebelled and caused him to be banished.

The most fervent of his disciples followed him to Massawa. There, on the beach, they said: "We would go with thee, O our Father! What matters it if thy ship cannot hold us all? Did not St. Takla Haymanot extend his cloak over the waters and so travel to Jerusalem? We have faith in God, and in His wondrous works. Do thou entreat Him, and He will bid the sea to bear us all around thy ship!"

Moallim Petros prostrated himself with his face to the sand. He shed tears and remained long in ecstasy. Then he arose and said to his disciples: "Not so! You shall stay here. Without you the furrows would close again." He stretched out his hands to heaven and said: "O God, if I have taught the truth, make manifest the injustice of my persecutors! If my mouth has propagated lies or error, may this sea close over me, and let me be devoured by the monsters of the deep!"

He embarked upon the ship alone, saluted his disciples for the last time, and pronounced these words: "My brothers, meditate on the effect of the anointing that Our Lord Jesus Christ received in the waters of Jordan."

And the ship sailed away. It was these last words that gave birth to all the doubts, the troubles and endless disputes that divide the people of Ethiopia still today.

Moallim Petros's disciples remained, but the furrows he had ploughed did close again.

Portugal has long ago forgotten Prester John, and Prester John only remembers Portugal in legends which are like a people's dreams. Lost among the mountains of that enigmatic land are descendants of the wanderer Pero da Covilham, and the heroes of Dom Cristóvão da Gama's army — black men whose ancestors were brought up at Dom Manuel's gorgeous court, whose earlier forefathers were Gothic kings.

But these lost pioneers have left more than their blood be-

The End of a Dream

hind. Their sojourn in the land is also marked by stone memorials. In the heart of Africa we still may find a concrete fragment of old Portugal that has survived centuries of sun and storm. There is something of the sadness of a vision that has fled that haunts the crenellated towers of the ruins at Gondar.

Notes

CHAPTER 1

[1] Azurza: *Chronica d'El-Rei Dom João I*, Parte III, p. 63.
[2] Diogo Gomes: *Relação do descobrimento da Guine*. (Published in *Bulletin* of the Sociedade de Geografia de Lisboa, 1898.)
[3] See "*Do sigilo nacional sobre os descobrimentos*," by Jaime Cortesao, in *Lusitania*, January 1924.
[4] Castanheda: *Historia do Descobrimento e Conquista da India pelos Portugueses*. Liv. I, Cap. i.

CHAPTER 2

[1] Gaspar Correa.
[2] Francisco Alvares: *Verdadeira Informação das terras do Preste João*, p. 100.
[3] *Ibid.*, p. 127.
[4] Gaspar Correa: *Lendas da India*, III, p. 49.

CHAPTER 3

[1] *Comentarios*, Parte I, Cap. liv.
[2] *Cartas de Afonso*. Com. Parte II, Cap. xlix. Correa: *Lendas*, II, p. 139. De Albuquerque, I, p. 277.
[3] Translations of this letter, with slight variations, are to be found in F. Alvares, Castanheda, and Damião de Gois.
[4] *Cartas*, I, p. 302.
[5] *Cartas*.
[6] *Cartas de Afonso de Albuquerque*, V, p. 412.
[7] *Ibid.*, I, p. 302.
[8] *Ibid.*, VII, p. 194.
[9] *Ibid.*, VII, p. 67.
[10] *Lendas da India*, II, p. 327.
[11] See *Lendas da India*; also *Cartas*, I.
[12] Damião de Gois: *Cronica do Felicissimo Rei D. Emanuel*, p. 196.

Notes

CHAPTER 5

1 *Cartas*, III, p. 167.

CHAPTER 9

1 *Alvares Verd.*, Inf., Cap. cxiii, p. 148.
2 Ibid., p. 157.
3 Castanhoso: *Historia*, Cap. vi.
4 *Cartas*, I, p. 350.
5 This letter is published in Fr. Francisco de S. Luiz's notes to *Andrade's Vida de D. João de Castro*, p. 442. Esteves Pereira also reproduces it among the appendices to his edition of Castanhoso.
6 See letters of D. Cristóvão da Gama, published in Esteves Pereira's edition of Castanhoso.
7 Anonymous report dated from Goa, December 8, 1541, published in Vol. X of *Rerum Æthiopicarum Scriptores Occidentales*, edited by Beccari.
8 Diogo do Couto: *Decada*, V.
9 Anonymous report. Gaspar Correa calls him Antonio de Sousa.
10 Correa: *Lendas*, IV.
11 Diogo do Couto: *Decada*, V.

CHAPTER 10

1 Castro: *Roteiro de Goa até Soez*, p. 246.
2 Correa: *Lendas da India*, IV.

CHAPTER 20

1 *Beccari*, XII, p. 54.

CHAPTER 21

1 This was written before the outbreak of the present war. Since then deliverance has come to Abyssinia, and a new chapter, quite as exciting as any of the past, has been written in the story of that strange land.

Chronology

Part I

Conquest of Ceuta, which marks the real beginning of Portugal's quest
    for India and for Prester John, August 21, 1415.
Death of Infante Dom Henrique, who first started the quest, 1460.
Envoy from Benin arrives in Portugal and tells the tale of Ogané, 1486.
Bartolomeu Dias sailed to discover Cape of Good Hope, 1486.
Afonso de Paiva and Pero da Covilham set out for Ethiopia overland,
    May 7, 1487.
Death of Afonso de Paiva at Cairo, ?
Pero da Covilham reached Abyssinia, 1492 or 1493.
Departure of João Gomes, João Sanches, and Sid Mohammed for the
    land of Prester John, April 5, 1506.
Arrival at Malindi, February or March 1507.
Picked up, still at Malindi, by Francisco de Tavora, April 4, 1508.
Landed near Guardafui, April 18, 1508.
Arrived in Abyssinia, ?
Matthew dispatched with letter for Dom Manuel, 1510(?)
Arrival at Dabul and imprisoned, November 1512.
Rescued and brought to Goa, December 1512.
Left Goa for Cannanore, before December 16, 1512.
Sailed from Cannanore for Portugal, 3rd or 4th week January 1513.
Arrived in Lisbon, February 24, 1514.
Sailed with Duarte Galvão's embassy, April 7, 1515.
Arrived at Goa, September 2, 1515.
Sailed with Lopo Soares for the Red Sea, February 1517.
Death of Duarte Galvão on Kamaran Island, June 9, 1517.
Matthew and Francisco Alvares arrived back in India, August or Sep-
    tember 1517.

Chronology

Arrival of Diogo Lopes Sequeira as Governor, September 7, 1518.
Diogo Lopes sailed for Red Sea, taking Matthew and Francisco Alvares, January 8, 1520.
Arrived at Massawa, April 7, 1520.
Meeting of Diogo Lopes and Bahr Nagach, April 17, 1520.
Instructions issued by Dom Rodrigo de Lima as ambassador to Prester John, April 25, 1520.
Departure of embassy, April 30, 1520.
Death of Matthew at Bizan, May 23, 1520.
Arrival of embassy at Debaroa, June 28, 1520.
Entered province of Tigré, July 29, 1520.
Met Saga Zaab, August 1520.
Entertained by Ras of Angote, September 14, 1520.
Arrived at Emperor's camp, October 10, 1520.
Received at court, October 20, 1520.
Personal interview with the Emperor, November 19, 1520.
First dispatch of embassy, February 1521.
Returned to court, April 1521.
Arrival of letters from Dom Luiz de Menezes with news of Dom Manuel's death, April 15, 1523.
Sailed at last from Massawa, taking Saga Zaab as ambassador to Portugal, April 28, 1526.
Arrived at Goa, November 25, 1526.
Sailed from Cannanore for Portugal, January 4, 1527.
Arrived in Lisbon, July 24, 1527.

PART II

Invasion of Ethiopia by Ahmed Granyé, 1527.
Father Francisco Alvares was sent to Rome, September 1531.
Dom João Bermudez appointed Patriarch and sent to Europe, 1535.
Arrived in Lisbon (probably), 1537.
Viceroy Dom Garcia de Noronha sailed for India, 1538.
Dom João Bermudez sailed, 1539.
Dom Garcia died at Cochin, 1540.
Dom Estevão da Gama succeeded him as Governor and sailed for the Red Sea, 1541.
Fleet arrived at Massawa, February 16, 1541.
Returned to Massawa from Suez, May 22, 1541.
Departure of Dom Cristóvão da Gama's expedition, June 9, 1541.
Arrival at Debaroa, June 18, 1541.
Departure from Debaroa with Queen, December 15, 1541.
Capture of Amba Sanayt, February 2, 1542.
Arrival of letters from Massawa, end of February 1542.

Chronology

First battle with Granyé, April 4, 1542.
Second battle with Granyé, April 16, 1542.
Capture of Simen mountains, August 1542.
Dom Cristóvão's last battle, August 28, 1542.
Arrival of Emperor Galawdewos, September or October 1542.
Emperor's army marched, February 6, 1543.
Defeat and death of Granyé, February 22, 1543.
Castanhoso decided to leave Abyssinia after Christmas 1543.
Sailed from Massawa, February 16, 1544.
Arrived in India, April 19, 1544.

PART III

Letter of Dom João III to Galawdewos, promising to send him a new and better Patriarch, March 13, 1546.
Arrival of Padre Gonçalo Rodrigues in Abyssinia to prepare the ground, May 16, 1555.
Patriarch Dom João Nunes Barreto arrived at Goa with Bishop Dom André de Oviedo, September 13, 1556.
Bishop arrived in Ethiopia, March 25, 1557.
Death of Galawdewos, May 23, 1559.
Brother Fulgencio Freire attempts to reach Ethiopia, 1560.
Rebellion of Bahr Nagach, 1561.
André Gualdames killed by Turks at Massawa, 1562.
Death of Patriarch at Goa, 1562.
Death of Dom João Bermudez in Lisbon, 1570.
Death of Dom André de Oviedo at Fremona, 1577.
Departure of Fathers Antonio de Monserrate and Pero Paes for Abyssinia, February 3, 1588.
Captured by Arabs off Dofar, February 14, 1589.
Left King Omar's realm, June 27, 1589.
Reached Sana, in Yemen, July 1589.
Transferred to Turkish galley at Mocha, 1594.
Ransomed and returned to India, 1595.
Departure and death of Father Abraham de Georgis, 1595.
Death of last Jesuit left in Abyssinia, 1597.
New departure of Pero Paes for Abyssinia, March 22, 1603.
Arrived at Massawa, April 26, 1603.
Reached Fremona, May 15, 1603.
Emperor Za Danguil wrote to the King of Portugal, June 26, 1604.
Arrival of Fathers Antonio Fernandes and Francisco Antonio de Angelis, July 13, 1604.
Arrival of Fathers Luiz de Azevedo and Lourenço Romano, July 6, 1605.
Accession of Emperor Susenyos, 1605.

239

Chronology

Conversion of Susenyos's brother, Ras Seela Krestos, 1610.

Father Antonio Fernandes goes to seek Malindi route, March 1613.

Returned to Abyssinian court, September 1614.

Theological debate which convinced the Emperor, 1615.

Arrival of Fathers Diogo de Matos and Antonio Bruno, June 11, 1620.

Complete conversion of Emperor, beginning of 1622.

Death of Father Pero Paes, May 23, 1622.

Nomination of Patriarch Dom Afonso Mendes, July 1622.

Death of Father Francisco Antonio de Angelis, October 21, 1622.

Arrival of Fathers Manuel Barradas, Luiz Cardeira, Francisco de Carvalho, and Manuel de Almeida, 1623.

Arrival of Patriarch at Goa, May 28, 1624.

Arrival in Ethiopia accompanied by six other Jesuits, June 21, 1625.

Emperor's public submission to the Church of Rome, February 11, 1626.

Revolutions and unrest, 1628–32.

Battle against rebels of Lasta, followed by restoration of national church, June 1632.

Death of Susenyos, September 1632.

Expulsion of Jesuits, 1634.

Bibliography

(Dates given are those of earliest and last editions)

PART I

AFONSO DE ALBUQUERQUE: *Cartas seguidas de documentos que as elucidam.* 7 vols. (Published by Academia das Ciencias de Lisboa, 1884–1935.) Documents with reference to Prester John are to be found in every volume of this series.

Alguns Documentos do Archivo Nacional da Torre do Tombo. (Lisboa, 1892.)

BRAZ DE ALBUQUERQUE: *Comentarios do Grande Afonso de Albuquerque.* (Lisboa, 1557. Coimbra, 1923.)

Carta das novis que vieram a el Rey Nosso Senhor do Descobrimento do Preste Ioham. (Lisboa, 1521. London, British Museum, 1938.)

CASTANHEDA: *Historia do Descobrimento e Conquista da India pelos Portugueses,* I, II, III, IV. (Lisboa, 1551. Coimbra, 1924.)

DAMIÃO DE GOIS: *Cronica do Felicissimo Rei D. Emanuel.* (Lisboa, 1566. Coimbra, 1923.)

——: *Legatio magni indorum imperatoris Presbyteri Ioannis ad Emanuelem Lusitaniae Regem. Anno Domini MDXIII.* (Antwerp, 1532.)

——: *Fides, religio, moresque Æthiopum sub Imperio Preciosi Ioannis.* (Louvain, 1540.)

Documentos Arabicos para a historia portugueza copiados doa originaes da Torre do Yombo e vertidos em portugues por João de Souza. (Lisboa, 1720.)

FRANCISCO ALVARES: *Verdadeira Informação das Terras do Preste João das Indias.* (Lisboa, 1540, and 1889.)

GASPAR CORREA: *Lendas da India,* II, III, IV. Written between 1512

Bibliography

and 1561. (Published, Lisbon, 1858–66. Reprinted, Coimbra, 1924.)

João de Barros: *Decadas da Asia*, I, II. (Lisboa, 1552. Last complete edition, 1778.)

Part II

Miguel de Castanhoso: *Historia das cousas que o muy esforcado capitao D. Christóvão da Gama fez nos Reynos do Preste João* (Lisboa, 1564.) An edition in modernized spelling has been brought out by A. C. Pires de Lima (Porto, 1936). Another version taken from a manuscript in the Biblioteca da Ajuda was published by Esteves Pereira (Lisboa, 1896), entitled: *Dos Feitos de D. Christóvão da Gama, tratado composto por Miguel de Castanhoso*. This edition has very useful notes and appendices.

Dom João Bermudez: *Breve Relacion de embaxada que o Patriarcha do João Bermudez trouxe do Emperador de Ethiopia, vulgarmente chamada Preste João*. (Lisboa, 1565. Reprinted, 1844.)

Gaspar Correa: *Lendas da India*, IV.

Diogo do Couto: *Decadas*, V, VI. (Lisboa, 1602, 1778.)

Dom João de Castro: *Roteiro de Goa a Suez*.

An account of Dom Cristóvão da Gama's expedition is also to be found in the *History of Ethiopia* by Pero Paes, and Baltasar Teles reproduces it in his *Historia de Etiopia a Alta*. He says that Pero Paes heard it from the sons of the survivors of the famous expedition. Paes's narrative, however, is no more than a paraphrase of that of Miguel de Castanhoso, as are also the accounts given by Diogo do Couto and Gaspar Correa. Castanhoso and Bermudez are the only eyewitnesses who have recorded their experiences – almost the only ones who ever got away to tell the tale – and between the incoherent self-glorification of the pseudo-patriarch and Castanhoso's modest and straightforward narrative it is impossible to hesitate. Castanhoso's account has, moreover, the advantage of having been written immediately after the events that it describes. Gaspar Correa, who met him in India in 1544, says that he brought the manuscript with him. Correa's own story must have been the next one to be written. He reproduces Castanhoso almost word for word, and any extra details that he puts in cannot have been derived from any other source, since no one else had yet returned from Abyssinia.

Diogo do Couto does no more than repeat Castanhoso with a few additions that he may have heard from a certain Diogo Dias, one of Dom Cristóvão's old companions, who reached India after many years. Diogo do Couto knew this man, and says that he vouched for the accuracy of Castanhoso's book.

Bibliography

That is more than anybody has ventured to do for Dom João Bermudez's rather confused narrative, written twenty years after the events. The clearest impression that it leaves the reader is what a fine fellow João Bermudez felt himself to be. Dom Cristóvão da Gama — that very capable young man, who had been commanding ships and handling men five or six years before he met João Bermudez — is represented as an irresponsible boy entrusted by his brother to the Patriarch's care; and it is the ex-physician and improvised priest who teaches Vasco da Gama's son how battles should be fought!

PART III

BALTASAR TELES: *Historia de Etiopia a Alta.* Coimbra, 1660.
A valuable compilation which incorporates large portions of Almeida and Paes, as well as a number of contemporary letters. An abridged edition has been published by A. de Magalhãis Basto. Porto, 1936.
Cronica de Susenyos. Translated by Esteves Pereira. Lisbon, 1900. This work has especially valuable notes.
DAMIÃO DE GOIS: *Fides, religio. moresque Æthiopum sub imperio Pretori Joannis.* Louvain, 1540. Coimbra, 1741.
DIOGO DO COUTO: *Decadas,* VI, VII.
Rerum Æthiopicarum Scriptores Occidentales inediti a sæculis XVI ad XIX. 16 vols. Published by Beccari, Rome, 1903–15.
This monumental series includes the histories of Manuel de Almeida and Pero Paes, the works of Manuel Barrades and Afonso Mendes, besides most of the correspondence of the Jesuits.

Two very useful modern works embracing the whole period are:
Conde de Ficalho: *Viagens de Pero da Covilham.* Lisbon, 1896.
C. F. Rey: *Romance of the Portuguese in Abyssinia.* London, 1929.

English translations of the narratives of Francisco Alvares Castanhoso and Bermudez have been made by the Hakluyt Society, as also of the *Commentaries* of Bras de Albuquerque. I have not made use of any of these, however, and the translations that are given here are mine. Living, as I do, in Portugal, I have had no opportunity to see the English editions of these books.

A NOTE ON THE TYPE

The text of this book has been set in Caledonia, a Linotype face designed by W. A. Dwiggins. Caledonia belongs to the family of printing types called "modern" by printers — a term used to mark the change in style of types that occurred about the year 1800. Caledonia borders on the general design of Scotch Modern, but is more freely drawn than that letter.

The book was composed, printed, and bound by The Plimpton Press, Norwood, Massachusetts.

HERE is the story of Prester John, the legendary ruler of an undiscovered country of the Far East, a region as strangely fascinating to the Europeans of that day as the mountains of the moon and — as over a century of exploration was to prove — nearly as inaccessible. Here too is the whole history of the relationship between Portugal and Ethiopia from the arrival in 1442 of the first Portuguese to venture into the territory to the expulsion in 1634 of the Portuguese Jesuits.

It was not until late in the fifteenth century that Prester John passed from the realm of legend to assume tremendous stature as a potential ally against the heathen, and the lost kingdom, the stronghold of the Abyssinian Negus, was found to have its roots not in Asia but in Africa.

The chronicling of this period has been highlighted by fabulous tales — of a glamorous queen marooned in a mountain fortress approachable only by means of a pulley basket; of magnificent battle actions replete with sword clashings and the roar of the arquebusiers, of a lofty hermitage inhabited only by mummies. But, more than this, it is a revealing story of sixteenth-century Jesuitism, of soldiers and priests tireless in their efforts to Christianize the Ethiopians according to the precepts of the Church of Rome, defeated by the peculiarly stubborn Abyssinian brand of Catholicism.

Drawing for her source material upon the wealth of contemporary record, the author has created a rich and colorful picture of an extraordinary era of European exploration and missionary endeavor — one worthy of comparison with Marco Polo's account of his famous journey.

Printed in the United Kingdom by
Lightning Source UK Ltd., Milton Keynes
141584UK00001B/66/A

9 781406 728101